MEN OF ACTION

Also by Ed Robertson

The Fugitive Recaptured: The 30th Anniversary Companion to a Television Classic
Maverick: Legend of the West
45 Years of The Rockford Files
The Case of the Alliterative Attorney: A Guide to the Perry Mason TV Series and TV Movies (with Bill Sullivan)
The FBI Dossier: A Guide to the Classic TV Series (with Bill Sullivan)

MEN OF ACTION

BEHIND-THE-SCENES OF
FOUR CLASSIC TV SERIES

ED ROBERTSON

CUTTING EDGE

Copyright © 2024 by Ed Robertson

No part of this book may be reproduced, or stored in a retrieval system, or transmitted in any form or by any means, electronic, mechanical, photocopying, recording, or otherwise, without express written permission of the publisher.

ISBN-13: 978-1-962896-35-1 (Paperback)
ISBN-13: 978-1-962896-38-2 (Hardcover)

Published by
Cutting Edge Books
PO Box 8212
Calabasas, CA 91372
www.cuttingedgebooks.com

AUTHOR'S NOTE

Television Chronicles was a short-lived, but fondly remembered quarterly print publication best described as *"Filmfax* meets classic television." Twelve editions were published between April 1995 and January 1998, followed by a brief attempt to resurrect the magazine online in 2006. Each issue featured long-form retrospectives of notable shows that originally aired during the first three decades of network TV and left their mark on either their particular genre or the medium in general. Each profile provided the back story of how these shows got on the air, exclusive interviews with stars and key behind-the-series personnel of each show, and an episode guide.

In an era that predated the Internet—not to mention the vast number of social media outlets, websites, eBooks, episode recaps, and the various niche cable and digital channels that allow virtually every TV series today to remain in the public consciousness one way or another, regardless of how long it aired—*Television Chronicles* was a boon to classic TV fans from all walks of life. One such fan was esteemed film and TV critic Leonard Maltin, whose ringing endorsement appeared on the inside cover of most issues. "I really like *Television Chronicles*," Maltin said. "[It is] lots of fun and full of information that's hard to find elsewhere."

The four series chronicled in this book—*The Magician, The Untouchables, Harry O,* and *Run For Your Life*—were all subjects of articles that I wrote for *Television Chronicles*. Here's what made each of these shows special:

- *The Magician* (NBC, 1973-1974) was the first network series to integrate stage magic into episodic TV drama (Anthony Blake, the character played by Bill Bixby, was a professional magician who moonlighted as a detective), as well as the first to incorporate the Magic Castle, the legendary private club for stage magicians and magic enthusiasts, into a weekly series. While the concept of "troubleshooting magician" has been revisited (most notably, *Blacke's Magic* and *Deception*), *The Magician* was arguably the most successful attempt, given that it has held up and found new audiences more than fifty years later. Last, but not least, *The Magician* was also the series that launched the career of future Emmy Award-winning writer/producer David Chase (*The Rockford Files, The Sopranos*)
- *The Untouchables* (ABC, 1959-1963) put Quinn Martin in the foreground of network TV producers, while Eliot Ness (as played by Robert Stack) was the first TV hero who played straight man to the villains—meaning, the guest stars in each episode had the more colorful roles, in contrast to the straight-shooting Ness. This was five years before *Batman* did the same thing, and more than ten years before *Columbo*. The short-lived reimagining of *The Untouchables* (Syndicated, 1993-1994) then took that idea a step further by adding layers to the Al Capone character that made him almost heroic. This was five years before the debut of *The Sopranos*, the iconic HBO series that ushered in the era of anti-hero protagonists that have populated television over the past twenty-five years. In that respect, one could argue that the new *Untouchables* was ahead of its time.

MEN OF ACTION

- *Harry O* (ABC, 1974-1976) was the first network episodic drama to take a novelistic approach to storytelling, more than twenty years before HBO virtually patented the same approach. It was also one of the few network series that made it on the air even though its original pilot did not sell (*Star Trek* is the most famous example, followed closely by *Columbo*), not to mention one of the few network TV detective series to use voice-over narration successfully. Finally, Harry Orwell was among the first, if not the first, bohemian private eyes on television.
- *Run For Your Life* (NBC, 1965-1968), like *Harry O*, portrayed existential ideas at a time when most American TV series did not do that. Paul Bryan, the character played by Ben Gazzara, suddenly learns that he has a terminal disease, with no more than two years to live. Rather than drown himself in self-pity, he threw himself into living every remaining moment of his life as fully as possible. That makes the show a statement on what it means to live.

The episode guides that appear at the end of each series profile all follow the *Television Chronicles* format: They each contain the episode title, original air date, a one-sentence "log line" synopsis, guest casts (listed by actor name only), the "written by" and "directed by" credits, and miscellaneous information regarding awards, additional adaptations of the same material, and other items of interest. Except for the 1993-1994 revival of *The Untouchables*—a syndicated series that aired at different times, and on different dates of the week, in the markets that carried the show—the episodes for each series are listed according to their original date of broadcast.

I have also updated each retrospective with new quotes from actors or other personnel from each series, drawing from interviews that I've done in the twenty-five years since these articles were originally published.

My thanks to Lee Goldberg and the entire staff at Cutting Edge Books for letting me revisit each of these four series. I believe you will find the journey as satisfying as I did.

Ed Robertson
October 2024

THE MAGICIAN (NBC, 1973-1974)

Twenty-one episodes, plus 90-minute pilot

Starring   Bill Bixby as Anthony Blake ("Anthony Dorian" in the pilot)

Also Starring   Keene Curtis as Max Pomeroy (first twelve episodes)
Joe Sirola as Dominick (last nine episodes)

With   Jim Watkins as Jerry Anderson
Todd Crespi as Dennis Pomeroy (first five episodes)
Mark Wilson as Himself (last nine episodes)
Greg Wilson as Himself (last nine episodes)
Camiey Gwyn Sebring, Sheila English as Blake's assistants (various episodes)

Announcer: Bill Baldwin

Executive Producer: Laurence Heath (episodes 1-12)
Bruce Lansbury (episodes 13-21)

Created by: Bruce Lansbury

Produced by: Barry Crane (episodes 1-5)
Alan Armer (episodes 6-12),
Paul Playdon (episodes 13-21)
Theme by Patrick Williams

MEN OF ACTION

Time has certainly been kind to *The Magician* (NBC, 1973-1974), the offbeat action drama starring Bill Bixby as a troubleshooting illusionist. Despite its intriguing premise, the series was a marginal success at best, lasting only twenty-one episodes.

The failure of *The Magician* can be attributed in part to several factors. The premise of the series required the writers and the producers to find plausible ways to involve Bixby's character in matters that were normally under the domain of police officers or professional investigators. In addition, because magic was to be used in the context of the show, the writers had the added challenge of working it into the stories in an interesting, intelligent, and ultimately entertaining way. The sheer nature of episodic television (a volume-oriented yet speed-driven industry) made that difficult enough. Factor in the Writers Guild strike of 1973, which wiped out nearly four months of prep time for the 1973-1974 season—as well as some fundamental differences among the show's key participants as to what the series should be—and that made producing *The Magician* even more of a challenge. Viewed in that light, the series was an ambitious project that never really had a chance to succeed.

And yet, *The Magician* has lived on since its cancellation, finding new audiences via overseas syndication, cable television, and the release of the series on DVD in 2017, while also sparking a renewed interest in the performance of magic. While some professional magicians remain critical of the series, others have credited it for ushering in the so-called "golden age" of magic from which David Copperfield, David Blaine, Criss Angel, Siegfried & Roy, Penn & Teller, and other contemporary illusionists have emerged. In that respect, despite its limited number of episodes, *The Magician* continues to have the kind of far-reaching impact that few television shows ever achieve.

In *The Magician*, Bixby played Anthony Blake, a renowned illusionist/escape artist who had been imprisoned in a brutal South American jail on a false espionage charge. Blake befriended an old man in prison and later escaped with him two years later. The old man died shortly thereafter escape, leaving Blake his considerable fortune. Blake then became a sort of modern-day Count of Monte Cristo, putting his wealth and skills to the use of other victims of injustice. In contrast to most other TV crime stoppers, Blake didn't carry a gun—in fact, he abhorred violence and instead relied on his skills as a magician as his only arsenal against evil. "[With his magic], he overcomes brutality with dexterity and intelligence, and shows that compassion and intellect are stronger than brawn and brute force," proclaimed a spokesman for the show in 1973.

The concept of *The Magician* originated with Bruce Lansbury (*Mission: Impossible, Fantastic Journey, Murder She Wrote*). The younger brother of Angela Lansbury, Bruce Lansbury was the executive in charge of the television department at Paramount Pictures, where *The Magician* was produced. A longtime magic buff, Lansbury had previously developed *Escape*, a pilot about a James Bond-like professional escape artist (played by Christopher George) who moonlights as a private eye. *Escape* aired in April 1971, but never went to series.

Sometime in 1972, Lansbury approached writer/producer Joseph Stefano (*Psycho, The Outer Limits*) to develop the idea into a pilot. Here's his recollection of how it evolved:

> JOSEPH STEFANO: I had a meeting with some of the executives at Paramount, and I remember their saying that they wanted 'a magician who would also be a detective.' This was not on paper—this was what was said to me at the meeting. I'm quite sure there wasn't any book or outline. If there was, I don't remember seeing it, or perhaps reading it. Sometimes when people call me

MEN OF ACTION

in and say they have an idea for a movie they want to do, which happens a lot in television (and I did a lot of TV-movies in the '70s)—they'll say, 'Well, we'd love to do something like this,' and if I liked the idea, I'd just go away and create it. And even if Paramount had any material on the 'magician' idea, I really wasn't interested in seeing it, because that, to me, would just amount to research—and it also might, on the other hand, amount to sharing a credit with somebody. So I always felt that I would start from scratch, so that I could be able to sit back afterward and honestly say, 'Yes, I created this from scratch'—whereas, if I'd read something, I wouldn't be able to say that. I didn't feel that mixing the magician and the detective was a good idea, unless, I said, one of those jobs would have to be an avocation. So what does he do? Is he a detective all day, and then goes to clubs at night? I didn't see how I could have gotten those two things involved. But, I figured if he's a magician, *period*— and you call it *The Magician*—and he then gets involved in situations which he solves, or where he helps somebody... In the pilot story, for example, he didn't even know the people that he would be dealing with. It wasn't as if anyone came into his room and said, 'I'm having trouble with my ex-husband,' or anything like that. The way I saw the show developing was that, each week, the situation would always come at him.'[1]

Stefano began drafting the story treatment for the pilot, developing the back story for the Magician, as well as his motivation for helping people. What Stefano had in mind was a series similar in style and tone to *Journey Into Fear* (1942), a gritty, darkly photographed film written by and starring Joseph Cotten

---
1   As a rule, this is how the stories in the series played out.

as an American gun engineer who slowly finds himself embroiled in international intrigue. (Coincidentally, one of the minor characters in the film is a stage magician, Oo Lang Sang, played by accomplished character actor Hans Conried.)

"*Journey Into Fear* is a very dark, and kind of fabulous, movie," Stefano explained. "In my mind, I saw *The Magician* as being that kind of show every week, and so I went for oddness in the story that I developed."

When Stefano finished his story, however, he found that the studio had something much different in mind for *The Magician*. Indeed, a 1973 press release from Paramount described the series as a "modern swashbuckling adventure, a show full of pure entertainment made for the enjoyment of its audience."

"Bruce had one word for that series," said Sutton Roley, who directed four episodes. "If you ever wanted to make it a little more serious, or do something a little more dramatic with the show, he would always say, 'Remember, I want this series 'picaresque.' That's what he wanted it to be—and it certainly was that. *The Magician* had that kind of volatile, tongue-in-cheek feel to it."[2]

The opening title sequence of *The Magician*, with its splashy colors, accompanied by Patrick Williams' upbeat theme music, provides an excellent picture of what Lansbury and the studio had in mind. A pair of animated hands performing basic feats of prestidigitation (such as changing three ordinary balls into three flying doves) is superimposed against live-action footage of Bixby. The hands also twist an ordinary handkerchief, which then takes the shape of a curvaceous woman, underscoring the element of romance that the studio also wanted in the show (the

---

2 "Picaresque" is a literary term used to describe fiction in which the adventures of a rogue are narrated in humorous or satiric scenes. Just as the heroes in picaresque novels tend to get by life more through cunning than hard work, so the Magician would use his wits to "dazzle" his opponents into submission.

Magician, rogue that he was, would be something of a ladies' man). The catchy theme music, with its stirring trumpet solo at the outset, conveys the sense of wonder and spectacle often associated with the circus. The animated hands, by the way, also became a regular feature of the first ten broadcast episodes of the series. Besides appearing in the opening titles of these shows, each act of the first ten episodes opened and closed with a silhouette of the hands waving on and off the action.

"The pilot was very bright and colorful, but, in my mind, it was nothing that represented what I would have done had I stayed with the show," Stefano said. "After they read my story, the studio and I had a lot of disagreement over the direction the series was going to go. Once I had an idea of what they wanted to do, I divorced myself from the project completely."

Ironically, although Paramount rejected Stefano's tone for the series, the studio ultimately decided to use the story he had written—Laurence Heath *(Mission: Impossible)* wrote the teleplay, based on Stefano's story—and even incorporated the back story of the Magician's brutal prison experience, which supposedly had no place within the format of a light-and-airy series.

It's possible, however, that the studio may have initially "rejected" the story because of a provision in Stefano's contract that would have paid him a fee for each episode produced, in the event the pilot went to series. But with Stefano out of the picture, Paramount could then assign the teleplay to another writer who did not have that particular stipulation written into his contract. In any event, Stefano was paid for the story alone when the studio elected to use it as the basis for the *Magician* pilot.

Although Bill Bixby was an accomplished amateur magician himself (he was a member of the Academy of Magical Arts, the international society of magicians), he still seemed like an odd choice to play the lead. After all, *The Magician* was an action/adventure series, while Bixby's *forte*, to that point, was light comedy/drama (*My Favorite Martian, The Courtship of Eddie's*

Father). But both NBC and Paramount wanted Bixby from the outset because they believed he would be an audience draw—and, fresh from the success of the critically acclaimed *Eddie's Father*, Bixby was quite a popular fixture in television at the time.

A sixth-generation San Franciscan, Wilfred Bailey Bixby became interested in the theater while in high school, where he won numerous trophies for debating. As a student at San Francisco City College, and later at the University of California/Berkeley (where he studied law), he continued to perform in student productions. Four credits shy of his degree, Bixby quit school and joined the Army; while in the service, he decided to embark on a professional acting career, allowing himself five years to succeed (failing that, he vowed to return to his law studies).

After moving to Hollywood, Bixby worked many odd jobs at a hotel, where he was approached by a Detroit advertising executive and offered a commercial acting opportunity. He moved to Detroit for four months, appeared in several industrial films, and later made his stage debut in the Detroit Civic Theater's production of *The Boyfriend*. He studied drama upon his return to L.A., and was eventually discovered by an agent, who got him his first television acting assignment in an episode of *The Many Loves of Dobie Gillis*. After finding additional guest roles in such programs as *The Andy Griffith Show* and *The Danny Thomas Show*, he eventually won a regular part on *The Joey Bishop Show*. Bixby's next big break came in 1963, when he played a young newspaper reporter who befriends an anthropologist from Mars (played by *Damn Yankees* star Ray Walston) in *My Favorite Martian* (CBS, 1963-1966). After *Martian* ended, Bixby appeared in a couple of Elvis Presley movies *(Clambake, Speedway)*, and continued to work on stage *(The Paisley Convertible, Sunday in New York, Come Blow Your Horn)* before embarking on a three-year run as the widower father of a precocious young boy (played by Brandon Cruz) in the TV adaptation of *The Courtship of Eddie's Father* (ABC, 1969-1972).

While doing *The Magician* may not have come easily to Bixby (as he would soon discover, there are some fundamental differences between preparing a half-hour sitcom and a one-hour action series), playing the Magician was another story. "The show is larger than life in many aspects, but Anthony Blake is a man who can feel a great deal of compassion for his fellow man," Bixby explained in 1973. "He is a man I would like if I met him—and that is of no small importance. Doing a television series is something like living with someone. You must like his character in order to assume his identity."

Co-starring with Bixby was distinguished Broadway actor Keene Curtis, a Tony Award-winner in 1971 for Best Supporting Actor in *The Rothschilds*, and a founding member of New York's famed repertory company, The Association of Producing Artists. An established star of the New York stage, Curtis had appeared in productions of such classics as *The Cocktail Party, School for Scandal, The Misanthrope, Hamlet, A Midsummer's Night Dream, Twelfth Night, King Lear, War and Peace,* and *Man and Superman.*

As originally conceived, Curtis' character Max Pomeroy was a highly respected, if somewhat unconventional, newspaper columnist whose endless research files provided the Magician with a wealth of information needed for his investigations. "I read through the pilot script, and I thought it was an incredible part," Curtis recalled in an interview with me in 1996. "He was a person who could speak six different languages, who always had a hawk perched on his shoulder, and who also kept a leopard in his den as a pet. He was decidedly flamboyant. He was an international raconteur, an international author as well as a renowned journalist, and he was someone who knew all the important people all over the world. It sounded like a very fun part to do."

Max made his home in an elegant three-story Victorian manor in San Francisco, where he lived with his paraplegic son Dennis (Todd Crespi), and Lulu (Joan Caulfield), a woman "who is all things to me [including the mother of his child] but a wife." Crespi also appeared in the first five episodes of the series. Rounding out the cast was Blaxploitation film actor Jim Watkins (*Black Gunn*) in the role of Jerry Anderson, the chief pilot of *The Spirit*, the Boeing 747 airplane where Blake also lived and worked.

Blake drove a white 1974 Chevy Corvette T-top with the personalized license plate SPIRIT. Among the car's features was a built-in telephone—a rare item at the time. "Not many people had phones in their cars before the '80s because the satellite time was so prohibitively expensive," noted TV historian Billy Ingram. "I was just learning to drive when this show came on, so I naturally wanted a car just like the Magician's. In one episode, Tony comes back out to his car and some thugs have smashed it all up. I was more shocked by that than anything else I can remember seeing on television. They even ripped the phone out!"

The 90-minute pilot aired on March 17, 1973. On the basis of good reviews in the trade papers, and positive audience response in both test showings and the Nielsen television ratings, NBC scheduled *The Magician* as part of its Tuesday night lineup for the 1973-1974 season. That's when many of the problems that would eventually sink the series really began to surface.

Everyone involved had high hopes for *The Magician*. "Paramount had been prepared to launch a substantial marketing campaign for the show," reported magician Dustin Stinett in a profile of *The Magician* published in *Genii: The Conjurors' Magazine* in 2004. Central to the campaign was a nationwide tour featuring Bixby and the *Spirit* plane that, had it transpired, likely would have generated tremendous interest in *The Magician* in the weeks leading up to the show's premiere. According to Stinett, despite the demands it would have placed on his schedule, Bixby had been looking forward to the tour and was greatly disappointed when it was eventually scuttled on account of the Writers Guild strike.

Meanwhile, executive producer Laurence Heath and producer Barry Crane wanted to approach each episode of *The Magician* as a "mini-movie" for television that would adapt the quality of movement and visual action usually reserved for the big screen. Apparently, Heath and Crane wanted *The Magician* to be similar, at least in terms of style and production, to *Mission: Impossible*, a series frequently noted for the "movie-like" quality of its episodes throughout its seven-year run on CBS (1966-1973). Not surprisingly, many of the key members of *The Magician*'s staff and crew were, like Heath and Crane themselves, alumni of *Mission: Impossible*, including executive story consultant Steve Kandel, staff writer Walter Brough, director of photography Ronald Browne, set decorator Lucien Hafley, and assistant producer Dale Tarter. In addition, many of the writers (Harold Livingston, Richard Hesse) and directors (Sutton Roley, Reza Badiyi, Paul Krasny) recruited for the show also had ties to *Mission*.

Heath and Crane understood that both the studio and the network wanted *The Magician* to be an action/adventure series. But Bixby had his own ideas about the show, specifically about how the magic would be presented each week. Among other things, he insisted that the illusions he performed on each show be filmed in one take, without trick photography, so that the audience would not think that it was being tricked or fooled. "Bill's ideas weren't bad; they were just a little different from what NBC had in mind," said Heath. "Bill wanted a show that had some sort of an imaginative quality that had more of an aesthetic appeal, than the action/adventure appeal. And that's all to his credit—except that it clashed very badly with the network, right from the start."

Technical consultant Mark Wilson, the world-renowned stage magician who himself was a veteran of such television series as *The Magic Land of Allakazam* and *Magic Circus*, agreed that Bixby, Crane, and Heath were not always on the same page during the early stages of production. "They had written the story and then tried to work the magic into it," he told *Genii: The Conjurors' Magazine* in 2004. "You have to do it the other way around. [But the producers] did not understand the concept of the show. They did not understand the importance of the magic Bill did on the show."

Even under ordinary circumstances, the first year of producing a television series is often the most difficult. It usually takes a few shows for the producer, the writers, and the actors to figure out what works and what doesn't work about a series, or the kinds of stories that they want it to tell. Even in cases such as *The Magician*, where major differences existed between the producers and the lead as to what the series should be, there is usually time to work things out, either during the early months of script preparation (which, for series set to premiere in September, normally begins around March or April) or during the first few weeks of filming (which usually commences sometime in mid-June).

But the circumstances surrounding *The Magician*, as well as every other show scheduled to air in the fall of 1973, were far from ordinary because of a Writers Guild strike that halted production throughout the entire television industry. The strike commenced in the spring and wasn't settled until late in the summer. That effectively wiped out the early months of preparation that are often critical to working out the kinks in a new series.

"The differences between Bill and Barry and myself over the show might have been worked out during those early months of prep time, and we all might have been able to experiment with the concept of the show, with different kinds of scripts, until we were all on the same track," said Heath. "But that was totally impossible during all those months of the strike. The writers and I were forbidden to do anything—of course, we did talk over the phone and things like that, but, basically, we were unable to do anything, with regard to resolving our differences in how to look at the series, until after the strike was settled. When we came back, we were simply trying to get the scripts written as quickly as we could so that we could get the sets built, and the things filmed, and all of that, because we were still scheduled to premiere in the fall."

Of course, some actors, even they if own a piece of the show they're starring in, don't want to bother with any of the creative aspects of a show; they leave those matters in the hands of the producers, the writers, and the directors. This isn't meant as a slight against Bixby—after all, his own production company (B & B Productions) made the show in conjunction with Paramount, so he probably felt entitled to have some say in the overall production of the series. Still, because the production schedule had been thrown out of whack due to the strike, it was particularly important for everyone involved in the series to maintain a spirit of cooperation to work themselves out of the hole and keep the series on schedule.

Bixby was a very meticulous performer—he worked very hard with Wilson on mastering the particular illusions for each episode before actually performing them on-camera. Because Bixby insisted on filming the magic in one take, without any camera cuts, these scenes often required several takes until that one, flawless shot needed for the episode was finally captured on film. This meant that the days on which these sequences were filmed were often very long—requiring the studio to pay the crew overtime, which in turn made the show even more expensive to produce. "The crew was working till 11 or 12 at night on those days, and the costs were horrendous [for that time], running up all that overtime," said Heath. "The studio was always on our necks about that, and that was creating its own pressures."

Although Bixby was occasionally difficult to deal with, Heath felt that his biggest problem as producer was not with the star, but the situation brought on by the strike. "The strike was certainly an insurmountable obstacle with *The Magician*, because we were not able to get the tone in sync, where everybody knew what the objective was, and was working toward the same end," he said. "Again, in the normal course of things, we would have found out about that right away. But we never had a chance, because we were never all able to get together during the time of the strike."As a result, Heath, Crane, and Bixby were never quite on the same wavelength, which made producing an already difficult series under extraordinary circumstances even tougher.

Though no one knew it at the time, the WGA work stoppage of 1973 yielded one development that would benefit *The Magician* in the short run and, ultimately, television drama in the long run. One day, while on picket duty for the Guild, a young writer member named David Chase met writer/producer Paul Playdon (*Mission: Impossible, Banacek, Cannon*). Though he had sold a script for an episode of *The Bold Ones* that was produced in 1971, Chase had no other screen credits at the time of the strike and was, by his admission, still struggling to find his way in television. "Paul and I got along really well," Chase recalled in an interview for the Television Academy. "We had a lot of fun just on picket duty, sort of goofing on it and, you know, trying to dodge the harder parts of it. I told him I had a script. And he said, 'Well, you should send it to my agent.' So I sent it to his agent when the strike was over, and his agent wanted to represent me—probably, I think, because Paul was one of his star clients and an up-and-coming young guy. So the agent said, 'I'll represent you.' Well, when the strike was over, Paul Playdon took over the back nine of a show called *The Magician*, with Bill Bixby, and he brought me on as a staff writer." The experience that Chase gained on *The Magician* provided the foundation for an Emmy Award-winning career as a writer and producer that included such groundbreaking series as *The Rockford Files* and *The Sopranos*.

Meanwhile, *The Magician* proved to be a difficult show to write "because of this very problem: how do you get this altruistic magician involved in situations he has no business being in?" noted staff writer Walter Brough, who eventually penned four of the show's first ten scripts. "When I came on board, I met with Larry Heath and Steve Kandel, and I pitched a story with the following premise: 'The Magician has a girlfriend—and that girlfriend is going to be killed right in front of his eyes.' That was the plot [for the third episode, 'Illusion in Terror'], and it knocked them off their chairs, because I knew they were sweating that problem out: you had to find a way of getting him involved. Well, I figured, if he had a girlfriend, and the girlfriend is killed right in front of his eyes, but he thinks something's wrong, and then he spends the rest of the episode trying to prove she isn't killed..."[3]

Another highlight of Illusion in Terror is the spectacular closing sequence, set in Blake's workshop, where the Magician literally uses every trick at his disposal to thwart the two bad guys who are chasing him. That particular sequence was filmed at a Hollywood warehouse owned by Mark Wilson. "Mark was much more than the technical consultant for Bill Bixby," said Brough. "Mark was incredibly helpful to Larry and Steve and me. He sat with us frequently, and would tell us about magic tricks, and how the illusion is created, so that you could interpolate it into the story. For example, he helped me set up the sequence in Illusion in Terror in which Bill had to pull off a Houdini-like escape from a burning barn. Mark was always available to us. Any time you needed to ask, 'Can I do this, can I do that, could he catch a speeding bullet?' and so on, he was there."

---

[3] The girlfriend was played by Brenda Benet, who was also Bixby's wife at the time.

On that point, Wilson agreed. "For the first couple of shows, the initial script would often just say, 'Tony does a trick,' and I would have to come up with something to fit into the scene," Wilson told *Genii: The Conjurors' Magazine* in 2004. "When it comes to magic, television writers will run through their stock of what they know very quickly: pulling rabbits from hats, sawing women in half, escapes through trunks, and that's about it. They don't realize what a great reservoir of material we really have." So instead of inserting the magic into an already written story, "I would supply [the writers] with the ideas that they could use for the magic, and they would write the story around them, which was terrific. Of course, the conclusion of every episode was for Tony to get into some terrible trouble—some action sequence—and solve the problem with magic. *Our* kind of magic."

Even with Wilson's help, the writers were still faced with the problem of keeping the action moving in a show that was essentially non-violent. Since magic was Blake's only tool, the magic itself had to be dazzling or otherwise interesting to watch. But it often wasn't, as many critics of the show (TV reviewers and magicians alike) have pointed out. Although occasionally (as in the pilot, as well as the episodes LADY IN A TRAP and BLACK GOLD), we would see Blake use firecrackers or smoke pellets to cause a diversion that enabled him to escape, as a rule, he tended to resort to card tricks or basic sleight-of-hand to distract his opponents. While Bixby had learned to become quite adept at these displays of prestidigitation, they were not exactly "visually exciting," cinematically speaking.

Another part of the problem with the magic—if it indeed could be called a "problem"—stemmed from the particular philosophy that Wilson and Bixby had with regard to magic.

"I think there are basically two schools of magic," explained Anthony Maddox, a former professional magician currently based in Northern California. "One of the kind of 'pure,' 'show-biz entertainer' kind of thing, which is the 'Vegas style' of magic that you see whenever you watch David Copperfield or Siegfried & Roy. Magic is a sort of production number, where the illusions are part of a big set production number. These kinds of magicians want you to 'suspend your disbelief' and pretend that you're really seeing magic. They don't ever want you to think, 'Oh, I'm being fooled.' They think that you should be enjoying the illusion. Mark Wilson, who is a really good magician, comes from that kind of school of thought—where the thinking is, if you expose a trick, or even show how anything is done, you are somehow hurting magic. In fact, the thinking goes, you should never under any circumstances, discuss a trick as a 'trick.' 'It's not a trick, it's an *illusion*,' and you should never talk about how it's done, or anything like that.

"This is in contrast to guys like Penn and Teller, and Harry Anderson, who come from a sort of 'carnival' school of thought," continued Maddox. "Instead of doing this whole show-biz production kind of thing, they're kind of like hucksters, or cheats. They're the folks who say, 'It's a *trick*—everyone knows it's a trick, so why pretend it's not. People enjoy it anyway, so let's not insult their intelligence by pretending it's otherwise.' And so, if something is exposed, or if they expose minimal things along the way to create a better illusion overall, then they'll use that in their act, and they'll use it intelligently. Their shtick isn't necessarily 'Hey, come and see magicians exposed,' but if they can use that to set up something bigger, then it's another tool."

So while Wilson's presence as technical consultant was very helpful to the production staff, at the same time it put them in a bind because of his strong beliefs about how magic should be used on the show.

"I know that, as part of the deal that the studio made with Mark, it was agreed that we wouldn't 'give away ancient secrets of the trade,'" Brough said. "I don't know whether that was a deal-breaker or not, but it was understood that we weren't going to go behind the scenes and show how tricks were put together, although sometimes we did show how Bill would set up an illusion. But it was an illusion, and that's the way we operated. You wanted to keep the illusion that he was a magician, not a magician who's telling you about his trade." However, Brough, who himself was an admirer of both "schools" of magic, also believed that the philosophy behind how magic should be portrayed was not the biggest problem *The Magician* faced.[4]

On the other hand, while the magic on the show may not have been spectacular, there were a few instances (such as in the pilot, as well as in THE CURIOUS COUNTERFEIT and THE EVIL SPIKES) in which Blake used the principle of how an illusion worked, if not the actual illusion itself, to resolve a situation. However, these stories didn't always work, either, because of another basic problem with the series: viewers found it difficult to connect themselves with Bixby's character (a problem that was reflected in the show's low Nielsen ratings throughout the first half of the season). Just as you rarely got a peek inside Blake's head as a magician, you also rarely got a sense of who he was as a person.

"One of the problems that a lot of magicians have, which is talked about often in magic publications and books on the trade, is that there are certain kinds of people who don't like to be fooled," said Maddox. "They think that you're making them look stupid, or calling them stupid, or that magic is a contest of wits. The problem is, if you have a guy in a tuxedo, standing across from you, and he's just fooling you and fooling you and fooling you, how is it that you empathize or connect with that character? You probably don't a lot, because there's a wall between you—he's the guy who's fooling you, and there's nothing really tying you

---

4 In the *Genii* article from 2004, Wilson noted that while the show held firm to the rule of not revealing how a trick was done, exceptions were made in the case of the director of each episode. From a practical standpoint, the director had to understand the workings of a particular trick or illusion in order to stage it properly on film.

together. The thing that may interest you is the magic itself—you might be interested because something amazing, or funny, happens, but you're not really tied very strongly or emotionally to the person across from you at the table.

"That's what you've got going on with *The Magician*. He's not the kind of magician you're likely to feel any empathy for, so who cares?"

It is certainly difficult to find empathy with a character who is reluctant to reveal much about himself. Blake was a man of few words who usually left it to Max to explain his motivations. For example, early in the pilot, a bewildered Nora Duggan (Kim Hunter) suddenly becomes alarmed upon noticing the horrid scars on Blake's wrists, a remnant of his imprisonment. "You know, I really don't know a thing about you," she says. "I don't understand why I trust you."

"One mustn't study a magician too closely," replies Blake. "Never look up his sleeve, and never look under his hat. Just sit back, Mrs. Duggan, and let him do his act." Compounding the matter was Bixby's own low-keyed, mannered style of acting, which occasionally gave the viewer the impression that the Magician, who was supposed to be a man of compassion, was actually someone who preferred to remain emotionally detached from the situation.

It was also very difficult for viewers to relate to a man who lived and operated out of his own sumptuously furnished private airplane—particularly when you consider that *The Magician* aired at a time when the entire country was feeling the impact of the oil crisis. "I know that the staff had a conference about the fact that Bill Bixby was this one person on this huge plane, eating up all that gas, while nearly everyone else across the country was standing in line for hours just to get a gallon of gas for their cars," Keene Curtis recalled in 1996. "The producers thought that that was hurting the show, and so they decided to get rid of the airplane [when the series was revamped in midseason]."

Despite the wrench thrown into the publicity campaign by the Writers Guild strike, Paramount did its best to promote the show. Besides running full-page ads in major trade publications, the story arranged for a cover story in *TV Guide*, as well as a photo feature in the December 1973 edition of *Playboy* in which Bixby performed tricks with the help of bikini-clad models. The studio also commissioned magician Marshall Brodien to produce *The Magician Magic Set*, a licensed tie-in that hit the stores shortly after the show's premiere on October 2, 1973.

NBC opened the series with THE MANHUNTERS, the second episode filmed, featuring a fast-paced climax in which Blake clings to the top of an ambulance driven by the man who's trying to assassinate Max.

"We shot that in the back of the Ambassador Hotel, here in L.A.," recalled director Sutton Roley, whose work in television is often recognized for the kind of visual excitement that Paramount wanted *The Magician* to have. "There were a lot of storage places and delivery areas that we could use to stage the scene where the ambulance drove in and out of the building. Actually, it wasn't much of a drivethrough—it was really more like a storage house, but we made it look like a much longer drivethrough than it actually was by repeating that footage several times. I also used a couple of large bags of feathers, and I had the driver drive right into them, so that the bags would burst open and there'd be feathers flying all over the place. I remember the camera operator thought that was pretty funny—and Bruce Lansbury, when he saw the dailies, loved that sequence, too. He loved all the feathers, because they made it look like the ambulance was going even faster."

Despite Roley's efforts, however, the trade papers panned THE MANHUNTERS, noting that it featured very little by way of magic, spectacular or otherwise. This, as Wilson noted earlier, was symptomatic of many of the early shows.

Even more devastating than the early reviews was the fact that *The Magician* was getting pounded in the ratings. During its first three months on the air, the series faced stiff competition in its Tuesday 9:00 p.m. time slot—*Hawaii Five-O* (the third-highest-rated show in television heading into 1973-1974) and *The ABC Tuesday Movie of the Week* (No. 17). Meanwhile, Alan Armer replaced Barry Crane as producer five episodes into production. Armer was a solid, experienced, take-charge producer with an excellent sense of storytelling (he won an Emmy in 1966 for producing *The Fugitive*), as well as a track record in producing shows with offbeat or difficult concepts *(The Invaders, The Name of the Game)*. Ironically, Crane returned to *The Magician* later in the year, but in another capacity: he directed episode 10, OVATION FOR MURDER. Crane remained one of TV's most active directors until he died in 1985.

The Magician continued to be plagued with problems behind the scenes. When production of the series began, Keene Curtis was dismayed to learn that his character had been stripped of nearly all its color. While the pilot established Max Pomeroy as Blake's best friend and most trusted cohort, by the time the series commenced filming, Max had become a two-dimensional character whose primary function was to "sell the concept" of the series.

"Selling the concept" means reiterating a critical element of the premise (such as why the Magician involves himself in the lives of people in trouble) throughout the first few episodes of a new series, for the benefit of those viewers who might be watching the show for the first time. However, after about three or four episodes, it became less and less necessary to repeat that particular story point. That, in turn, made Max more and more of a dramatic non-entity.

"By the time we got the first script [THE VANISHING LADY, parts of which were filmed on location in Las Vegas], all of the spectacular coloring of my character had gone out the window," Curtis recalled in 1996. "The director of that show felt that no one was going to believe the hawk on Max's shoulder, or that I could speak six different languages, and he felt that those things would get in the way of the show. So all of that went out, and when it did, the kind of phantasmagorical aspect of Max's character had been cut to a two-dimensional size.

"Still, since I had never done episodic television before, working on the show was a new and interesting experience, and I kind of enjoyed it at first. But, after a few shows, when there was less of a need for me to explain what the Magician was doing, I was given less to do, and it was no longer fun for me, and I became kind of disgruntled."

On the one hand, given the difficulties that Heath, Crane and the writing staff had in developing scripts to begin with (about establishing the Magician's motivation for becoming involved, as well as working in the magic in a logical but interesting way), the series was hard enough to make, so perhaps it became necessary to alter Max's character to facilitate production. However, one can certainly understand Curtis' frustrations as well. After twelve episodes, Curtis sent a letter to the studio stating that he was not happy. "I said that this was not what I had come out from New York for," he explained, "and so I asked to be released from the series." Given the problems the show was experiencing, both with its format and with the ratings, changes were likely to be made anyway. The producers were willing to accommodate Curtis, making it an amicable parting.

NBC obviously wanted *The Magician* to succeed—otherwise, the network probably would have canceled it immediately. The network not only moved the series to a new time slot (Mondays, 8pm), but brought forth so many other changes that, by the time the Monday night episodes started airing in January 1974, it was as if *The Magician* were a brand-new series. Bruce Lansbury took over the series from Heath, who continued to be listed as executive producer for the remainder of the season, and replaced producer Alan Armer with Paul Playdon. Lansbury and Playdon worked together before on *Mission: Impossible* and had tapped him to write the pilot for *Escape*, Lansbury's previous attempt at a series about a crime-fighting illusionist.

Playdon brought in a new set of writers, including Larry Brody (*Police Story*), David Moessinger (*Quincy, Murder She Wrote*), and David Chase (*The Rockford Files, The Sopranos*). Meanwhile, with Blake's airplane out of the picture, our hero took up residence at the legendary Magic Castle in Hollywood, where he performed on-camera along with other real-life magicians (including technical consultant Mark Wilson, who appeared regularly as himself throughout the second half of the season). The Magic Castle theater was recreated as a set; these scenes were filmed on a soundstage at Paramount, although exterior footage filmed for THE ILLUSION OF THE CURIOUS COUNTERFEIT was also edited into subsequent episodes for use as an establishing shot. In addition, the opening title sequence was completely changed. The animated hands were dropped; instead, the titles and clips from earlier episodes were matted onto a deck of playing cards that Bill Bixby held up to the camera.

Joe Sirola replaced Keene Curtis, albeit as a new character: Dominick, the owner of the Magic Castle. Unlike Max Pomeroy, however, Dominick was more a functionary than a full-fledged character: his main purpose was to introduce Blake and the other magicians who performed at the Castle (although, as a recurring gag, Dominick was constantly trying to guess how Blake performed one trick or another). The series also became somewhat more action-oriented.

"Playdon's idea was to forget about reality and make the villains as over the top as the hero, which I loved," Brody told Ed Gross of *Closer Weekly* in 2019. "I was a kid in my mid-twenties, and this was my first staff gig, so I looked forward to what seemed like pure fun, letting my imagination roam and bringing the medium something. The good news was that we did indeed to get use our wildest imagination. The bad news was that because this was a mid-season revamp, we had absolutely no time to properly prepare. We had to jump in and turn out script after script pretty much in real time."

As noted earlier, *The Magician* marked David Chase's first real entry into network television. In many respects, it was trial by fire. "Every day I was driving in onto the Paramount lot to work and go into production meetings and going onto the stage and watching as it was being shot and participating in story conferences with [Paul Playdon and] splitting scripts up with him," Chase recalled in an interview with the Television Academy. "We were like four hours ahead of camera and the whole thing was a mess…. We would write until three or four o'clock in the morning—get some pages for the scenes that were going to be shot the next day, those would be sent down to the set, and they'd be shot. The show was failing, [but, for me] it was a huge education, and then everything fell into place for me in my head as to how it worked."

According to magician Dustin Stinett, author of the profile of *The Magician* published in *Genii: The Conjurors' Magazine* in 2004, Playdon approached Wilson about developing a nontraditional weapon for Blake—something only a magician might carry for protection, while staying true to the character's aversion to violence. The solution was a set of steel cards (introduced in episode 17, THE ILLUSION OF THE DEADLY CONGLOMERATE) that enabled Blake to slice through pipe, disable lights, and create other distractions that could extricate him from harm. Besides adding a level of excitement to the final five episodes of the season, the cards managed to level the playing field somewhat for the Magician when it came to hand-to-hand combat. After all, despite his athleticism, the slightly-built Blake was never going to get the best of the burly henchmen he usually had to face; in two episodes in particular (THE ILLUSION OF STAINLESS STEEL

Lady, The Illusion of the Lost Dragon), he absorbs a brutal beating before finally subduing his foe.

Meanwhile, the relocation to the Magic Castle, along with the frequent on-camera appearances of Wilson and other actual magicians (including Larry Anderson, Peter Pit, Ron Wilson, Dai Vernon, Andre Kole, and Mark Wilson's son, Greg), was more in tune with Bixby's aesthetic vision for the series. In addition, no doubt to underscore the notion that Blake operated in a world of illusion, each of the episodes produced by Playdon carried the uniform title "The Illusion of…" (such as The Illusion of the Curious Counterfeit, The Illusion of the Stainless Steel Lady, The Illusion of the Fatal Arrow, and so forth).

But, even with all the aesthetic changes, *The Magician* could not quite overcome the chaotic nature of script production for the last nine episodes. According to Larry Brody, Bixby's aloofness did not help.

LARRY BRODY: Before this show, I'd liked Bixby as an actor, because, to me, he had the perfect combination of comic timing and 'serious drama actor' looks," Brody told Ed Gross of *Closer Weekly* in 2019. "I think he made the best he could of his talents, but he couldn't really light up the screen, because of the script situation. Bixby made his contempt for the writing staff known throughout the half-season by never even bothering to learn a lot of the dialog, preferring to ad-lib and encouraging the other actors to do the same. The result was that key information—the reason a scene even existed—often got omitted during the filming, which meant that we had to try and shoehorn it into the next set of pages and hope the info reached the screen the next day.

I don't believe that this was entirely Bixby's fault, by the way. Paul Playdon had experience as a writer on

Mission: Impossible, but as far as I know, he'd never produced before.[5] And David Chase and I were pretty much noobs to the industry. Bixby didn't reach out to us with his concerns, and we didn't know how to reach out to him. In terms of the storylines, and what we used to call the 'all running, jumping, and no standing still' look of *The Magician*, the series was solid, but with more communication and genuine collaboration between the writing staff and the star, it could have been much, much better.

Meanwhile, despite its new night, *The Magician* faced the same problem it had in its original Tuesday time period: competing against two Top 20 shows (in this case, *Gunsmoke* and *The Rookies*). Nevertheless, according to Mark Wilson, *The Magician* performed well enough on Monday nights to merit serious consideration on the part of NBC to order a second season. Reportedly, the outlook for renewal was so sunny that elaborate plans were made for Bixby to promote the series during the summer of 1974.

"If the show was going to be renewed—as we thought it was—Bill was going to appear in Las Vegas as a magician," Wilson told *Genii: The Conjurors' Magazine* in 2004. "We were working on that show when we found out we were canceled." According to Wilson, NBC dropped *The Magician* not because of ratings, but because of demographics. "Bixby said that NBC's 'mad programmer' was not looking at ratings for those shows he considered borderline. The demographics were the deciding factor. I never

---

5   According to IMDb, though Playdon had previous experience as an associate producer on *Banacek* and *Cannon*, *The Magician* marked his first experience as a show runner.

did find exactly what demographic we had or were failing to capture."⁶

Anthony Blake disappeared from NBC in May 1974, although he did not vanish completely from television. ABC aired reruns of *The Magician* on *ABC Late Night* for six months in 1976, while the series also enjoyed a lengthy run on Britain's ITV throughout the mid-1970s. According to Dustin Stinett, who profiled *The Magician* in 2004 for *Genii: The Conjurors' Magazine*, the popularity of the reruns in the U.K. led to the publication of *The Magician Annual* (Brown Watson, 1975), "a hardbound comic book featuring stories and simple magic tricks." *The Magician* also enjoyed renewed interest throughout the '90s, from a passing reference in a 1994 episode of *The X-Files* to frequent airings on The Sci-Fi Channel (and later, TV Land) between 1993 and 1998. The Sci-Fi Channel airings included special wrap-around interviews featuring staff writers Walter Brough, Steven Kandel, Shimon Wincelberg, and director Sutton Roley.

"I think what happened with *The Magician* is a story of people with high hopes, and with a high concept, who were working against tremendous odds," observed Laurence Heath, whose later credits include *Murder, She Wrote*. "I think the pilot film was good—I basically used the story by Joe Stefano, which was a very good story, and the film came out well. We got good reviews in *Variety*, and so forth, and that's why the show went on that fall. Of course, that was all before the strike. But after that, it was a mess."

---

6   The "mad programmer" is a reference to Marvin Antonowsky, NBC's vice-president of programming in the mid-1970s. Antonowsky became forever known as such following an infamous appearance by Lee Grant on *The Tonight Show with Johnny Carson* in October 1975. Moments before joining Carson on the air, Grant was informed of NBC's decision to cancel her series, *Fay*, after only three broadcasts. Once Grant took the stage, she proceeded to lambaste Antonowsky, denouncing him as "the mad programmer" while reportedly conveying her anger by way of a familiar obscene gesture.

"What happened with that show was a very unfortunate situation," adds Joseph Stefano. "I think that it was doomed from the start."

NBC gave the concept of a troubleshooting magician another try in 1986 with *Blacke's Magic*, starring Hal Linden and Harry Morgan, but that series went poof after six months. In the meantime, real-life magicians such as David Copperfield and Penn & Teller have fared much better on network and cable television. An abundance of magic extravaganzas have aired on prime time over the past five decades, including a few specials hosted by Bixby himself in the mid-1970s. No other network, however, attempted to incorporate magic in a scripted series until 2016, when ABC ordered a pilot for *Deception*, an hour-long drama about a high-profile magician who helps the FBI solve crimes after a scandal ruins his stage career. Jack Cutmore-Scott played the illusionist and Greg Berlanti (*Brothers and Sisters, Everwood*) was the executive producer. ABC not only ordered thirteen series, but gave the series a prominent time slot: Sundays at 10pm, where *Brothers and Sisters* had thrived. *Deception*, however, fared even worse than *Blacke's Magic*. The series premiered in March 2018 and was canceled two months later.

Bill Bixby's next venture into dramatic series television yielded much better results: *The Incredible Hulk* (CBS, 1978-1982), which later spawned three TV-movie sequels. Bixby also enjoyed a successful parallel career as a director, with numerous series episodes and TV-movies among his credits, including *Rich Man, Poor Man, Goodnight, Beantown* (his final series, co-starring Mariette Hartley, which ran in 1984-1985), *Blossom*, and *The Incredible Hulk*. Bixby died of cancer in 1994.

"Bill was one of the most generous guys I ever knew," recalled Walter Brough. "I remember receiving a letter from Bill and

Brenda after we made ILLUSION IN TERROR—it was one of the few fan letters I've even gotten from an actor. They both loved that show, because, of course, they worked together on that show, and they were just so happy to be able to do that. His life was so sad, at the very end. It's a shame he died so soon, and so young, because he really did so many wonderful things in his career."

"Bill Bixby was one of the funniest people I've ever known," added Keene Curtis in 1996. "He was absolutely hilarious. He had a great, great sense of humor, and he was just fun to be around, because you were laughing the whole time. And he also taught me how to make the best martini I've ever had, I'll tell you that!"

Curtis returned to the stage after *The Magician,* starring in such productions as *La Cage Aux Folles, Saint Joan, You Can't Take It with You,* and *Annie* (in which he played Daddy Warbucks). But he also found steady work in television, including regular roles in *One in a Million, Amanda's By the Sea,* and *Empire,* plus guest appearances on such popular network shows as *Cheers, Coach, Caroline in the City, The Pretender, Beverly Hills 90210, Ally McBeal, Star Trek: Voyager* and *The Drew Carey Show.* He also appeared in such motion pictures as *I.Q.,* starring Walter Matthau and Tim Robbins; *Sliver,* starring Sharon Stone; and *Legalese,* starring James Garner. In later years, he endowed a scholarship at his alma mater, the University of Utah, to help graduates embark on their acting careers; in addition, he donated his Tony Award, theatre memorabilia, and many of his personal files to the university's Marriott Library. Keene Curtis passed away on October 13, 2002.

In 2017, Visual Entertainment Incorporated released *The Magician: The Complete Collection,* a four-disc DVD set including all twenty-one episodes, plus the 90-minute pilot. Other than what has been already discussed above, the pilot does not differ much from the series, except for one detail: the name of the Magician was originally Anthony Dorian. According to Dustin Stinett, who interviewed Mark Wilson in 2004 for *Genii: The*

Conjurors' Magazine, Wilson urged Paramount to change the character's name before the pilot went into production because of a potential problem: there was at the time an actual stage magician whose last name was Dorian. Though the studio originally scoffed at the notion, it changed its mind after the real Dorian voiced a complaint shortly after the pilot aired.

As for the series itself, the best episode in our opinion is THE MAN WHO LOST HIMSELF, a charming story in which the situation really does "come right at" Blake (Joe Flynn of *McHale's Navy* plays an ex-con who loses his memory after crashing into the Magician at a rehearsal for a charity bazaar). Marion Hargrove's script features some interesting dialogue, while Sutton Roley's offbeat direction adds to the fun. Other episodes of note include THE QUEEN'S GAMBIT, the only episode featuring both Curtis and Sirola (although the segment was filmed while Curtis was still on board, it was not broadcast until after the series had been revamped; thus, a scene with Sirola was filmed and edited into the beginning of the show); LADY IN A TRAP, featuring Robert Webber as Zelman, the man who had Blake imprisoned in South America (the show also features Kristina Holland, Bixby's co-star on *The Courtship of Eddie's Father*); and THE ILLUSION OF THE EVIL SPIKES, the final episode of the series (directed by Bixby), in which Blake uses footage illustrating his escape from a submerged safe to unmask the identity of the man responsible for the death of a fellow illusionist.

Familiar faces to look for include Mark Hamill, Anthony Zerbe, William Shatner, Yvonne Craig, Carl Betz, Joseph Campanella, Lloyd Nolan, Carol Lynley, Jessica Walter, Lew Ayres, France Nuyen, Macdonald Carey, and Eric Braeden, as well as nightclub singer Amanda McBroom, NFL quarterback Craig Morton, prizefighter Jerry Quarry, and Pamela Britton (Bixby's co-star on *My Favorite Martian*).

THE MAGICIAN EPISODE GUIDE

Opening narration (written by Mark Wilson):

All of the magic you are about to see is performed, without trick photography of any kind, by Bill Bixby... THE MAGICIAN.

THE MAGICIAN (90-minute pilot) (3/17/73)
Anthony Dorian looks into a possible conspiracy involving a plane crash, which he suspects has been staged
Kim Hunter, Elizabeth Ashley, Barry Sullivan, Anne Lockhart, Signe Hasso, Joan Caulfield, Allen Case, Robert Mandan, Richard Van Fleet, Jeff Morris, Tol Avery, Bill Quinn, Holly Irving, Arline Anderson, Don Brit Reid, Dale Tarter, Johnny Haymer, Bruce Watson, Nancy Stephens, Edward Knight, David Moses, Michael Clark
Teleplay by Laurence Heath, story by Joseph Stefano; Directed by Marvin J. Chomsky

THE MANHUNTERS (10/2/73)
Max is marked for murder when he is about to expose a corrupt gambling syndicate
Marlyn Mason, Stephen McNally, Vincent Beck, Scott Walker, Mort Thompson, Lenore Stephens, David Brandon, Marcia Mae Jones, Tony Cristino, Sandra Wirth, Jerry Quarry
Written by Jimmy Sangster; Directed by Sutton Roley

THE VANISHING LADY (10/9/73)
A singer appearing on the same Vegas bill with Tony is kidnapped and held for ransom
Peter Brown, Amanda McBroom, Ramon Bieri, John Karlen, Lilyan Chauvin, Lenore Kasdorf, Byron Mare, Patti Elder, Craig Morton
Written by Harold Livingston; Directed by Marvin Chomsky

ILLUSION IN TERROR (10/23/73)
Tony's new love is struck by a hit-and-run driver, but the ambulance that carries her away never arrives at the hospital
Cameron Mitchell, Brenda Benét, Macdonald Carey, Tom Geas, Bill Zuckert, Barbara Collentine, Carleton Young, John Pickard, Jerry Strickler, Claudio Martinez, Sonja Dunson
Written by Walter Brough; Directed by Paul Krasny

LIGHTNING ON A DRY DAY (10/30/73)
Tony visits a backwoods community to learn the secret behind a young boy's frightened withdrawal into silence
Neville Brand, Geoffrey Deuel, Beah Richards, Mark Hamill, Susan Foster, Frances Reid, Quinn Redeker, George Wallace, Kurt Grayson, Leigh Hamilton
Written by Walter Brough; Directed by Reza S. Badiyi

OVATION FOR MURDER (11/6/73)
Tony comes to the aid of a party host he saw fire a gun at a man, but who can't remember killing him
Jack Kruschen, Susan Oliver, Walter Brooke, Roy Jenson, Wesley Lau, Sid Grossfeld, Dennis Cross, John Craig, Eddy C. Dyer
Written by Walter Brough; Directed by Barry Crane

MAN ON FIRE (11/20/73)
Tony helps a young magician break a blackmailer's hold on the boy's father

Carl Betz, Lloyd Bochner, Brad David, Jane Merrow, Eric Holland, Wayne Heffley, Miguel Landa, Barry Cahill
Teleplay by Sam Roeca, James L. Henderson, and Juanita Bartlett, story by Sam Roeca and James L. Henderson; Directed by Reza S. Badiyi

LADY IN A TRAP (11/27/73)
Tony "reads" a man's mind to locate a rare book stolen from a museum
Robert Webber, Kristina Holland, William Jordan, Anthony Eisley, Rob Townsend, Brad Trumbull, Tom Dever, Gayle B. Cameron
Teleplay by Frank Telford and Marion Hargrove, story by Frank Telford; Directed by Leslie H. Martinson

THE MAN WHO LOST HIMSELF (12/11/73)
While helping an amnesiac try to regain his memory, Tony discovers that the man was involved in a long-unsolved crime
Joe Flynn, Yvonne Craig, George Murdock, Hal Williams, Pamela Britton, John Milford, Yuki Shimoda, Russell Thorson, Joe Perry, Johnny Lee, Allen Joseph
Written by Marion Hargrove; Directed by Sutton Roley

Adam West notes in his memoir, *Back to the Batcave* (Berkley Books, 1994), that Yvonne Craig and Bill Bixby were dating each other in 1967, the year she played Batgirl on *Batman*.

NIGHTMARE IN STEEL (12/18/73)
The estranged husband of Tony's assistant is involved with modern-day pirates, and holds the key to why attempts have been made on the woman's life
Leif Ericson, Christopher Stone, Robyn Millan, Frank Christi, Anne Randall, Charles Picerni, Robert J. Priest, J.P. Burns, Jim Driskill, Glenn R. Wilder, Bob Herron

Teleplay by Walter Brough and Shimon Wincelberg, story by Shimon Wincelberg; Directed by Reza S. Badiyi

SHATTERED IMAGE (1/8/74)
Tony is recruited to help when a little girl's father becomes a fugitive from both the police and the mob after killing a prominent gangster
Joseph Campanella, Leslie Parrish, Edmund Gilbert, Wesley Lau, Tara Talboy, Tommy Madden, Betty Anne Rees, Bob Hoy
Written by Richard Hesse; Directed by Michael O'Herlihy

THE ILLUSION OF THE CURIOUS COUNTERFEIT (AKA RIP-OFF) (2 parts, 1/14/74, 1/21/74)
A crooked prison official holds hostage the daughter of a reformed criminal to force his aid in a scheme involving millions in foreign currency
John Colicos, Carol Lynley, L.Q. Jones, Lloyd Nolan, Joe Maross, Joan Shawlee, Barbara Rhodes, John Devlin, Jack Perkins, Charles Picerni, Eddy Donno, Lassie Ahern, Dai Vernon, Cherie Latimer, Larry Watson
Written by Laurence Heath; Directed by Sutton Roley

Carol Lynley (*The Poseidon Adventure, The Night Stalker, Bunny Lake is Missing*) previously co-starred with Bill Bixby in LAST RITES FOR A DEAD DRUID, a segment episode of *Rod Serling's Night Gallery* that aired in January 1972. "Billy Bixby and I had the same business manager and we knew each other through him," Lynley said to Tom Lisanti in an interview for his book *Carol Lynley: Her Film & TV Career in Thrillers, Fantasy & Suspense* (Bear Manor Media, 2020). "Working with Bill was a pleasure. He was very polite and gracious to the other actors. He was also a funny guy and I liked him a lot."

The Illusion of the Stainless Steel Lady (1/28/74)
A young lady claiming to be the granddaughter of a reclusive film star, who happens to be a friend of Tony's, asks his help in contacting her
Anthony Zerbe, Beth Brickell, Nina Foch, Edward Winter, Mark Lenard, Ian Wolfe, John Ragin, Dolores Quinton, Penny Santon, Biff Elliott, Jim Burk
Teleplay by Richard Hesse and Paul Playdon, story by Richard Hesse; Directed by Alexander Singer

The Illusion of the Queen's Gambit (2/4/74)
While Tony performs at a benefit aboard the Queen Mary, a group of thieves is stealing the proceeds
William Shatner, Katherine Justice, Brooke Bundy, Paul Mantee, Byron Morrow, William Vaughn, Jack Rader, Heath Jobes, Barry Brooks, Ron Wilson, Peter Pit, R.J. O'Hara
Written by Edward J. Lakso; Directed by Don Weis

The Illusion of the Black Gold (2/11/74)
Blake sets out to rescue a scientist who was mysteriously kidnapped moments after defecting to the U.S.
Eric Braeden, Lynda Day George, Milton Selzer, Normann Burton, Curt Lowens, David Cryer, Michael Ivan Cristofer, Ben Andrews, Abraham Sofaer, Peter Hellmann, Anthony Mason, Bob Okazaki, Michael St. Angel, Bob Golden, Ed Fury, Wallace Earl, Richard Reed, George Jordan, Robert Beau-Geste, Glen Wilder, Alan Gibbs
Written by Edward J. Lakso; Directed by Arnold Laven

The Illusion of the Lost Dragon (2/18/74)
Tony takes on a modern-day Chinese warlord to help a friend retrieve a valuable jade dragon

Joseph Wiseman, France Nuyen, Philip Ahn, Soon-Taik Oh, Nobu McCarthy, Frank Michael Liu, Pat Li, Lester Fletcher, Adele Yoshioka, Joycelyne Lew, Ruth Ko, Susan Ikeda, Larry Anderson

Written by Howard Berk; Directed by Alexander Singer

The Illusion of the Deadly Conglomerate (2/25/74)

At the request of a down-on-his-luck former magician, Blake investigates the disappearance of a man from skid row

Eugene Roche, Jack Ging, William Sylvester, Michele Marsh, Peggy Rea, Bill McLean, Crane Jackson, Russ Grieve, Charles Wagenheim, Damon Douglas, Ralph Montgomery, Larry Anderson

Written and Directed by David Moessinger

The Illusion of the Fatal Arrow (3/4/74)

A pair of archers commit a murder, after which a psychic assures Tony that more will follow

Jeremy Slate, Tim Matheson, Murray Matheson, Pamela Franklin, Fred Sadoff, Grace Gaynor, James Victor, Greg Wilson, Nino, NaniDarnell, Larry Anderson, Robert Ruth, Ford Lile, Billy Livingston, Michele Livingston

Written by Paul Playdon and David Chase; Directed by Leslie H. Martinson

The Illusion of the Lethal Playthings (3/18/74)

A murderous toymaker sets his sights on Tony Blake when he interferes with the madman's plans

Louis Hayward, Joanna Miles, Scott Hylands, Simon Scott, Richard O'Brien, Ivor Francis, John Devlin, Argentina Brunetti, Andy Albin, Peggy Doyle, R.J. O'Hara, Larry Anderson, Charles Picerni, The Bob Baker Marionettes

Written by Larry Brody; Directed by Jack Arnold

THE ILLUSION OF THE CAT'S EYE (3/25/74)
Tony is called in to investigate the theft of a missing art treasure—a solid silver cat—from a museum with tight security
John Dehner, Don Gordon, Marianna Hill, Claudette Nevins, Joseph Ruskin, David Frankham, Joseph Mell, J. Jay Saunders, Vic Vallaro, Larry Anderson, Philip David
Written by David Chase and Paul Playdon; Directed by Paul Stanley

This episode marked a reunion of sorts: David Frankham provided the voice of Sergeant Tibs in the animated Disney classic *101 Dalmations* (where he first met and became friends with Angela Lansbury), while Bruce Lansbury, Angela's younger brother, was the showrunner of *The Magician* at the time Frankham appeared in this episode.

"When I got the script, a key scene called for a leopard to kill my character up on a landing," Frankham recalled in his memoir, *Which One is David?* (Bear Manor Media, 2012). "As I read the script, I thought, 'Oh, they'll do this with process photography.' I got to the set and there was the landing with some stairs. Up at the top of the landing was a cage with a real black leopard inside! I thought the scene would be done in two shots, one of me reacting, and one of the leopard jumping without me in the actual shot. The director, Paul Stanley, said, 'No, we need you on camera as the leopard leaps toward you.' I was very apprehensive about the idea, so the big cat's trainer led me upstairs and put my hand into the cage. 'He's very tame,' the trainer told me.

"Ye gods, but I was nervous as the leopard paced up and down. He seemed to be tame enough. 'He's trained to do this,' the trainer explained. 'You'll be on the camera, and I'll be off camera to the left. At a sign, I make a move, and the leopard will toward yet over you.'

"The shot had to be done in one take for realism and for the leopard's sake since he was trained to do it from the start," Frankham continued. "If I botched my role, the mistake would impact the leopard's work. The trainer clicked his fingers. I looked startled as that huge animal leaped right over my head and into the arm of the trainer. He was like a pussycat. It looked very real on camera. Even though I was absolutely petrified, the shot worked beautifully just as the trainer said it would." Franklin's other screen credits include *Master of the World, Return of the Fly* (both directed by Roger Corman), and Is THERE IN TRUTH NO BEAUTY, one of the most famous episodes of the original *Star Trek*.

THE ILLUSION OF THE EVIL SPIKES (4/15/74)
While shooting a movie, an escape artist is killed performing his signature trick
Jessica Walter, Lew Ayres, Richard Evans, Robert Burr, Tom Rosqui, Herbert Anderson, Frederic Down, George Wyner, Virginia Hawkins, Dale Tarter, Mel Allen, Larry Anderson, Denise Demirjian, Andre Kole
Written by David Moessinger; Directed by Bill Bixby

THE UNTOUCHABLES ORIGINAL SERIES (ABC, 1959-1963)

118 episodes, plus two-hour pilot

Starring	Robert Stack as Eliot Ness
Also Starring	Nicholas Georgiade as Enrico Rossi
	Abel Fernandez as William Youngfellow
	Anthony Zerbe as Lt. K.C. Trench
	Jerry Paris as Marvin Flaherty (first season)
	Anthony George as Cam Allison
	Paul Picerni as Lee Hobson (beginning with the second season)
	Steve London as Jack Rossman
and	Bruce Gordon as Frank Nitti (recurring)
Narrator:	Walter Winchell
Executive Producer:	Desi Arnaz
Based on the book	*The Untouchables* by Eliot Ness and Oscar Fraley

Produced by: Quinn Martin (first season)
Alan Armer (second and third seasons)
Alvin Cooperman (fourth season)
Leonard Freeman (fourth season)
Theme by Nelson Riddle

MEN OF ACTION

This ground-breaking series won four Emmy Awards, jump-started the television careers of at least fifteen people, and kept ABC on the map when the network was still struggling. It made icons out of a true American hero and the man who played him.

It also prompted a torrent of protests from the Italian-American community, irritated two federal agencies, and set off three Congressional investigations.

It was a morality play of the good guys taking on the bad guys, against incredible odds, and winning. Yet it was also considered part of the "vast wasteland" of network television.

Made with a boldness and style not seen in television before, it prompted other shows to upgrade the quality of their product just to compete.

It was also a kind of prime-time paradox, criticized by many who could not, or would not, comprehend its humongous success. After all, something has to be "pretty good," and "pretty well made," to have had the phenomenal effect *The Untouchables* had on television audiences during its four years on ABC (1959-1963). The story of Eliot Ness has been imitated and duplicated many times since, but none of the others—not even the blockbuster movie version of 1987—have come close to matching the tremendous widespread impact the original still carries today.

Simply put, *The Untouchables* was simultaneously the most loved and most despised television show of its time.

From the time he first read the adventures of Sherlock Holmes as a teenager, Eliot Ness had wanted to be a detective, a desire which heightened after his sister married an FBI agent named Alexander Jamie. After graduating from the University of Chicago, he found work as an investigator with a credit company before landing a post with the Prohibition Bureau of the U.S. Department of Justice.

But Ness soon found that he was "a white knight on a broken horse." The vast, powerful booze syndicate run by Alphonse "Scarface Al" Capone in the late 1920s existed partially because nearly every politician—and more than a few law enforcement officials—were on Capone's payroll. This angered Ness no end, to the point where he became determined to do something about it.

In 1929, Jamie brought Ness to a meeting of "the Secret Six," a special citizens committee formed by the Chicago Chamber of Commerce devoted to fighting crime. That gave Ness the impetus to take the matter into his own hands. He wanted the Bureau to form a small, select group of agents who were above reproach. Each would be investigated thoroughly; some would even be recruited from other cities to ensure that they had no connections with the Chicago mob. Ness presented his case to United States District Attorney George E.Q. Johnson, who not only approved the idea but named the twenty-six-year-old leader of the special squad.

Ness selected ten agents: Marty Lahart, "an Irishman with a perpetual devil- may-care grin," and an avid sports buff "who could, and did, quote batting averages, football scores and fight results by the hour if given the chance"; Sam Seager, a former prison guard at Sing Sing who was "absolutely fearless until he got into a hotel bathroom" (he wouldn't get into a strange bathtub without first cleaning it with a disinfectant he always carried in his suitcase); Barney Cloonan, a barrel-chested giant who was always "a stalwart when it came to physical action;" Lyle Chapman, a former college football player, and a meticulous man with a keen analytical mind (he often told Ness "he was happiest when working on a difficult office problem"); Tom Friel, a onetime Pennsylvania State Trooper; Joe Leeson, "a genius with an automobile" whose exploits at tailing a suspect's car were legendary; Paul Robsky, a telephone expert from New Jersey; Mike King, a man "who could sit in a room with half a dozen people and be the last one you would notice," but who also had a mind like a sponge; Mike Gardner, a college football All-American; and Frank Basile, Ness' personal driver, a former convict whom Ness had reformed.

Once, after an incident in which Lahart and Seager defiantly refused yet another hefty bribe from Capone's men, Ness decided to hold a press conference designed to "tell the world—and 'Scarface Al' Capone—that Eliot Ness and his men couldn't be bought." Every newspaper and motion picture company in town covered the event. By the next day, Ness and his squad were known in the press, and by the rest of the world, as "The Untouchables."

The battle continued for the next two years, until Ness finally nailed Capone on charges of income tax evasion in October 1931. After several failed appeals, Capone began an 11-year sentence at the federal penitentiary in Atlanta in May 1932; he was later moved to the facility on Alcatraz Island near San Francisco, where he died in 1947.

Although the likes of Bugs Moran, Klondike O'Donnell, Machine Gun Jack McGurn, Bomber Belcastro, Tough Tony Capezio, and the Terrible Touhys were still very much at large in 1932, Ness believed none of them, dangerous though they all were, ever belonged in the same class as Capone. "Those who remained were only muscle hoodlums, certain to be exterminated in their own feuds or by the revolver of the newest rookie policemen," Ness wrote in the concluding chapter of his book. "None possessed the genius for organization which had made Al Capone criminal czar of a captive city. The other men of violence would try...but they would be conquered by the workaday channels of the law." Believing that their work was done, Ness disbanded his team of Untouchables shortly after Capone was transported to Atlanta.

In 1955, Ness began writing his memoirs of the Capone case. Co-authored by veteran UPI reporter Oscar Fraley, *The Untouchables* is a straightforward, page-turning account of the battle which Ness frequently likened to a football game of epic proportions. The best-seller also captures the essence of Eliot Ness—a brilliant tactician respected by his peers, and a man of quiet courage, ever mindful of the possibility that sudden death was always around the corner. But Ness never lived to enjoy the book's success. He died of a heart attack on May 16, 1957, at age fifty-four, shortly before *The Untouchables* went to press.

In early 1959, Desi Arnaz announced that Desilu Productions had purchased the movie and TV rights to *The Untouchables* and that it would adapt Ness' memoirs as a two-hour drama to be broadcast on consecutive weeks on its anthology series, *The Desilu/Westinghouse Playhouse*. Although *The Untouchables* would "premiere" on American television, it was actually filmed for the big screen, because Arnaz planned on releasing the film theatrically in Europe. Budgeted at nearly $600,000—far above the $250,000 fee Arnaz would receive from CBS for the broadcast rights—Arnaz figured he would easily earn back his investment, plus another $1 million-to-2 million profit, from the box-office receipts overseas. (The film was, in fact, distributed internationally in late 1959, under the title *The Scarface Mob*.)

Emmy-nominee Paul Monash wrote the script, which was helmed by motion picture director Phil Karlson (*Kansas City Confidential, The Brothers Rico, Walking Tall*). The producer was Quinn Martin, a former sound editor whom Arnaz had given his first break in television.

Apparently, Arnaz had once given thought to casting himself as Eliot Ness. "Desi sprung that idea on me," recalled former Desilu and CBS executive Martin Leeds in *Desilu: The Story of Lucille Ball and Desi Arnaz* (William Morrow & Co., Inc., 1993). "I asked him, 'Des, do you really believe that the world is waiting for Ricky Ricardo to pull the plug on Al Capone?' He started to laugh and said, 'Okay, not such a good idea, sport.'"

Arnaz then sought film star Van Heflin, then later Van Johnson, for the lead role. Johnson initially accepted, and the four-week-long shoot was set to begin on March 16, 1959. However, three days before the start of production, Johnson backed out of the deal after his wife (who was also his agent) asked for more money. Arnaz then put out a mad scramble to locate his next choice, Robert Stack.

Although he had done some television, mostly in such prestigious anthology series as *Playhouse 90, Producers Showcase, Celanese Theater*, and *Schlitz Playhouse of Stars*, Stack was primarily a motion picture actor, with nearly thirty films under his belt at the time. He was, of course, "the boy who gave Deanna Durbin her first screen kiss" in *First Love*; his other films included *A Date with Judy, To Be or Not To Be, Bullfighter and the Lady, The High and the Mighty, Good Morning, Miss Dove*, and *John Paul Jones*. He received the 1957 Academy Award nomination for Best Supporting Actor for his role as Lauren Bacall's maniacal husband in *Written on the Wind*.

Arnaz located Stack late on Saturday night, with shooting still scheduled to commence the following Monday morning. Stack initially declined, but changed his mind after some intense lobbying by his agent Bill Shiffrin.

Although the real Ness was flanked by ten men, Stack would have just seven at his side for the two-parter—Lamaar Kane (Peter Leeds), a law school graduate; Eric Hansen (Eddie Firestone), an ex-prison guard at San Quentin; Martin Flaherty (Bill Williams, father of *Greatest American Hero* William Katt), a former Boston cop with an excellent bureau arrest record; Jack Rossman (Paul Dobov), Ness' wiretapping expert; William Youngfellow (Abel Fernandez), a former All-American gridiron hero; Tom Kopka (Robert Osterloh), an ex-Pennsylvania State Trooper; and ex-con Joe Fuselli (Keenan Wynn), Ness' closest friend. Monash patterned these characters very closely after the actual Untouchables, although he did exercise some poetic license in making Lamaar Kane a husband with two children. In his book, Ness states that he deliberately selected men who did not have wives and/or families because he knew "the job was too hazardous for a man with marital responsibilities."

Neville Brand was cast as Capone, with Bruce Gordon as his first lieutenant Frank "The Enforcer" Nitti. Patricia Crowley played Betty Anderson, Ness' fiancé. Also featured, albeit as "bad guys," were future *Untouchables* Paul Picerni and Nicholas Georgiade.

As Abel Fernandez recalled, the actors playing the T-men "clicked" from the very beginning:

> ABEL FERNANDEZ: None of the eight of us had ever worked together before that show—we'd known each other, but we'd never worked together. On the first day of shooting, we filmed the scene where we all meet for the first time. We're all in the big room, and then Keenan Wynn comes in. Bob tells everyone that Keenan's an ex-con, and all that, and that somebody's got to get inside Capone's operation so we could tap the phones. We run through all the dialogue—Phil Karlson, of course, was directing us, and Paul Monash was also on the set, watching. At one point during the sequence, one of us says, "Somebody's got to get in there, so we could tap his phones." Now, you couldn't have planned what happened next. Everybody looks at each other, and then Bill Williams says, "Well, I don't mind playing in Capone's backyard. Who's gonna loan me a nickel for the phone?" Instinctively, everybody looked at each other, and we all reached into our pockets at the same time. And Phil Karlson just went crazy! He said, "Cut—print that thing, right now!" And Paul Monash said, "I couldn't have written that any better!"
>
> That was the first day—the first thing we did. So we knew something big was going to happen.

Producer Quinn Martin was responsible for much of the show's unique visual style. Within ten minutes of Part One, you'll recognize many of the features that would become staples of the eventual *Untouchables* series as well as the shows that Martin would later make as an independent producer: the movie-like quality of the editing, the artsy camera angles; the night-for-night shooting, and the staccato narration of Walter Winchell.

Because the story was unveiled in a semi-documentary style, akin to the motion picture newsreels of the 1930s, Desi Arnaz's selection of Winchell as narrator was a master stroke.

"He gave the viewers the feeling that *The Untouchables* was 'Honest to God' real," said Alan Armer, who produced the series for three seasons. "Now, most people today (especially younger people) don't remember who Walter Winchell is, but at that time he had a nationwide radio show, and he was a syndicated newspaper columnist. His voice and his name were recognized all over the country. And that voice, and that manner, gave *The Untouchables* a feeling of legitimacy. He gave it the smell of reality."

Some of the narrations did not come easily to Winchell.

"He had a problem with sibilance," said Alvin Cooperman, who produced half of the fourth-year episodes. "We used to record him once a month. When we had all our narrations written out, he'd come in, always with his hat (and usually with a pretty girl). He had false teeth, and because of that, he had problems saying his S's. He'd have to read things like 'On Saturday, September Second, Eliot Ness and his Untouchables...,' and he'd have to do it over and over and over! But, of course, he was wonderful."

The first half of the two-parter aired on April 22, 1959—ironically, less than a week after the premiere of another Prohibition drama, *The Lawless Years*, based on the exploits of New York undercover cop Barney Ruditsky (James Gregory). But while Ruditsky never caught on with the viewers, Eliot Ness and *The*

Untouchables hit it big, scoring a 31.8 rating. Buoyed by excellent reviews, Part Two finished even better at 37.6—meaning that nearly 40 percent of the entire national television audience watched Ness and his men put away Capone for good.

The tremendous response prompted CBS to explore the possibility of turning *The Untouchables* into a weekly series. Just because the real Ness broke up the team at the end of the Capone case, the TV Ness didn't necessarily have to follow suit. After all, there was still plenty of material from the era waiting to be exploited.

There was one minor obstacle, though. Stack had no interest in doing a series—indeed, considering that nothing of the kind had ever been mentioned in his original contract, he was quite surprised when the matter came up. But the forty-year-old star changed his mind after Arnaz offered him a hefty salary, plus a percentage of the show's profits.

Stack and Fernandez were the only Untouchables actors from the original two-parter who reprised their roles for the series. Jerry Paris assumed the role of Flaherty, while Nick Georgiade played Enrico Rossi, a material witness to a gangland execution whom Ness protects, and later recruits, in the first episode of the series (THE EMPTY CHAIR) as the team's driver. Charlie Hicks appeared in several of the early episodes as Lamar Kane.

About halfway through the season, Paris left the show and was replaced by Anthony George (*Checkmate*) as agent Cam Allison. Paris went on to co-star in *The Dick Van Dyke Show* and later became a prominent TV director.

Cam Allison was killed off in the last episode of the first season (THE FRANK NITTI STORY) and was replaced by agent Lee Hobson, played by Paul Picerni, for the remainder of the series. Steve London also joined the show in the second year, playing Jack Rossman on a recurring basis.

The Untouchables premiered on October 15, 1959—on ABC, which had aced out CBS for the rights to the show. THE EMPTY

CHAIR picks up right where the two-parter had left off. Capone's conviction leaves a void at the top of Chicago's crime world, and both Nitti (again played by Bruce Gordon) and bookkeeper Jake "Greasy Thumbs" Guzik (Nehemiah Persoff) battle each other over who should rightfully succeed him as head of the organization. Nitti became Eliot Ness' most frequent adversary.

"Bruce was wonderful," said George Eckstein, who began as a casting director on the show, then later wrote nine episodes. "Bruce was great to write for, because he brought so much energy, and vitality, and excitement to the screen. He was a little 'over the top' sometimes, but always entertainingly so."

Gordon was so popular that he managed to continue appearing on *The Untouchables* even after Nitti had been gunned down at the end of the first season (in THE FRANK NITTI STORY).

"Dorothy Brown, who was the head of continuity acceptance at ABC [i.e., she was the censor], absolutely loved Nitti," recalled Alan Armer. "He was her favorite character, and she always bugged us to put him in more shows simply because she loved him! She thought he had humor, and that he had—well, she never used the word 'balls,' but she always thought there was a lot of testosterone working in that character. Another reason we were able to do that with Nitti was simply because of the way the series was done. The stories were not told in chronological order. One week the story might have taken place in 1934, the next week in 1928, the next week in 1932, so that even if Nitti was killed in a show that took place in 1934, we could always go back to an earlier year, and he would be very much alive. And that's what we did."

Gordon's agreement with the series required him to appear in at least four episodes a year. He would eventually star in a total of twenty-four shows.

Although the stories on *The Untouchables* were clearly fictional, the smell of reality was so overwhelming that many viewers—including quite a few in high places—took it very,

very seriously. The FBI, for example, took exception to THE MA BARKER STORY, in which Ness apprehends the legendary gangstress, even though the real Ness had nothing to do with the case. James Barrett, head of the U.S. Bureau of Prisons at the time, was so horrified by the first hour of THE BIG TRAIN, a two-parter in which Capone forges an elaborate escape plan with the help of a crooked prison guard, that he threatened to have the licenses of ten ABC affiliates revoked unless they refused to air the second half of the show. Although the stations refused to capitulate, ABC did air a disclaimer at the start of Part Two, emphasizing that the story was completely fictitious: "Nothing herein is intended to reflect unfavorably on the courageous and responsible prison guards who supervised Al Capone during his internment in the Federal Penitentiary in Atlanta, and during his transfer from Atlanta to Alcatraz."

Some real-life mobsters took it seriously, too. Alvin Cooperman had planned to take a crew to Chicago to film exteriors during his tenure with the show in 1962. "We had sent out a press release to that effect," he recalled. "About a week later, my secretary buzzed me and said, 'There's a gentleman on the phone who wants to speak with you, but he won't give his name.' Well, I talk to everybody, so it didn't matter to me whether he gave his name. I picked up the phone. The voice said, 'Mr. Cooperman?' I said, 'Yes.' He said, 'I understand yer plannin' to come to Chicago to shoot some film for *The Untouchables*.' I said, 'Oh, yes, that's right.' He said, 'I'm warnin' ya—Don't.' And he hung up. So I went back to the powers that be. They didn't think it was a good idea... So we canceled it."

Desi Arnaz also received numerous crank calls and thinly veiled "death threats" throughout the run of the series. According to the *Desilu* book, underworld assassin "Jimmy the Weasel" Fratianno once claimed that Arnaz was the target of a Mafia "hit" ordered by Sam Giancana because of the "bad publicity" the show gave to Al Capone and Frank Nitti. When told that the hit was canceled because Fratianno "couldn't get close enough," Arnaz responded, "I don't know how the hell they couldn't get me. I always drive to the studio by myself, and I've never had a bodyguard in my life."

Arnaz did have to resolve another kind of emotional conflict when he decided to make *The Untouchables*. He'd grown up with Capone's son, who pleaded with him not to do the show. Arnaz, though, figured that even if he passed on the show, someone else would inevitably make it. The newspaper editorials denouncing Capone belonged to the public domain. Capone's son unsuccessfully filed suit against Desilu Productions for defamation.

Some "gangster-types," on the other hand, found *The Untouchables* kind of amusing. "Sometimes when I was in Vegas," said Nick Georgiade, "I'd meet some of these guys who were considered of 'ill repute,' and they would tell me 'the real way' those stories occurred."

The Italian-American community, however, was not amused—they felt *The Untouchables* persisted in the stereotype that "all gangsters are Italians, and all Italians are gangsters." That certainly wasn't the case. Although some of the villains on the show were of Italian descent (because the gangsters pursued by the real Ness were also Italian), an equal number of "Italian characters" were portrayed as shopkeepers, businessmen, and other honorable occupations. In fact, one of the Untouchables (Enrico Rossi) was Italian. Still, many prominent Italian-Americans fought hard for the demise of the show.

Yet, for all the different organizations that rallied against *The Untouchables*, millions of viewers loved the show. After a slow start, *The Untouchables* quickly caught fire—by the end of its first season, it was consistently finishing among the Top 20 shows on television, as determined by the Nielsen rating service.

It was also a "marquee" show that a lot of actors from stage, screen, and television wanted to do, because the gangsters were such plum roles to play. The guest stars had the best lines, and usually the majority of the screen time.[7]

Like the great anthology shows, *The Untouchables* showcased many of the finest performers of our time every week: Barbara Stanwyck, Thomas Mitchell, Ruth Roman, J. Carrol Naish, Dan Dailey, Jack Warden, Martin Balsam, Cloris Leachman, Robert Vaughn, Dick York, Jim Backus, Mike Connors, Jack Klugman, Lee Marvin, Nehemiah Persoff, Keenan Wynn, William Bendix, Dane Clark, Martin Landau, Victor Jory, Vic Morrow, Barry Morse, Claire Trevor, Cliff Robertson, Anne Francis, Elizabeth Montgomery, Arthur Hill, Lloyd Nolan, Vince Edwards, Peter Falk, Nita Talbot, Brian Keith, Jack Elam, Michael Ansara, Clu Gulager, Patsy Kelly, Frank Sutton, Harry Guardino, Sam Jaffe, Joseph Wiseman, Henry Silva, Dorothy Malone, Murvyn Vye, Herschel Bernardi, James Gregory, and Patricia Neal.

The series also attracted many motion picture directors, such as Howard W. Koch, Tay Garnett, Jerry Hopper, Robert Florey, Richard Whorf, and Ida Lupino, and screenwriters such as Ben Maddow, Harry Essex, and John Mantley.

The production values were certainly "movie-like" in quality, from the costumes to the vintage automobiles, to how the episodes were filmed and edited. "We tried to make every one of the *Untouchables* special," said Walter Grauman, who directed nineteen episodes. "We tried to make them like 'features,' instead of 'television shows.' We used special effects, and had

---

7 This was about five years before *Batman* (ABC, 1966-1968) did the same thing, and more than ten years before *Columbo* (NBC, 1971-1978). In the case of *Batman*, the contrast between the colorful arch-villains and the straight-laced Batman and Robin was even more exaggerated, given the camp format of the show. In the case of *Columbo*, the guest murderers not only had more screen time, but almost always had the first act of the show to themselves. By design, Columbo usually did not appear until about twenty minutes into the episode.

huge, elaborate sets, which you didn't see on any of the other shows that were on at the time."

The show had other kinds of standards that you didn't often see in television. Most of the action on *The Untouchables* takes place at night. Whereas most TV shows back then would film those sequences during daylight hours (using black muslin over the lens, so that when filmed it would appear darker than it was), Quinn Martin insisted on shooting those scenes during the evening hours, when it actually was dark, to achieve a more gritty (and more realistic) cinematic effect. The results were stunning. Martin's "night-for-night" shooting (or "QM in the PM," as it was known colloquially) forced other TV shows to upgrade their quality of production if they wanted to compete with the look of *The Untouchables*.

"Night-for-night" also meant that days were long and that costs were high (because of all the overtime that had to be paid to the crew for working late hours). That was one reason why *The Untouchables* was one of the most expensive shows of its time. It was also one of the most grueling—eighteen-hour-long shooting days were not unusual. In fact, after one of the show's camera operators was felled by a heart attack, a law was passed in California that limited the number of overtime hours in television production.

In its first season, *The Untouchables* won four Emmy Awards: two for the series (Robert Stack as Best Actor, Ben Ray and Robert Swanson for Outstanding Achievement in Film Editing), and two for the original *Desilu Playhouse* episodes (Charles Swanson for Cinematography, Ralph Berger and Frank Smith for Art Direction and Scenic Design). Also honored with Emmy nominations that year were Phil Karlson, for his work on the Desilu two-parter; and the series itself, as Outstanding Dramatic Program. The series won several other honors, including the *Look* magazine award for Best Dramatic Show.

Stack's accomplishment is particularly remarkable, considering what he had to work with. Because the series was written to showcase the gangsters, as a rule, Stack's dialogue didn't present him with many "dramatic" opportunities.[8] In fact, most of his scenes "were terribly expositionary—he was always on stakeout, or at his desk," said George Eckstein. "But Bob made those scenes work because of the intensity he brought to Eliot Ness. That's the thing that made him stand out, and which made the show stand out from all the other cop shows on TV at the time. Bob, as Ness, didn't just 'not like' the bad guys—he had a pathological hatred for them. And it was that intensity that drew the audience in every week."

Stack recognized that he would have to play Ness as a "counterpuncher"—i.e., as a stark contrast against the gaudy flamboyance of the guest villains. He often likened Ness to "a pot boiling with the lid flipping on top." Although a man who usually kept his cool in the face of disappointment, Ness could also explode at a moment's notice. It was that unique combination of quiet strength and unpredictability, Stack determined, that made Ness an extraordinarily powerful character.

An outgoing man, Stack could be searingly funny right until the very moment he heard the word "Action!" Once he went completely into the character he was playing, though, he was just about unflappable.

> PAUL PICERNI: In one of the shows directed by Paul Wendkos, Bob and I had a scene together where we're at the morgue, and there's a body on a gurney covered with a sheet. Ness is supposed to throw back the sheet and identify the body.
>
> Now, the previous weekend, I'd gone fishing with a friend of mine, and we'd caught a 15-foot-long blue shark off the waters of Santa Cruz Island. I cut off the

---

[8] Efrem Zimbalist, Jr. faced a similar challenge about five years later, when he began playing Inspector Erskine on *The FBI* (1965-1974).

head of the shark, and I brought it to the set that day, thinking I'd use it to play a joke on Bob. So I told our prop man about it, and I told Wendkos, and we put the shark's head on the gurney where the head of the "stiff" would be. Pretty soon everybody on the set knew what was going on—except for Bob.

So, we rolled the cameras, Wendkos says 'Action!' and we walked into the room. Bob pulls back the sheet... and without batting an eye, he said, 'Yeah, that's him!'

While the gangsters were the most colorful characters on *The Untouchables*, they were also the most brutal. More bullets were fired, knives wielded, cars exploded, and corpses gathered per episode than on any other television show at the time. Ironically, although the series would be ultimately blasted for its frequent depictions of violence, it probably would have been criticized for being unrealistic had it not done so.

ALAN ARMER: If you do the research on that period of history (or any period, for that matter, dealing with crime syndicates and/or the Mafia), you'll find that these people did a lot of terrible, horrifying things. They stuck people with icepicks. They drenched people with gasoline and set fire to them. And so, if you're going to tell stories about these kinds of people, you cannot do so with any honesty without inserting a certain amount of violence. Whether we went over the line... well, that's something you could debate for hours.

I'll say this, though: the programming people at ABC were always very damn nice to us. They pretty much let us do whatever we wanted to do, in terms of shaping the series.

I first came on board in the second season. Jerry Thorpe [who replaced Quinn Martin as executive producer that year] and I met with the people from Standards and Practices (the censors), who cautioned us about violence. Because there had been terrible rumbles in Washington with the P.T.A., and with the Italian-American society, the censors said, "We will be watching you. You've got to be careful. We can't kill too many people. The show can't be too violent...."

Then, the next day, Jerry and I had lunch with the programming people. They kind of winked at us, and said, "We know you've had a meeting with the network censors, and we know that they all have jobs to do. But, just between us, we know that the audiences will expect, and even demand, a certain amount of violence every week. Violence is what made this series successful. Therefore..."

Now, they didn't say this in so many words, but they were actually encouraging us to use as much violence as they felt we could get away with."

Ironically, as shocking as *The Untouchables* was in its day, the brutality of the show is practically mild, and certainly not nearly as graphic, when compared to some of the acts of violence regularly depicted in contemporary movies and television shows. At the same time, however, because *The Untouchables* had to adhere to the standards of its time, the violence of the show was presented in a style that was actually more effective, in terms of having an impact on the audience. Unlike much of the cinematic violence of today, *The Untouchables* leaves a lot to the viewer's imagination.

WALTER GRAUMAN: The first show I directed was THE NOISE OF DEATH, written by Ben Maddow. That was also one of the first shows ever made, and I don't think the censors were as apprehensive about the show at that point as they would eventually become after it first aired.

Ben wrote a scene early on in which a woman discovers her husband's body hanging from a meat hook in a walk-in freezer. I filmed a two-shot of Bob and Jerry Paris as they walk in the freezer; Bob strikes a match, and they notice something off to the side. The audience doesn't know what they've seen, but they can tell from their reactions it's not pretty. Then Norma Crane, who played the wife, enters the freezer. Bob blocks the door and tells her, "Don't go in there!" But she pushes her way through. She, of course, becomes horrified by what she sees. At that point, I cut to the body, which I shot from about the waist down, but you can see that it's suspended from a meat hook. So we played that scene mostly off the actors' reactions.

I did something similar with THE WHITE SLAVERS, with Dick York. That script had a scene in which Dick and his brother bring a truckload of Mexican prostitutes across the border, but when they discover Ness is waiting for them, they take the girls into the woods and shoot them. The girls have no idea what's going to happen to them—they're poor, uneducated women, who think they're going to Hollywood to become movie stars.

By that point, the censors were scrutinizing the show very closely. After Dorothy Brown read the script, she said to me, "Walter, you cannot show these poor innocent girls being killed. We can't allow it. It's much too violent." I said, "Dorothy, let me see what I can do."

Now, as it turns out, Dick York's character is really a sort of "reluctant" heavy. So I had Dick leaning against a tree, so that he sees—and we see—the girls in the center of a circle of killers with submachine guns, and then we see their guns firing from all sorts of angles. Then I cut to a close angle of Dick as he watches, and he starts to vomit. We played the killing of all these girls off of his retching against the side of the tree.

Grauman directed many of the best episodes of the entire series, including THE ANTIDOTE (with Joseph Wiseman), THE MASTERPIECE (with Rip Torn), THE PURPLE GANG (with Werner Klemperer), and THE RUSTY HELLER STORY (for which Elizabeth Montgomery received an Emmy nomination).

ALAN ARMER: The network censors sat on us, and we often had fights with them. For example, they'd let us hurt or kill people, but we couldn't hurt any animals. We once had a scene in a show where a pair of pet rats were killed; we had to change that. Also, they never seemed to mind whenever we had people shot or blown up, but they frowned upon having people killed with 'personal' instruments, like knives, because (1) using a knife is more painful and personal than using a gun, and (2) they didn't want us to show killings done with objects that could easily be found in every home. Apparently, there was another ABC show in which a character was strangled with a coat hanger; because there were a number of 'coat hanger stranglings' that occurred throughout the country within months of that broadcast, the network initiated that particular policy.

Sometimes when they reviewed the script or the film, and recognized problem areas, their suggestions were very helpful. Dorothy Brown was particularly helpful in that regard. We did a show called 'The Organization' in which a character was stabbed in an icehouse. At first, Dorothy objected, because of the network's stance on using 'personal' instruments. But we needed the stabbing in order to make the story work. Dorothy came over to the editing room, and she went over that one scene with the cutter and me for about ninety minutes until we found a solution that we both found acceptable.

Dorothy was a very gutsy lady, and it was not unusual for her to work with us in that way.

Yet even the most intense moments on-screen were not as frightening as some of the actual attacks leveled against the show. *The Untouchables* was the target of three Congressional investigations: the Senate Subcommittee on Violence on Television, the Subcommittee on Juvenile Delinquency, and the Subcommittee on Communications. ABC programming president Thomas Moore was subpoenaed three times to testify before the juvenile delinquency panel.

Executive producer Jerry Thorpe was also summoned to Washington, as a witness before the committee on violence.

"Jerry told me he'd never been so frightened before in all his life," said Armer. "Those committees were determined to crucify the people who produced that series. They subpoenaed all our files, including all the confidential memos Quinn had written to his staff. It was a pretty scary time."

Indeed, *The Untouchables* was blamed for causing practically every social ill imaginable—even though it was fundamentally a moral show that regularly presented mankind (as personified by Ness) in an uplifting light. Sure, the gangsters lived the good life, with custom-made suits, flashy cars, beautiful women, piles of money, and, of course, plenty of booze readily at their disposal. They were also morally bankrupt, in contrast to the prototypical hero, Eliot Ness—a truly untouchable man who cannot be tempted by evil because he knows it has absolutely nothing to offer him.

The stories on *The Untouchables* were quintessential morality plays of right triumphing over wrong, with no gray shadings. No matter how clever the bad guys were (and they often came up with ingenious stratagems), they were always brought down at the end. The guest characters almost always had an Achilles heel (greed, arrogance, lust) which Ness would inevitably use against them. "In every promotional appearance we did, the first thing people asked was, 'Do you think *The Untouchables* is the reason why kids are on the streets picking up guns, and all of that?'" said Abel Fernandez. "I still work with youth groups, and I'm often asked the same question. My answer has always been the same: We were the good guys. We always showed that good prevails over evil. No matter how smart the bad guys were, they always went out crying."

Still, Newton Minow, then-chairman of the Federal Communications Commission, blasted *The Untouchables* in May 1961 in his now infamous speech denouncing television as "a vast wasteland." In addition, the Italian-American community continued to mount its campaign against the show. It organized protests outside ABC's headquarters in New York City. It coordinated nationwide boycotts of the products that sponsored the show (and eventually convinced the Liggett & Myers Tobacco Company, one of the major sponsors, to withdraw its participation in the show). It pressured ABC to issue a new disclaimer at the end of each episode stating that "certain portions of this story have been fictionalized."

Finally, representatives for both ABC and Desilu Productions announced a pact made with the National Italian-American League to Combat Anti-Defamation regarding the content of future episodes of the show. The major points of the agreement were as follows:

(1) The series would no longer give Italian names to any of its fictional hoodlums.
(2) Enrico Rossi would be given a more prominent role in the show.
(3) The show would seek opportunities to feature characters with Italian names that would reflect "the great contributions which the millions of American citizens of

Italian extraction are making to advance the American way of life."

What did the producers do? "Obviously, we had to shift gears," said Armer. "There were, in fact, other groups involved in organized crime at that time. There was a Jewish Mafia in New York. The Irish were also heavily involved. So we used Jewish names, Irish names, German names, Dutch names, Greek names, and Spanish names. And what happened, of course, is that by the end of the second season, we managed to offend just about every ethnic group except the Italians." (In fact, by the time Armer left the series at the end of the third year, about the only names the show could use without offending anyone were nondescript, like Smith and Jones.)

However, despite all the controversies that dogged the show during its second season, *The Untouchables* continued to attract big names and even bigger Nielsen ratings. The series consistently ranked among the Top 20 shows (and eventually finished as No. 8); by the end of the year, nearly 40 percent of every television household in the country watched it every week. Stack, Montgomery, and the show itself all were honored with Emmy nominations. The continued success of *The Untouchables*, not surprisingly, begat several other "crimebuster dramas," most notably *The Roaring Twenties*, *The Asphalt Jungle* (based on the W.R. Burnett novel, and the 1950 film adaptation by Ben Maddow), *Cain's Hundred* (created and produced by Paul Monash), *Target: The Corruptors*, and *The New Breed* (Quinn Martin's first series as an independent producer). While some captured the style of the original better than others, none came close to drawing the same kind of audience numbers. All of these shows were gone by the time *The Untouchables* began its fourth season in September 1962.

The fourth year brought a new producing team—Leonard Freeman and Alvin Cooperman—and a new approach that would change the scope of the series. The storylines had less violence and more complex characterizations; Ness in particular was explored more fully as a "rounded personality," as *Variety* reported at the time. Not only would Ness actually lose some cases (as in THE NIGHT THEY SHOT SANTA CLAUS, wherein a murderer he tracks down is acquitted at the end of the show), he would be made vulnerable in other ways (he is blinded and held hostage by a psychotic in A TASTE OF PINEAPPLE). Freeman promised that the violence in the fourth-year shows would not be "without motivation. In fact, in some shows, we will have no killings at all."

> ALVIN COOPERMAN: Lenny and I came in at the tail end of the controversy surrounding the show over the violence and the complaints from the Italian-Americans. So we looked for other kinds of stories that we thought were dramatically interesting. We decided to show Eliot Ness was human. We did shows like A TASTE OF PINEAPPLE—which the people at Desilu hated because they never wanted Eliot Ness to be hurt or shot.[9] But we felt kind of "trapped" by that point, in that we couldn't go "the full route" in terms of telling stories about organized crime."

The new producers also brought in a second-unit production team that would shoot new location footage for use on the show.

---

9 Given this observation, it's worth noting that ABC held A TASTE OF PINEAPPLE for broadcast until the end of the 1962-1963 season—long after Cooperman and Freeman had been replaced as producers of the series. (Like all television networks, ABC determined the order in which each episode of *The Untouchables* aired and could withhold a show from being broadcast for any reason.) Therefore, it's quite possible that ABC didn't think much of PINEAPPLE, either. The network finally aired the episode on May 21, 1963 as the last first-run show of the series.

COOPERMAN: We thought about what we could do to change the "look" of the show, and make it more exciting, without having to deal with more violence. At the time, we had the old RKO "New York" street at Desilu. We'd change the signs, or paint over the storefronts, but it was still the same street. So I had the bright idea of saying, "Why don't we put a second unit on film?" That hadn't been done before on the show. We shot all over Los Angeles we found warehouses and streets and skylines and things like that. Bob Butler was one of the second-unit directors who shot exteriors for me; later that year, he directed some of our shows.

Freeman and Cooperman also brought in jazz artist Pete Rugolo to compose new music to complement the original orchestrations by Nelson Riddle.

Desilu also announced early in the campaign that several of the fourth-year episodes would double as pilots for prospective series. Barbara Stanwyck played a missing persons investigator in ELEGY and SEARCH FOR A DEAD MAN, both of which were designed to launch a show called *The Seekers*. The episodes with Dane Clark (BIRD IN THE HAND, JAKE DANCE) were pilots for a possible spinoff entitled *The White Knights*, while THE FLOYD GIBBONS STORY was a vehicle for a potential Scott Brady series called *Floyd Gibbons: Reporter*.

"I don't like spinoffs unless the show involved fits into the series in which it's seen," said Desi Arnaz at the time. "We don't want to weaken *The Untouchables*, but these properties do integrate into the series." It also didn't hurt that the show was still an audience draw (it placed in the Top 20 late in the 1961-1962 season).

While the new music and visuals enhanced the look of the show, the thematic changes were in sharp contrast to the basic morality play that made *The Untouchables* the success it was.

No matter how many bullets were fired each week, the audience knew that Eliot Ness, and all that he stood for, was going to win in the end. When that was taken away from him, the viewers left the series in droves. By the middle of the season, Freeman and Cooperman were gone; Alan Armer was brought back as executive producer for the balance of the year.

Two other Freeman/Cooperman shows are worth noting, though. COME AND KILL ME includes an authentic recreation of a horse race at Arlington Park. THE SNOWBALL, written by George Eckstein, has become known as "the Robert Redford episode." Indeed, THE SNOWBALL was the episode shown at the Museum of Broadcasting History's tribute to *The Untouchables* held in Los Angeles in 1993—an event in which Stack, Georgiade, Picerni, Fernandez, Armer, Grauman, Eckstein, and Cooperman all participated. (Stack also appeared at the special screening of *The Scarface Mob*, sponsored by American Cinematheque, that took place at the Raleigh Theater at Paramount Studios in 1996.)

Compounding the ratings problem: the grueling production pace of the series finally took its toll on star Robert Stack, who was sidelined for several weeks after hemorrhaging a vocal cord. Not surprisingly, he declined an offer to return for a fifth year (although the ratings were down, ABC was still interested in continuing the show). Eliot Ness and *The Untouchables* retired at the end of the 1962-1963 season, although the reruns have continued to air throughout the world ever since. In addition, Columbia House released fifty-four of the 118 series episodes, as well as the original *Desilu Playhouse* two-parter, on VHS in the late 1980s. CBS Paramount released all four seasons of *The Untouchables* on DVD in 2016.

Stack completed several motion pictures before returning to television in 1968 in *The Name of the Game*. He also starred in two other series (*Most Wanted*, *Strike Force*), as well as several more features and TV-movies, before becoming host and narrator of *Unsolved Mysteries* in 1987, a role he maintained through the end of the series in 2002. Although best known for his dramatic roles, Stack also did a lot of lighter fare in his twilight years, including *Beavis and Butt-Head in America*, *King of the Hill*, and *BASEketball*, not to mention his memorable turns in *Airplane!* and *Caddyshack II*.

Stack also sent up his most famous role in LUCY AND THE GUN MOLL, a 1966 segment of *The Lucy Show* that parodied *The Untouchables*. Normally, of course, whenever he examined a bottle of booze, Stack as Ness would take a sip from the bottle, then immediately spit it out. But in LUCY AND THE GUN MOLL, Eliot Ness got *drunk*.[10]

---

10 The *Lucy* episode also features Bruce "Frank Nitti" Gordon, who also headlined his own series in 1966: *Run, Buddy, Run*, a parody of *The Fugitive* co-starring fellow *Untouchables* alum Nick Georgiade.

THE UNTOUCHABLES MOVIE

In 1962, Desilu Productions announced plans for a motion picture feature called *The Story of Eliot Ness* that would star Robert Stack. Although that project never materialized, the company re-edited the two-part episodes THE UNHIRED ASSASSIN and THE BIG TRAIN and released them theatrically across the country (as *The Guns of Zangara* and *Alcatraz Express,* respectively). *The Scarface Mob* was also distributed to American theaters for the first time later that year.

But Paramount Pictures, which purchased Desilu Productions in 1967, continued to kick around the idea of an *Untouchables* movie for many years. Nothing ever developed, though, until 1985, when Ned Tanen, then-president of Paramount's Motion Picture Group, and producer Art Linson *(Fast Times at Ridgemont High)* made a deal to bring the story of Ness and Capone to the big screen.

Linson approached Pulitzer Prize winning playwright David Mamet *(Glengarry Glen Ross, American Buffalo)* to write the script. Mamet had been a fan of the TV series, but after re screening the original two-parter, he decided to go in an entirely different direction. "Just because something is true, that doesn't necessarily make it interesting," he told *Time magazine* in 1987. "Ness and Capone never met, and Capone went to jail for income tax evasion, which is not a very dramatic climax. So I made up a story about two of the guys—Ness and Jimmy Malone, the idealist and the pragmatist."

After three drafts, Linson sent Mamet's script to director Brian DePalma *(Phantom of the Paradise, Carrie, Dressed to*

Kill, Blow Out). While DePalma was intrigued by the notion of doing a period piece, he envisioned *The Untouchables* not as a "gangster" movie, but as a kind of Western in the tradition of *The Wild Bunch, The Searchers,* and *The Magnificent Seven.* In fact, DePalma included an homage to those films in the final cut—the scene in which the Untouchables are on horseback as they thwart a liquor smuggling operation near the Canadian border.

What DePalma liked most about Mamet's script is that he found himself caring about the characters. "Our Eliot Ness is a gentle family man required to get tough to get Al Capone," he told Gene Siskel in 1987. "In the TV show, he already was tough—a sort of stern father figure, as played by Robert Stack. But our version is closer to the truth."

Actually, that's not the case. While the real Ness was a gentle family man who strived to keep his work from interfering with his home life, he did not marry the former Elizabeth Anderson until long after the Untouchables disbanded. As noted earlier, Ness selected men who were not encumbered with wives and families because he knew the matter at hand was far too dangerous for someone with marital responsibilities. Nor did Ness need to "get tough" to take on Al Capone. He already had the fortitude to turn down bribery money at a time when nearly every other law enforcement official in town was on the take. He never underestimated the opposition or the degree of danger in any situation. These characteristics, of course, were at the core of the Eliot Ness brought to life by Robert Stack in the original series.[11]

Paramount also claimed authenticity for their incarnation of Ness by having an eighty-five-year-old former Federal agent

---

11 Stack's interpretation of Ness was also validated by none other than Elizabeth Ness herself. In a personal letter to Stack (and, later, in an article published in *TV Guide*), Mrs. Ness commended the actor for capturing the essential qualities and mannerisms of her husband, such as "his quietness of voice—the same gentle quality that characterized Eliot."

named Al Wolff, who was supposedly the last of the actual Untouchables still alive at the time, act as a special consultant to Kevin Costner. However, while Ness and Fraley may have changed the names of the actual agents for privacy purposes, there is no mention of anyone named "Al Wolff" in the original book.

The movie Ness is "closer to the truth" in one respect: his age. The real Eliot Ness was twenty-six at the time he formed the Untouchables. By comparison, Costner was thirty-one when the movie was in production, while Stack was forty when he first played Ness in 1959.

William Hurt, Harrison Ford, and Mel Gibson were among those initially considered for the movie Ness. But the role went to Costner, fresh off his first big-screen success (Jake in *Silverado*), who captured the combination of "naivete, earnestness and strength" that Linson and DePalma sought.

Sean Connery was cast as Malone, the crusty beat cop who teaches Ness "the Chicago way." Connery would later win the Academy Award for Best Supporting Actor. Rounding out the rest of the Untouchables are Andy Garcia (as rookie cop George Stone) and Charles Martin Smith (as Oscar Wallace, the accountant who originates the idea to nail Capone on tax evasion charges).

Robert DeNiro had been Linson's original choice for Capone, but when the two-time Oscar winner wouldn't commit to the role, Linson hired Bob Hoskins instead. When DeNiro finally said yes, Hoskins was released. DeNiro then disappeared for most of the first ten weeks of the three-month-long shoot. When he returned, he displayed many of the lengths he'd gone to prepare himself to play Scarface Al—he gained twenty-five pounds, wore nose plugs to broaden his nose, and endured several long days in a barber's chair while hair stylists meticulously patterned his head to match photographs of the real Capone. DeNiro also had his wardrobe styled after Capone's, right down to his underwear:

he ordered silk boxers from A. Sulka & Co., the same company that custom-made Capone's shorts.

While the basic storyline of the *Untouchables* movie—the good guys versus the bad guys, a few good men against the world of gangland corruption—is unchanged from that of the original memoir and TV series, the DePalma/Mamet rendition of Eliot Ness, as noted earlier, is considerably different. When Malone is gunned down by a Capone underling, Ness changes from a man who operates within the boundaries of the system to an avenger determined to get the job done by any means possible—even cold blooded murder, as depicted in the climactic scene where Ness dispatches Frank Nitti after a dramatic rooftop confrontation. This particular characterization, more than anything else in the movie, undercuts the tremendous integrity of the real Eliot Ness.

Costner had concerns about this portrayal of Ness. Although Mamet and DePalma told him his fears were unfounded, by the end of the production the actor was convinced he was right. "Could I win the audience by the end of the movie? It's a big hole to climb out of," he told *Time magazine* in 1987. "People are always saying they don't want another Rambo. Well, here's Ness. He doesn't have all the answers. He doesn't do his thinking with a gun. He's troubled. He's naive. The critics are begging for something different. When you give it to them, they don't like it."

As big-budget ($24 million) entertainment, though, the film delivered at the box office, grossing $16 million in its first week alone. Everything was done on a grand scale, from location shooting in Chicago to costumes by Giorgio Armani, and an elaborately recreated section of LaSalle Street designed by Patrizia von Brandenstein (*Amadeus*). It's also a lot bloodier than the original *Untouchables* ever could have been. The legendary sequence in which Capone pummels three men to death with a baseball bat—a scene from Ness' memoirs that ABC would never allow in the TV series—is brought to life in the movie in all its brutality.

Another signature of the *Untouchables* movie is the dialogue-free scene in which Ness protects a key witness (Capone's bookkeeper) from an assassination attempt at Union Station. Filmed in slow motion, DePalma modeled the suspenseful sequence after the famous "Odessa steps" montage of Sergei Eisenstein's *The Battleship Potemkin*. This scene was not in the original script—DePalma improvised the whole thing after the studio refused to pay $200,000 for a vintage train. As it was, though, it still "wasn't easy to get Paramount to pay for the scene," DePalma said in 1987. "It cost about $20,000 alone simply to light the set. You need a lot of extra light to shoot in slow motion. And we shot the scene in six days, which cost another $100,000."

The film also received Oscar nominations for Best Art Decoration (von Brandenstein and Hal Gausman), Best Original Score (Ennio Morricone), and Best Costume Design (Marilyn VanceStryker).

After filming was completed, Linson had a chance meeting with none other than Robert Stack on the plane ride back to Los Angeles. Although Stack was skeptical about some of the changes made to Ness' character, he did offer the producer a word of encouragement: "If *The Untouchables* does as well for you guys as it's done for me, you'll be very, very happy." The movie was one of the Top 20 grossing films of 1987.

Coincidentally, *The Untouchables* was also the focus of controversy (albeit indirectly) as a result of an incident in a Maryland theater that happened to be showing the film. A man who had asked a noisy patron to lower his voice was severely beaten, along with his brother, by ten men—while none of the other forty moviegoers in the house did anything about it. Neither the police nor the complainants, however, indicated that the assailants' violent outburst was triggered in any way by the contents of the movie.

Paramount also reissued the original *Untouchables* book in 1987 to coincide with the release of the movie. *The Untouchables* is presently available both on DVD and Blu-ray.

INTERVIEW WITH ROBERT STACK

Ed Robertson (ER): It seems to me that you and the real Eliot Ness had at least one thing in common as a character trait.

Robert Stack (RS): What would that be?

ER: Well, I know from reading your book [*Straight Shooting*; Macmillan, 1980] that one of the values you learned as a kid and as a young man was teamwork, and all that comes with teamwork—loyalty, playing within the rules, reliance upon other members of the team. Having also read the original book by Oscar Fraley, that's the essence of Eliot Ness.

RS: Yes. I knew Oscar Fraley. He was a friend.

ER: I also understand that you based how you played Ness on three people.

RS: Right. You're talking about the three bravest men I ever knew: Audie Murphy; Carey Loftin, the dean of Hollywood stuntmen, and an old chum of mine; and Buck Mazza, my Navy roommate, and a decorated dive-bomber pilot. They were all the best in their fields, and they never bragged.

ER: I realize I'm probably the 1,000th person to say this to you, but you certainly had the intensity of Eliot Ness nailed to a tee.

RS: I made up my mind early on that the man had to be a counterpuncher. I could not be like Gene Barry with a cane in *Bat Masterson*. I could not be out there competing with the flashy guys in the pin-striped suits—the gangsters.

The real irony (and this may have been kicked around a thousand times) is the fact that, after four years—although you don't realize that you're doing a show for four years—you "become" that character in the eyes of the audience. But I never thought I *was* Eliot Ness.

Prior to this, I got an Academy Award nomination [for *Written on the Wind*] for a part in which I'd played a maniac, and chewed the scenery, and beat up my wife, and tried to kill my best friend, and all of that. It was "over the top," if anything. And to go from that to being criticized for being "The Great Stone Face"... *[Laughs]* somehow, it doesn't fit!

ER: No, it's like night and day.

RS: But, see, when you play the same part 120 times, that's what you "become" in television. And so inadvertently, all of a sudden, I "became" Eliot Ness.

But the show worked well, particularly in the first two years. Our best directors were Wally Grauman and Stu Rosenberg. Johnny Peyser was good, too. But Walter was really our best director, because there was always an offbeat "Sword of Damocles" hanging over the head of every character in his shows. There was always a tempo—boom, bah-dah-dah, boom, bah-dah-dah—and that's the story. When someone sits down, and says, "Tell me what happened to you the last twenty years, Harry, and..." *Wrong!* Because, always in the wings, there's somebody with a knife, or a gun, or something. And that's what keeps people awake.

Essentially, the first two or three years, we had the best Jewish actors. We had the Actors Studio—we had

Joe Wiseman, Marty Balsam, Peter Falk. We had all the top actors on Broadway, coming in and doing our show as a lark. We had writers like Ben Maddow, who were motion picture writers—because this was a whole new breakthrough in a medium they didn't know the first thing about.

Now, after a while, you couldn't buy those guys any longer, because around the fourth year, they weren't available. In other words, we were getting people in the first few years who did it as a jaunt, as a tip of the hat. You go out in the open market back then and try to buy a Ben Maddow, good luck!

ER: I know there were three main studios that Desilu had at the time: Desilu/Cahuenga, Desilu/Gower [the old RKO studios], and Forty Acres. I also know there were several different producers over the course of each year, and different production crews, because you had a lot of shows to film each year—thirty or thirty-two shows a year, which is a lot, compared to today. Did you ever shoot more than one show at once?

RS: We did once—once or twice when we were losing one or two days each week. The shows started out five, then went to six, then went to seven days, and we were losing two days a week. All of a sudden, we started doing two at once. And I've got to tell you, man, that's when you're really going crazy—you don't know what your name is, where you're going.

We also filmed most of our stuff on the Forty Acres, and we shot occasionally, once maybe every week or ten days, at Gower. But most of the stuff was shot on our little Forty Acres "Chicago Street"—in fact, they used to call us "The Fanatics," because that's where we lived, practically.

ER: Yeah, and when you're working eighteen-hour days, you turn around, and it's three in the morning, and then you've got to be on the set at, what, seven or eight the next day…

RS: It was terrible. Now, it didn't begin like that, but once we won everything—as you know, we won six Emmy nominations, and four Emmy awards, that first year. And once you've got that fire in your belly, then you just keep trying to make it as good as you can. That's what winning an Emmy will do.

ER: The story of how the original pilot—I mean, the original two-parter on *The Desilu Playhouse*—and how you became Eliot Ness, is kind of strange.

RS: It's not strange at all, speaking as someone who comes from a motion picture background. We didn't do television.

But first, to get something straight—because you mentioned the word "pilot." You may or may not know (and I hope you do know) that this was never a pilot.

ER: Right—it was intended only as a one-time show, just as many of the segments on *Desilu Playhouse* were "one-time only" shows.

RS: That's right—because you're one of the very few who *do* know this. And the word "series" was never mentioned contractually, because they wouldn't have gotten anyone to do it.

ER: I understand that they wanted to ultimately release the two-parter as a feature in Europe.

RS: That's true, called *The Scarface Mob*—and that was going to be it. That's when Phil Karlson called me and said, "Kid, they're going to try to get you to do a series. Don't do it—you'll hate yourself in the morning. Say you're a film actor, and you don't do that kind of crap. It's terrible."

That's when I went to Desi Arnaz, and I said, "Is it gonna be anything good?"

And he said, "Amigo, we're gonna make it the best damn show in all of television."

I said, "Okay, but if you screw it up, I'm gonna come back and shoot you!" Because, believe me, I was scared to death, and I sat up all night with Rosemarie (my wife) before I decided to do the series. And then I thought I was taking a terrific risk, anyway, because Bob Taylor, Barbara Stanwyck (before she did *The Big Valley*), and Henry Fonda (*The Deputy*), all these big movie stars, had done television, and they'd all fallen flat on their face! So, film people were scared about TV.

So the image I want to get clarified quickly is that this was not something that was done with a proviso of doing a show, hoping it would go to series. They never had the guts to put into the contract anything having to do with a "series" —they wouldn't have gotten any actor to do it. And as it was, neither the director, Phil Karlson, nor two of the major actors, Keenan Wynn and Bill Williams—all of whom also came from film—ever did do the series.[12]

ER: I know that you owned 25 percent of the show, and it sounds like you had a lot to say about the overall makeup, production, and running of the show.

RS: That's correct, but the ownership doesn't have much to do with anything. You'll find that anybody who is the Big Daddy of any show in which they are the lead, without whom they cannot make the show, has an input. I like to think that I was brought up as a professional, by people like Clark Gable, and a few others, to be a pro, to do your job, and not to interfere and bastardize the author's intention. The thing I fought for was a quality. It was a very expensive show. We worked horrible hours—in fact, they

---

12 Stack's memory is mostly correct; neither Karlson nor Williams were involved in the *Untouchables* series. Wynn, however, played the title character in the second-season episode Augie "The Banker" Ciamino.

passed a labor law as a result of our show. We lost our camera operator, Wilbur Bradley, as a result of a heart attack. The show was a trial by fire. It was the most difficult television show at that time.

What Quinn Martin tried to do, at least the first year, was to make "motion pictures" for television, before that term was ever misused. For the first time, we brought motion picture technology (special effects, and stuff like that) to television, where it doesn't fit. It was like pouring a quart of water in a half-pint glass—clinically, you just cannot do that. And this is why everybody got sick, and ran down, and finally the show went off the air. I couldn't go a fifth year. I was just exhausted.

But we tried so damned hard after we won all those Emmys to make it special. And it was a very rare, breakthrough kind of a show that did not really work, or was designed for, television. At least, it didn't work in terms of "living with it," because it was not structurally viable. You could not long-run this show and work eighteen-hour days. But we tried so hard to make it good—and this is, I know, not a great story, but I can remember working till two, and three, and four in the morning.

ER: Although *The Untouchables* was considered one of the most shocking and violent shows on television of its time, by today's standards, it's kind of tame. But I think that's one of the reasons why the show still holds up—there's a definite style to the way the violence is portrayed, or dramatized, compared to the sheer "blood and gore" that you often see in movies and on TV today. What are your thoughts on this matter?

RS: I think portions of what you say are quite true. But I think that if you're going to get into the "violence on the show," we really ought to do it definitively. First of all, we should define what violence is, semantically. Some people call it "action," some people call it "violence." It's contingent upon the time frame, the mores, and the behaviors of the time. And as you say, as the years go by, things change. Now you have to go in there with *Die Hard 3,* or *Independence Day,* and unless you eviscerate and blow people's heads off, you're not going to get an audience.

Now, every time anybody gets into the cliché "violence on television," it gets into a semantic that has absolutely nothing to do with theater. It has to do with a clinical word which, again, if you use the proper rationale, can either be called "action" or whatever, so long as the audience is properly motivated to listen, or tune in, and empathize with the good guys winning.

I'll give you an example of what I'm talking about. I did a movie with John Belushi called *1941,* and he kept forgetting his lines. I said to him, "John, what's wrong?'

He said, "Mr. Stack, I—"

I said, "Don't call me Mr. Stack."

He said, "Okay, Bob. You know, my family was never around when I grew up. I mean, hell, you were the Man—the guy with the hat. You were Eliot Ness. You were my authority figure."

I said, "Really?"

He said, "Yeah, and the same thing goes for Chevy Chase. You were the Big Man. You were the good guy. You were beating the crap out of the bad guys!"

Now, if you've got "violence" with Capone winning and beating Eliot Ness, that's a dangerous premise. They had a long battle between psychiatrists claiming it was good and bad. Some said, "This is actually a catharsis for the average viewer — instead of his punching the boss out in the mouth, he goes home, and watches Eliot Ness beat up Al Capone, and he doesn't have to resort to physicality." I could spend two hours on this very subject, because I've been through it, chapter and verse. But you simplify it by using the word "violence," because that's only one small detail of the whole mishmash.

They once tried doing a story about gangsters, which failed. Same kind of premise. I told the producer the reason it doesn't work is that nobody gives a screw about the gangsters, or what happens to them, whether they lose their wives or kids—they're a bunch of assholes. It doesn't matter what happens to them. You've got to have an "Eliot Ness."

Now, you talk about violence—did you see the movie?

ER: Yes, I did.

RS: Okay. Remember when the brains and stuff were all over the wall? Remember the baseball bat sequence? Well, that's one scene we tried to get in our show for the better part of four years, and couldn't do it. They were marching to a different drummer. They were able to do all the things in the movie (because, of course, of it being a "motion picture") that we could not do on television because of Standards and Practices.

So you do have one point, in the nostalgic aspect of the fact that "it's an old-fashioned show and it ain't that violent" (except, obviously, for the machine guns and stuff). But the violence factor was vitiated, after much, much argument by psychologists and psychiatrists, as long as the end result was that the kids, or whoever was listening in, sided with the good guys against the forces of evil. I think that pretty much circumvents the "violence" factor. You cannot tell the story of Al Capone and do it with Chinese—you do it with Italians, *and you tell it like it was*. So long as you happen to side with Eliot Ness against Al Capone, then I think that's okay.

ER: You guys always won at the end. And the audience knew that was going to be the case every week.

RS: And a lot of people empathized with that. As I told you—I mentioned John Belushi, and I mentioned Chevy Chase. I mentioned others who found in this legendary, apocryphal character of Eliot Ness, the prototypical hero, that they "became" that character, in a sense, emotionally, and that they got their jollies out of psychologically kicking the crap out of Al Capone, as opposed to kicking the crap out of their boss, or their wives, or their kids, or whoever else... *[Laughs.]* At least, that's what one psychologist told me.

The only thing people seem to remember about *The Untouchables* is the so-called "violence." They forget the behavior pattern. They forget that entire bowling leagues were scheduled around the show.

ER: Right. It was one of those shows where people dropped what they were doing every Tuesday night so they could watch it.

RS: And that's the only real determinant: Does it "work"? Does it work for an audience?

ER: I understand that driving those vintage cars could be a lot of trouble if you didn't know exactly what you were doing.

RS: Even if you did know what you were doing, nobody had any idea that the show was going to run as long as it would. They could've bought that whole fleet of cars for nothing, but instead, they rented the damned things every year.

Some of the cars had no brakes. I remember one time racing toward the camera in my 1930 Buick when Boom! the brakes failed. All of a sudden, it was "We've got no brakes, hang on!" and *Bo-ing!* I went right through the sound stage wall.

Plus, some of the fellas who came out from New York had no idea of how to handle a stick shift. I remember one poor actor who'd been practicing all morning for his big scene—driving the getaway car. The bad guys ran out and jumped in the car, and he gunned the motor and put 'er in gear—only he'd stuck it so long, he put the car in reverse and proceeded to knock down the camera, scatter the crew, and run right over the foot of the director...! *[Laughs.]*

They weren't exactly "versed in action," as it were.

ER: Meaning, they weren't as accustomed to dealing with props and special effects and things like that, as film actors are.

RS: Right. But I must tell you, though, that those New York actors were also the greatest to work with. I'm not knocking Hollywood actors, but the stage actors were great because they always came prepared. We had little or no time for rehearsal because we had to be on camera most of the time. And I would tell every one of them—wonderful actors, like Steve Hill, who now does *Law and Order*—I'd say, "Look, it's up to you. You're Legs Diamond—you be good. The better you are, the better I'm gonna be. If you're lousy, I'm lousy. So, be wonderful—do your homework!"

And this is why we got these guys. They'd say, "This guy Stack is nuts, he'll let you go. He told us that we're the stars."

I'd say, "*You are* the stars. The guys in the pinstriped suits are the stars. I'm the guy that kind of comes around and counterpunches. So you've got to be wonderful."

And they all were! That's why I killed myself staying up nights, because I had to get ready to be one-on-one with some of the best actors in America.

ER: You had several interesting, dramatic experiences with actual criminals that took place around the time of the show.

RS: Some years ago, Rosemarie and I went up to Lake Tahoe to see a friend of ours, Phyllis McGuire, perform at Cal-Neva. I believe we knew that she was, at the time, the girlfriend of Sam Giancanna, a real-life "godfather" who was also a Public Enemy Number One. He was killed about six months after I indirectly met him.

After the show, we went backstage to visit Phyllis in her dressing room. At some point, we both had the same feeling that someone was watching us—and in fact, we did notice what looked to be an eyeball peering through a crack in the door. Although it puzzled us why anyone would want to eavesdrop on our conversation, we proceeded as if nothing were the matter. (After we'd gotten home, we heard a report that "a notorious crime boss" had been seen at the nightclub.)

Sometime later, when Phyllis dropped by to see us, Rosemarie told her we'd been aware that her boyfriend had spying on us all along. "I'm glad you didn't let on," Phyllis told us. "He would've turned purple if he knew you hadn't been fooled. As it was, that night he flew back to Chicago so he could tell all his friends that he'd really put one over on Eliot Ness!"

That gives you an idea of how slim the cleavage line between fantasy and reality sometimes is. The gangsters didn't believe *The Untouchables* was fiction. Because here you had a man who could literally strike fear in the hearts of even the toughest mobsters, yet he couldn't resist acting like a five-year-old just so he could impress his buddies in Chicago. "I spied on Eliot Ness!"

ER: Along the same lines, I know you once participated in an actual drug raid with the L.A.P.D. as part of a photo

	shoot for *Look* magazine—although I must admit, after reading about that in your book, it seemed odd to me that the editors asked you to do that.
RS:	Not really—because I come from a military family. My wife and I got the Jack Webb award last year for being supportive of the police department. My family's been in California for about 150 years, and we've always been supportive of all law enforcement, and/or the military.
	Jack Webb used to ride around in the cars with the guys, and I'm also very "pro-cop." And towards that end, the editors knew that about me, and that's the reason why. It doesn't mean, "Just because you're an actor who plays a cop, you therefore think you're a cop." It merely means that this is where your heart line is: You don't like crooks. I never put my arm around John Gotti. I never said hello to Bugsy Siegel. I don't hang around, like some actors do, with all the crumb-bum gangsters. I never liked them.
	And, as a consequence, it wasn't that difficult to play Eliot Ness. I never thought I *was* Eliot Ness—it's just that my empathy went toward him, as opposed to figuratively "putting my arm" around the character of Marlon Brando in *The Godfather*, that's all.
ER:	You recently received yet another honor for your association with the show.
RS:	Yes. I was in Europe earlier this summer, where the show is still quite respected. I was in the south of France, where I was presented with their "Golden Angel Award," predicated upon lifetime achievement in television—and that, in their case, is *Les Incorruptibles*, which still runs at one o'clock in the morning over there. They tend to dramatize and glorify their so-called "stars" until they are put away six feet under (which is not always what happens in this country).

ER: Well, over the past ten years, especially with the popularity of Nick at Nite, there's been a genuine resurgence of interest in shows from the '50s and '60s. It's very funny—things do have a way of coming back. It's very cyclical.

RS: This doesn't relate to anything to do with *The Untouchables* necessarily, but I find that the real interest in our profession, in terms of its "lifetime achievement," stems from the young. It stems, for instance, from the kids at UCLA/Film, who have much more interest and much more knowledge of film and television ... *[Laughs.]* than the people who've worked in it all their lives.

ER: It does stem from the young, who are also the ones behind the many books and retrospective magazines on television that have grown in number over the years. It's become a kind of growing genre.

RS: Yes. Like for collectors, I suppose, and things like that.

ER: What is the essence of *The Untouchables*? Why does it continue to appeal to audiences all over the world?

RS: It was a morality play—a vigilante story of seven guys against the world. And the reason it worked is because of the same reason that Clint Eastwood says, "Go ahead, make my day!" That's what Mr. Ness said to Mr. Capone. And these seven guys took on an impossible task—suicidal, if you will—of taking on Capone, who owned Chicago and all of the police.

That's the basic heartline of *The Untouchables*. It was a morality play of the good guys versus the bad guys—the diametric opposite of *The Godfather*, the most dangerous show ever made, that glorifies the gangsters. It was a story about the underdogs going in against City Hall and the crooks and the gangsters, and winning. That's what the story is about.

THE RETURN OF ELIOT NESS

Stack reprised his Emmy Awardwinning role in *The Return of Eliot Ness,* a two-hour TV-movie that aired on NBC on November 11, 1991. Charles Durning, Lisa Hartman, and Jack Coleman co-star in a story that has Ness coming out of retirement to probe the murder of a former colleague besmirched by allegations of having mob connections. Stack is the best part of *Return,* which otherwise lacks most of the elements that made the original *Untouchables* an international success—not the least of which is the frenetic pace that gave the TV show its distinctive energy.

The producers of the telefilm began with much higher aspirations. Those plans were scuttled, however, when Paramount Pictures threatened legal action. Having purchased the rights to not only the original series, but all three of Oscar Fraley's books—the original collaboration with Ness; *Four Against the Mob,* a biography of Ness; and *The Last of the Untouchables,* co-written by former squad member Paul Robsky—Paramount objected on the basis of ownership, even though, from a creative standpoint, *The Return of Eliot Ness* had absolutely nothing to do with either the books or the original TV series. Nonetheless, the studio threatened to sue the producers if the TV movie resembled anything even remotely connected to *The Untouchables,* including the use of the name. This accounts for why the title of the show is *The Return of Eliot Ness.*

Still, the telefilm succeeds in restoring the integrity of the actual Ness, much of which had been gutted as a result of the box-office characterization. This, of course, is due entirely to Stack himself, whose commanding presence makes *The Return of Eliot Ness* more compelling than it otherwise deserves to be. (The movie aired immediately after a special edition of *Unsolved Mysteries* featuring a story about Ness' investigation of a serial killer during the 1930s.)

THE UNTOUCHABLES, REIMAGINED

SECOND SERIES (SYNDICATED, 1993-1994)

Starring Tom Amandes as Eliot Ness
William Forsythe as Al Capone

Also Starring John Rhys-Davies as Mike Malone
Nicholas Georgiade as Enrico Rossi
Paul Regina as Frank Nitti
David James Elliott as Paul Robbins
Nancy Everhard as Catherine Ness
John Haymes Newton as Tony Pagano

Hynden Walch as Mae Capone
Michael Horse as George Steelman (first season)
Shea Farrell as Sean Quinlan
Jenna Lyn Ward as Dorrie Greene
Jack Thibeau as Bugs Moran
Valentino Cima as Frankie Rio
Dick Sasso as Jake Guzik
John Colella as Vito Stellini

Executive Producer: Christopher Crowe
Developed for television by Christopher Crowe

Based on the book *The Untouchables* by Eliot Ness and Oscar Fraley and the 1987 screenplay *The Untouchables* by David Mamet
Produced by: Christopher Crowe
Theme by Joel Goldsmith

A good story is always worth a second telling, so long as it's done well and stays within the basic framework of what made the original work. Despite the liberties taken with Ness' character in the feature motion picture, that version of *The Untouchables* worked because it never strayed from the heartline of the story: a classic morality play, with clearly defined good guys and bad guys.

The same cannot be said for the syndicated *Untouchables* series, which debuted on independent stations across the country the week of January 11, 1993. Despite impressive production values, interesting stories, and strong performances (particularly by co-leads Tom Amandes as Ness and William Forsythe as Capone), the new series ultimately failed precisely because it blurred the lines between good and evil.

Of course, the biggest challenge facing the new series was overcoming the inevitable comparisons with the original, particularly with regard to Eliot Ness. For nearly forty years, television audiences worldwide had automatically associated the character with Robert Stack.

> TOM AMANDES: That's very much true. And Stack, in my mind, was the definitive portrayal. I can't say that I really watched the original *Untouchables* much at all, though, so it wasn't as if I had a really strong image in my mind of what Stack had done with Eliot Ness. Although it was already in reruns by the time I was a kid [Amandes was born in 1959], it wasn't something that I watched.
>
> Now, I know a lot of people that are a few years older than me who remember watching it when it was first on—you know, they'd sit down with their dad, and it was a real "male bonding" experience for a lot of people. But I wasn't one of them, so it wasn't something that was a big burden for me to get past. Plus, in the theater, I've done a lot of roles that have been made famous by other people,

so in that respect, playing Ness wasn't that big a problem for me. But I think for a lot of viewers it was.

The new *Untouchables* claimed to be based on both the original ABC series and all three of Oscar Fraley's books. Aside from an apparent homage to Quinn Martin in the second season (each segment of those episodes begins with "Act I," "Act II," etc.), the style and content of the show were actually patterned very closely after the Mamet/DePalma film. One of the keys to the show, for example, was the symbiotic relationship between the dedicated but somewhat idealistic Ness and the crusty, pragmatic Mike Malone (now played by John Rhys-Davies). "My character was a very differently written Eliot Ness," says Amandes. "I had a lot of talks with [executive producer] Chris Crowe early on about where the character was going, and I think one of the reasons I got the role was that I had a real, natural understanding of what Chris was looking for—in terms of his morality, his conscience, and the demons that would plague him—in the Ness that he wanted to write."

Like the Kevin Costner characterization, the new TV Ness is an earnest young man who strives to balance his responsibilities as a husband and father with his obligations to the members of his team, as well as the sheer enormity of taking on Al Capone. Ness successfully manages this juggling act until midway through the second season, when he has a head-on confrontation with evil brought on by the assassination of Malone in the episode TILL DEATH DO US PART. Ness becomes so consumed with revenge that he nearly snaps entirely, stopping just short of gunning down Capone in cold blood. Ness regains his composure, but not without a price—his obsession with defeating Capone is so overwhelming that his wife, Catherine (played by Nancy Everhard), decides to leave him.

While purists are likely to blanch at this particular characterization of Ness, in truth it's not the biggest problem with the new

Untouchables. That stems from another central motif established in a flashback sequence from the two-hour series pilot: Because Ness and Capone grew up along parallel lines, the two characters have more in common than you'd otherwise think. In fact, the Al Capone of the new show—particularly in the first-year stories—is a character who comes across as almost... virtuous.

> TOM AMANDES: That, to me, was probably the thing that undermined the series, more than anything else The character of Capone, or of any great villain like that, is very seductive to writers—and I think that ultimately they were seduced, to the point that Capone became the character around which the series was focused. Certainly, it was a lot more fun to shoot his stuff than it was to shoot my stuff—we had these sparse offices that looked like basic, boring offices in the '30s, whereas Capone had these wonderful mansions in Chicago that we were shooting in. We were using, for the Capone scenes, actual Lewis Sullivan buildings and Frank Lloyd Wright designs, and all this incredible architecture, and set dressing, with beautiful women wearing these wonderful costumes (or, depending, on the scene, next to nothing...!) And so, from that standpoint, it was very difficult for the "good guys" to compete."

While the villains on the original series were also colorful and attractive, they were morally bankrupt—the polar opposites of the forthright Ness and his T-men. It was very black and white, cut-and-dried, and that's why the original series (and later, the movie) worked. There was no confusion as to who the good guys and bad guys were, nor any doubt that good would prevail in the end.

In contrast, the writers of the new show infused Capone with many interesting shades of gray, including an "ethical code" of sorts when it comes to cold-blooded murder (gunning down men is acceptable, but killing women and children is deplorable). In one episode (BETRAYAL IN BLACK AND TAN), he disassociates himself from a black operative (played by Cuba Gooding Jr.) upon learning that the man has sold out his own people. In the two-parter A TALE OF TWO FATHERS, Capone and Ness actually *join sides* temporarily to track down a serial child killer.

This approach, of course, goes against the basic morality play that is at the heart of *The Untouchables*. By making Capone too attractive a character, you risk undermining the built-in appeal of the archetypical hero, Eliot Ness. In fact, the biggest danger with this concept is that it practically makes Capone a kind of tragic figure—you almost hate to realize he's going to lose at the end. This is exactly what happened with the new series. "The roles of Ness and Capone became sort of twisted," says Amandes. "I mean, there were more than a few people that came up to me on the street and said, 'You leave him alone! You leave that man alone!'

"In a cops-and-robbers show, you want it to be very satisfying at the end of each episode, that good has prevailed, and I think we sort of undermined that." (This, of course, is the very reason that the original series stumbled during its fourth season.)

Crowe recognized the problem, and tried to remedy it during the second season—and the stories that year do attempt to restore the heroic image that is fundamental to the character of Eliot Ness. In fact, in Malone's last episode, he encourages his young friend to keep up the good fight: "One day you are going to be an authentic American hero, you know that? Every decent cop in this city, and every decent lawman in the country, will be proud to know you and know of you. 'Who was Eliot Ness?' they'll say. 'Eliot Ness was a man who got together a group of people to fight organized crime. They were moral, they were idealistic, they were dedicated, and they were incorruptible.' That is not a bad epitaph."

However, by that point, it was too late to sway the viewers back in Ness' favor. "The die was already cast," says Amandes. "It had gotten to the point where most of the audience watching the show weren't exactly pleased whenever things didn't work out well for Capone. That's a tough thing to work against."

One should bear in mind, however, that this was 1993—about five years before the debut of *The Sopranos* (HBO, 1999-2007), the ionic series that ushered in the era of anti-hero protagonists that have populated network, cable, and digital television over the past twenty-five years. This isn't to say that Crowe's vision of Al Capone would have succeeded had the reimagined *Untouchables* aired a decade later. But, one could argue that, in this respect, the Amandes version of *The Untouchables* may have been slightly ahead of its time.

One big advantage the new show had over the original was in the area of special effects, simply because of the technology that was not available in the late 1950s. In this respect, *The Untouchables* of 1993 is very much along the same scale as the 1987 film. "The look of the show was excellent," says Amandes. "As you know, TV is a real compromise over feature filmmaking—but I think, in looking back on some of those episodes, we did a darn good job of producing a look that rivaled a lot of film stuff. And it wasn't easy, because period stuff is really tough to get the look and the feel of. We had gorgeous costumes. Richard Bruno, who's done things like *Chinatown*, did an incredible job with the costumes—and, thankfully, he had the budget to do it. Paramount really didn't stint when it came to that, and I think that's one of the things that made the show irresistible to watch. You turned it on, and you'd say, '*Oooh... this looks great*, whatever it is.'

"I think that's one of the things that anybody who worked on that show is most proud of: The look of the show is excellent."

The sound of the show was pretty good, too. The pilot episode received an Emmy nomination for Outstanding Individual Achievement in Sound Editing for a Series.

The new *Untouchables* was also filmed almost entirely on location in Chicago. Amandes himself grew up (and still lives) in the Windy City, which made filming the series a pleasant experience. "In fact, it was very frequent that we would shoot in my own neighborhood," he laughs. "I remember one time when my trailer was right outside my front door! It was very strange, actually. I kind of hung out at home, and then someone would say. 'Okay, it's time to go to work!' and I'd walk across the sidewalk and into my trailer."

The new series also benefitted (so to speak) from the less stringent standards in television today. The brutality depicted was certainly more graphic than anything ever shown on the original. In PAGANO'S FOLLY, a young woman is kidnapped, stripped, whipped, beaten, raped, and drugged repeatedly until she finally submits to a life of prostitution. Several episodes feature shots to the head, with all the blood and gore oozing onto the screen in glorious color. After hordes of complaints, the series regularly aired "Viewer Discretion" advisories beginning with the second season. However, several parents' associations successfully lobbied their local stations to move *The Untouchables* out of prime time (where the series had successfully competed against established network shows during its first year) and into less desirable late-night time slots. Also like its ABC predecessor, the new *Untouchables* upset many Italian-American groups, who were likewise successful in getting major sponsors to withdraw from the show. Paramount eventually canceled the series at the end of the 1993-1994 season. Both seasons of the reimagined *Untouchables* are available on Blu-ray.

Amandes has since starred in the short-lived NBC sitcom *The Pursuit of Happiness,* and appears in Geena Davis' latest motion picture, *The Long Kiss Goodnight.* John Rhys-Davies *(Raiders of the Lost Ark, Indiana Jones and the Last Crusade)* currently stars on Fox-TV's *Sliders,* while fellow movie veteran Forsythe *(Dick Tracy, Raising Arizona, American Me)* was recently seen in HBO's *Gotti*. Flanking Amandes as the Untouchables: John Haymes Newton (*Superboy*) as Tony Pagano, David James Elliott (*JAG*) as Paul Robbins, and Michael Horse *(Twin Peaks)* as George Steelman. (Horse's character is also killed off during the second season.) Other familiar guest stars include Karen Valentine, Michael Parks, Ronny Cox, George Dzundza, Gina Gershon, Famke Janssen, and movie Untouchable Charles Martin Smith.

One final thing to look for as you watch the reruns of the show. While the marriage of Eliot and Catherine Ness had its problems, romance bloomed off-camera between Amandes and Everhard (they wed in the summer of 1996 and are still married today). "That's why I'll always have a soft spot at the bottom of my heart for *The Untouchables*," Amandes said with a smile.

THE UNTOUCHABLES

ORIGINAL SERIES: 118 EPISODES, ABC EPISODE GUIDE

Desilu Playhouse: THE UNTOUCHABLES (2-parts; 4/20/59,4/27/59)
Eliot Ness forms his squad of agents with one goal in mind: to end the criminal reign of Al Capone
Robert Stack, Neville Brand, Keenan Wynn, Barbara Nichols, Patricia Crowley, Bill Williams, Joe Mantell, Peter Leeds, Eddie Firestone, Robert Osterloh, Paul Dubov, John Beradino, Wolfe Barzell, Frank Wilcox, Peter Mamakos, Wally Cassell, Herman Rudin, Richard Benedict, Bern Hoffman, Frank de Kova, James Westerfield
Written by Paul Monash; Directed by Phil Karlson
Based on the book *The Untouchables* by Eliot Ness and Oscar Fraley
Released theatrically and to home video as *The Scarface Mob*

Season One: 1959-1960

THE EMPTY CHAIR (10/15/59)
Following the imprisonment of Al Capone, Frank Nitti and Jake Guzik clash over the leadership and future of the organization
Nehemiah Persoff, Bruce Gordon, Barbara Nichols, Betty Garde, Wally Carroll, Herman Rudin, Richard Benedict

Written by Ernest Kinoy; Directed by John Peyser

Nehemiah Persoff (*On the Waterfront, The Greatest Story Ever Told, Yentl*) filmed this episode a few months after the release of *Some Like It Hot* (1959), the classic comedy starring Jack Lemmon, Tony Curtis, and Marilyn Monroe in which Persoff played a Prohibition-era mobster named "Little Bonaparte." Coincidentally, also in 1959, Persoff starred opposite Rod Steiger in the biopic *Al Capone*; Steiger played Capone, while Persoff played Johnny Torrio, Capone's original mob boss and mentor.

Director John Peyser was the father of film and television actress Penny Peyser (*The In-Laws, All the President's Men, Crazy Like a Fox*).

MA BARKER AND HER BOYS (10/22/59)
A flashback reveals the events leading up to Ma Barker's showdown with Ness and the Untouchables
Claire Trevor, Adam Williams, Joe de Reda, Peter Baldwin, Robert Ivers, Vaughn Taylor, Louise Fletcher
Written by Jeremy Ross; Directed by Joe Parker

THE JAKE LINGLE KILLING (10/29/59)
Ness cooperates with an ex-con detective who's trying to solve the mob murder of a crooked news reporter
Charles McGraw, Jack Lord, Phillip Pine, John Beradino, Herb Vigran, H.M. Wynant, Frank Wilcox, Chuck Hicks
Written by Robert C. Dennis and Saul Levitt; Directed by Tay Garnett

THE GEORGE "BUGS" MORAN STORY (11/5/59)
Bugs Moran moves to take over a small but growing trucking union by kidnapping the son of the union's president

Lloyd Nolan, Jack Warden, Chuck Hicks, Harry Shannon, Peter Baldwin, Robin Warga, Miriam Nelson, Kern Dibbs, Barbara Stuart

Written by David Karp; Directed by Joe Parker

AIN'T WE GOT FUN? (11/12/59)

A gangster muscling his way into the nightclub scene lays claim to a young comedian's career as well

Cameron Mitchell, Joseph Buloff, Ted de Corsia, Phyllis Coates, Timothy Cary

Written by Abram S. Ginnes; Directed by Roger Kay

THE VINCENT "MAD DOG" COLL STORY (11/19/59)

Mad Dog Coll plans to abduct a thoroughbred racehorse as Ness tries to collar both him and Dutch Schultz

Lawrence Dobkin, Clu Gulager, Susan Storrs

Written by Charles Marion; Directed by Andrew McCullough

MEXICAN STAKEOUT (11/26/59)

Ness follows the trail of a missing witness to Mexico

Vince Edwards, Martin Landau, Joe Ruskin, Byron Foulger, Stafford Repp, David Renard

Written by Alvin Sapinsley and Robert C. Dennis; Directed by Tay Garnett

THE ARTICHOKE KING (12/3/59)

The Untouchables try to thwart gangster dominance of the wholesale produce market in New York

Jack Weston, Robert Ellenstein, Al Ruscio, Mike Mazurki, Selette Cole

Written by Harry Essex; Directed by Roger Kay

At the time she appeared in this episode, Selette Cole was dating Byron Kane, the associate producer on *Peter Gunn* (and who also appeared onscreen on *Gunn* as Barney, the bartender at Mother's), while George Eckstein was a casting director on *The Untouchables*. Cole married Kane in June 1960, but they divorced a few years later. In 1968, Cole married Eckstein, then a writer and producer with Quinn Martin Productions (and, later, Universal Television). Cole and Eckstein remained married until Eckstein died in 2009.

THE TRI-STATE GANG (12/10/59)
Ness lakes on a formidable hijacker-kidnapper
William Bendix, John Ward, Roxanne Berard, Alan Hale Jr., Gavin MacLeod, Jay Adler
Written by Joseph Petracca; Directed by Allen H. Miner

THE DUTCH SCHULTZ STORY (12/17/59)
Ness tries to nail Dutch Schultz on a tax case
Lawrence Dobkin, Mort Mills, Robert Carricart, Maggie Mahoney, Richard Reeves
Written by Jerome Ross and Robert C. Dennis; Directed by Jerry Hopper

YOU CAN'T PICK THE NUMBER (12/24/59)
Ness tries to use a collector and his son to smash the flourishing numbers racket
Darryl Hickman, Jay C. Flippen. Chuck Hicks, King Calder, Whit Bissell, Chris White, Doreen Lang, George Ramsey, Harry Tyler
Written by Henry Greenberg; Directed by Richard Whorf

UNDERGROUND RAILWAY (12/31/59)
Ness goes coast to coast in search of an escaped felon who has had plastic surgery to alter his appearance
Cliff Robertson, Virginia Vincent, Joe de Santis, Murray Roman, Bob Hopkins

Written by Leonard Kantor; Directed by Walter Grauman

Walter Grauman cast "about 99 percent" of the shows that he directed in television. "It always works the same way," he told me in 1996. "You have ideas of your own, and you give them to the casting people to check out on their availability, cost, and so forth. The casting people will come up with thoughts for you, and you'll say 'Yeah, I like that,' or 'No, I don't think that's right,' or 'Let me read them or audition them,' etc. The casting department, or casting personnel/casting director, really works with the director—or for the director, basically. The director, in both TV and films, has, with very few exceptions, control of the casting—I mean, if you take a picture with a star in it already, you know that that star is there. But, normally, the director has a Yea or Nay on casting."

SYNDICATE SANCTUARY (1/7/60)
One of the Untouchables goes undercover in the mob to root out the plot behind the assassination of a mayoral candidate
Mike Kellin, Anthony Caruso, Gail Kobe, Jack Elam, Frank Wolf, Douglas Dumbrille
Written by George F. Slavin; Directed by Paul Harrison

THE NOISE OF DEATH (1/14/60)
A district mob boss denies making what was obviously a mob hit
J. Carrol Naish, Rita Lynn, Chuck Hicks, Mike Kellin, Henry Silva, Karen Docker, Joi Lansing
Written by Ben Maddow; Directed by Walter Grauman

"NOISE OF DEATH was one of the best shows I've ever done, and also one of the best scripts I've ever seen," Walter Grauman told me in 1996. "That was written by Ben Maddow. That was also the first *Untouchables* that I did. When Quinn sent me the script, he called me one night and said, 'Listen, I saw an *Alcoa*

Goodyear you did, and I liked your work a lot. Would you read this script if I send it, and if you like it, would you do it?' He sent it, and I read it. And, I must say, my eyes jumped right out of my head, because that script was so good. I couldn't believe it."

Grauman not only went on to helm twenty-one episodes of *The Untouchables*, but became Martin's "go-to" director over the next two decades. He directed six pilots for Martin that went to series (including *The Fugitive*, *Barnaby Jones*, and *The Streets of San Francisco*), plus multiple episodes of virtually every other show that Martin produced. Not only that, but Grauman personally selected THE NOISE OF DEATH as one of two shows that were screened at the UCLA Film and Television Archive in March 2012 as part of a special evening honoring the director on the occasion of his ninetieth birthday. (The other was FEAR IN A DESERT CITY, the pilot episode for *The Fugitive*.)

STAR WITNESS (1/21/60)
When a bookkeeper for the mob finds retirement an unlikely option, Ness tries to turn him against the organization
Jim Backus, Marc Lawrence, Dorothy Morris, Jay Warren, Sal Armetta
Written by Charles O'Neal; Directed by Tay Garnett

THE ST. LOUIS STORY (1/28/60)
The Untouchables go after a St. Louis gang who robbed a U.S. Mail truck
David Brian, Leo Gordon, Tom Trout, Richard Bakalyan, Bernard Fine, Lillian Bronson, Rita Duncan, Percy Helton
Written by Joseph Retraces; Directed by Howard W. Koch

ONE-ARMED BANDIT (2/4/60)
An ex-con is blackmailed into joining a group of slot machine racketeers

MEN OF ACTION

Harry Guardino, John Beradino, Larry Gates
Written by E. Jack Neuman; Directed by Walter Grauman

LITTLE EGYPT (2/11/60)
Ness's newest agent goes undercover to solve the murder of an honest sheriff and mayor
Fred Clark, Susan Cummings, Bartlett Robinson, John Marley, Norm Alden, Miriam Goldini, Sam Oilman, James McCallion, Frank Bella
Written by Joseph Petracca; Directed by John Peyser

THE BIG SQUEEZE (2/18/60)
Ness tries to trip up a notorious bank robber
Dan O'Herlihy, Dody Heath, John Hoyt, Bill Forrester
Written by W.R. Burnett and Robert C. Dennis; Directed by Roger Kay

THE UNHIRED ASSASSIN (2 parts; 2/25/60, 3/3/60)
Ness steps in to protect the mayor after he rebuffs an effort by Nitti to move in on the World's Fair
Robert Middleton, Lee Van Cleef, Joe Mantell
Written by William Spier; Directed by Howard W. Koch
Released theatrically as The Guns of Zangara *(1962), this episode was not included in the syndication package*

THE WHITE SLAVERS (3/10/60)
Ness uses a reformed mobster to thwart a white slave racket
Betty Field, Dick York, Mike Kellin, Theona Bryant, Mona Knox, Jim Anderson
Written by Leonard Kantor; Directed by Walter Grauman

3,000 SUSPECTS (3/24/60)
Ness must put a second prisoner at risk after an informer is killed in jail

Leslie Nielsen, Peter Leeds, Benny Butt, James Flavin, Francis DeSales, Howie Storm
Written by Robert C. Dennis; Directed by John Peyser

Howard Storm (billed here as "Howie" Storm) began his showbiz career performing in nightclubs in New York, crossing paths with or working with such legends as Lenny Bruce, Shecky Greene, Judy Garland, and Woody Allen before segueing into television—first as an actor, then as a director, perhaps best known for his work on the first three seasons of *Mork & Mindy*,. At the time he appeared in this episode, Storm was a member of The Desilu Players, a group of young actors mentored by Lucille Ball that also included Robert Osbourne and Roger Perry.

THE DOREEN MANEY STORY (3/31/60)
A couple nicknamed "The Lovebirds" are connected to a series of armored truck robberies
Anne Francis, Connie Mines, Christopher Dark, George Mitchell
Written by Jerome Ross; Directed by Robert Florey

PORTRAIT OF A THIEF (4/7/60)
While working to smash bootleggers, Ness receives an unexpected lead that points to a scandal in a respected drug firm
Charles McGraw, Henry Jones, Frank Wilcox, Edward Andrews
Written by Herbert Abbott Spiro; Directed by Walter Grauman

THE UNDERWORLD BANK (4/14/60)
The romance between a disgruntled customer and the niece of a crooked banker gives Ness the leverage he needs to bust the operation
Thomas Mitchell, Peter Falk, Virginia Vincent, Ernest Sarracino, Tony Zagano, Penny Santon, Bernard Kates, Val Avery
Written by Aben Kandel; Directed by Stuart Rosenberg

MEN OF ACTION

HEAD OF FIRE, FEET OF CLAY (4/21/60)
Ness is put in jeopardy by an old school chum who has fallen in with the mob
Nehemiah Persoff, Jack Warden, Madlyn Rhue, Patsy Kelly, Virginia Christine, Leo Gordon Written by Ben Maddow; Directed by Walter Grauman

In his memoir, *The Many Faces of Nehemiah* (Autumn Road Company, 2021), Nehemiah Persoff wrote that he based the various characters that he played on *The Untouchables* (as well as Johnny Torrio in *Al Capone*) on a man known only as Kibbie, a street vendor who set up shop in the neighborhood in Brooklyn where Persoff grew up. "In the thirties in Brooklyn, almost everyone was a Dodger fan," Persoff recalled. "Kibbie was a rabid Dodger fan. He owned his own pushcart. He could afford to take a few hours off, spend a quarter, and go to see his favorite team. The Dodgers did not allow their games to be broadcast locally, so Kibbie, on his return to our block, brought us the first news we got about the game. If Kibbie turned the corner with his arms up dancing all the way, we knew that the Dodgers won. If he turned the corner with his nose dragging on the sidewalk, we knew that the Dodgers lost.

"One day in acting class [at the New Theater League, where Persoff studied the Method along with fellow students Shelley Winters and Martin Balsam], Lem Ward, the director, took charge for one session. When called upon, I did an imitation of Kibbie dancing down the street after a victory, Brooklyn accent and all. After I finished, Lem asked, 'This was particularly good. Who wrote your material?'

"I said, 'Nobody did. That's the way it happened.'" Needless to say, Ward was impressed.

THE FRANK NITTI STORY (4/28/60)
Frank Nitti is extorting money from theater operators, who would rather pay than cooperate with the law
Myron McCormick, Dick Foran, Frank Albertson, Phyllis Coates, Frank Wilcox
Teleplay by Blair Scott, story by Harry Essex; Directed by Howard W. Koch

Season Two: 1960-1961

THE RUSTY HELLER STORY (10/13/60)
A beautiful girl plays various mob elements against each other in her own quest for power
Elizabeth Montgomery, David White, Harold J. Stone, Linda Watkins, Norman Fell, John Duke
Written by Leonard Kantor; Directed by Waiter Grauman

THE JACK "LEGS" DIAMOND STORY (10/20/60)
The Untouchables go after Legs Diamond, who has hijacked a dope shipment for his own purposes
Steven Hill, Lawrence Dobkin, Robert Carricart, Suzanne Storrs, Norma Crane, Ted Berger
Written by Charles O'Neal; Directed by John Peyser
Remade for the second series

NICKY (10/20/60)
Ness gains a new enemy in the son of a bootlegger slain during a raid
Luther Adler, Michael Ansara, Mario Raccuzzo, Phillip Pine, Ronnie Haran, Malcolm Atterbury, Renata Vanni
Written by Joseph Petracca; Directed by Walter Grauman

THE WAXEY GORDON STORY (11/10/60)
Ness goes after the top bootlegger of the 1930s, but finds him to be elusive.

Nehemiah Persoff, Sam Oilman, Lisabeth Hush, Adam Becker, Terry Huntingdon, Frank De Kova
Written by Joseph Petracca; Directed by John Peyser
Remade for the second series

THE MARK OF CAIN (11/17/60)
Ness uses the power of the press to lean on dope pushers, but one minor member of the organization remains defiant
Henry Silva, Eduardo Cianelli, Paula Raymond, Will Kuluva, Wolfe Barzell
Written by David Z. Goodman; Directed by Walter Grauman

A SEAT ON THE FENCE (11/24/60)
Ness goes after a drug ring that steals narcotics from hospitals and drug stores
Frank Silvera, John McIntire, Arlene Sax, Olan Soule, Val Avery, Dan Barton
Written by William P. Templeton; Directed by Walter Grauman

THE PURPLE GANG (12/1/60)
A small-time hoodlum is abducted by mistake, and Nitti moves in when the mistake is corrected
Steve Cochran, Werner Klemperer, Steven Geray, Ilka Windish, Carl Milletaire
Written by John Mantley; Directed by Walter Grauman

THE PURPLE GANG includes an early example of "forced perspective," the innovative camera technique that became very popular among film and TV directors after Sidney Furie used it in *The Ipcress File* (1965). In this episode, director Walter Grauman has a sequence in which Werner Klemperer's character is leaning on his desk as he's speaking to Eliot Ness. Grauman shot the scene through the bend of Klemperer's arm. "I remember that shot very well," the director said to me in the summer of 1996. "I'll tell you the truth: I pre-planned 99-44/100 percent of those shots, in doing what I call 'blocking'—meaning, for several weeks, I would lay out every shot in the show in my mind, and then write it on paper, in my own shorthand, so that it was not just an accident you stumble upon. I thought everything through: the angle, the lenses, the relationship of the actors (one to the other), the relationship of the actors in their environment, the sets, or the locations. It was all pre-planned."

In other words, whenever Grauman sat down to read a script that he was scheduled to direct, he read it visually. "Exactly," he said. "As a matter of fact, it's still a problem for me today, to read quickly, because I stage in my head as I read."

KISS OF DEATH GIRL (12/8/60)
While working a hijacking case, Ness crosses paths with a girl whose boyfriends tend to meet untimely deaths
Jan Sterling, Mickey Shaughnessy, Robert H. Harris, David J. Stewart, John Conte
Written by Harry Kronman; Directed by John Peyser

THE LARRY FAY STORY (12/15/60)
Ness investigates strong-arm price-hiking of milk by racketeers
Sam Levene, Robert Emhardt, June Havoc, Tommy Cook, Robert Karnes, Larry Gates
Written by Harry Essex; Directed by Walter Grauman

THE OTTO FRICK STORY (12/22/60)
The Untouchables run into resistance from the State Department when it is learned that dope pushers have formed an alliance with the Nazi Bund
Francis Lederer, Richard Jaeckel, Jack Warden, Erika Paters, John Wengraf

Written by Leonard Kantor; Directed by John Peyser

THE TOMMY KARPELES STORY (12/29/60)
Ness isn't convinced of a known criminal's guilt when a jury convicts the man of a mail robbery
Joseph Wiseman, Harold J. Stone, Madlyn Rhue, Murray Hamilton, Vic Morrow, Joseph Julian, Vladimir Sokoloff
Written by George Bellak; Directed by Stuart Rosenberg

THE BIG TRAIN (2 parts; 1/5/61, 1/12/61)
While plans are made to transfer Al Capone to Alcatraz, Ness investigates some suspicious activity on the part of the mobster's gang
Neville Brand, Robert F. Simon, James Westerfield
Written by William Spier; Directed by John Peyser
Released theatrically as Alcatraz Express, *this episode was not included in the syndication package*

THE MASTERPIECE (1/19/61)
A hitman defies the Untouchables as he plans to carry out his latest assassination right under their noses
Robert Middleton, Rip Torn, George Voskovec, Joseph Ruskin, Harry Shannon, Addison Richards
Written by David Z. Goodman; Directed by Walter Grauman

An alumnus of The Actors Studio in New York, Rip Torn was a devotee of the Method, as taught by Lee Strasberg. While that made Torn a brilliant performer, it also made him difficult to direct sometimes. "Rip could be a really crazy sonuvabitch," Walter Grauman told me in 1996. "There were two things in [THE MASTERPIECE] that I remember. One was, early on, I wanted him to enter a room (or whatever the set was), and cross over to Ness. So I said, 'Okay, now, let's rehearse.' And Rip said, 'Now, why would I come in?' I said, 'Just come in the door.'

"'But *why*?' he said. [Meaning, what is my motivation for entering this room to talk to Ness in this particular scene.]

"And I said, '*Because you've got to get into the goddamn room, you sonuvabitch!*' And so, he finally came into the room.

"Now, later, in the scene where he has the gun under the table and he's going to kill George Voskovec, Rip is wearing this silly New Year's Eve hat. When I got to the angle across Rip to George Voskovec, every time I rolled the film, Rip would put his hand up and start playing with his hat—and every time he did that, it would block George Voskovec's face. And Rip was doing this deliberately, you know?

"Finally, I said, 'Rip, please don't play with the hat.'

"He said, 'Why not?'

"I said, 'Because I can't get George's face. I've got your shot, and now I want George over your shoulder.'"

"He'd say 'Okay'—and then he'd do it again, and again! Finally, I said, 'Cut!' We'd done maybe five takes.

"I said, 'Rip, I want to make something clear to you. It's now seven-thirty at night. I'm more stubborn than you are. I'm going to continue shooting this scene until you change your mind, or you forget to play with that hat! And when you do, that's the one I'm going to print—and if it takes us till eight o'clock tomorrow morning, I don't give a shit, we're still gonna be shooting it.'

"He didn't say anything... And then, about the second take after that, he suddenly didn't play with that, I said, 'Cut—*print!*' But I'll never forget it."

THE MASTERPIECE, by the way, was written by David Zelag Goodman, one of three writers on *The Untouchables* that Grauman singled out as being "unusually gifted writers." The other two? Ben Maddow and Leonard Kantor. Goodman later wrote the screenplays for several motion pictures, including *Straw Dogs*, *Lovers and Other Strangers*, and *The Eyes of Laura Mars*.

THE ORGANIZATION (1/26/61)
Ness attempts to thwart a gangster summit meeting that would establish a national crime organization
Richard Conte, Susan Oliver, Milton Selzer, Oscar Beregi, Richard Karlan, Thorn Carney
Written by Harry Kronman; Directed by Walter Grauman

JAMAICA GINGER (2/2/61)
The Untouchables try to shut down the smuggling into the country of a deadly drink from the Indies
Brian Keith, Michael Ansara, Alfred Ryder, James Coburn, June Dayton
Written by Joseph Petracca; Directed by John Peyser

AUGIE "THE BANKER"CIAMINO (2/9/61)
A ruthless bootlegger is concealing his operation by putting stills in the homes of frightened immigrants
Sam Jaffe, Keenan Wynn, Will Kuluva, Lee Philips, (Harry) Dean Stanton, Rebecca Welles, Bernard Kates
Written by Adrian Spies; Directed by Stuart Rosenberg

THE UNDERGROUND COURT (2/16/61)
A gangster with a million dollars stolen from the mob forces them to protect him from Ness as he takes a cross-country trip with an unsuspecting widow

Joan Blondell, Richard Devon, Eddie Firestone, Frank De Kova, Vic Perrin, Arthur Kendall, William Fawcett, Steve Conte, John Duke
Written by Leonard Kantor; Directed by Don Medford

THE NICK MOSES STORY (2/23/61)
After defying the code of the underworld, a mobster promises to eliminate Eliot Ness as the price for his actions
Harry Guardino, Joe De Santis, Michael Constantine, Dan Seymour, Herman Rudie, Nicki Marcelli
Teleplay by Tim Carlo and John Mantley, Story by T.L.P. Swicegood; Directed by Herman Hoffman

THE ANTIDOTE (3/9/61)
A bootlegging ring is using a new process to reclaim industrial alcohol that has been denatured
Telly Savalas, Joseph Wiseman, Jeff Corey, Gail Robbins
Written by David Z. Goodman; Directed by Walter Grauman

Joseph Wiseman (*Dr. No, Detective Story, Crime Story*) suffered a serious leg injury during the production of this episode. "A huge thermometer shattered in the big vat that was next to him, and it came down and caught him in his left leg," director Walter Grauman told me in 1996. "The glass sheared all of the muscle, and ligaments, and everything, from his knee all the way down to his ankle. It took a year for Joe to recover from all of that. It was really bad."

THE LILY DALLAS STORY (3/16/61)
Ness inserts an agent into the mob to exploit a disagreement over the protection of the young daughter of a gangland couple
June Vincent, Norma Crane, Barbara Parkins, Larry Parks, Dabbs Greer, Judy Strange, Linda Watkins
Written by Leonard Kantor; Directed by Don Medford

MEN OF ACTION

Murder Under Glass (3/23/61)
Ness unmasks a New Orleans importer who is using a respected family firm to smuggle narcotics
Luther Adler, Dennis Patrick, Carl Milletaire, Paul Burch
Written by Harry Kronman; Directed by Walter Grauman

Testimony of Evil (3/30/61)
Ness tries to locate a reluctant witness before the mob finds and eliminates him
David Brian, Fay Spain, John Marley, Jack Elam, Tom Fadden, Paul Genge
Written by Joseph Petracca; Directed by Paul Wendkos

Ring of Terror (4/13/61)
A blackmailed fight manager refuses to help Ness tie narcotics to the fight game
Viveca Lindfors, Harold J. Stone, John Crawford, Richard Karlan, Vaughn Taylor, Sheldon Allman, John Day, Frank Wilcox, Howard Caine, Walter Burke, Russell Collins, George Carver
Written by John Mantley; Directed by Walter Grauman

Mr. Moon (4/20/61)
A skillful counterfeiter has obtained enough government paper to print $100 million worth of phony bills
Victor Buono, Karl Swenson, Robert Osterloh, Olan Soule
Written by Charles O'Neal; Directed by Paul Wendkos

Death for Sale (4/27/61)
Ness takes on an underworld prodigy, who has exceeded the expectations of the mob
James MacArthur, Lou Polan, Ned Glass, Carol Eastman
Written by David Z. Goodman; Directed by Stuart Rosenberg

Stranglehold (5/4/61)
The price of fish soars in New York after the market is taken over by a racketeer
Ricardo Montalban, Philip Pine, Kevin Hagen, Trevor Bardette, Frank Puglia
Written by Harry Kronman; Directed by Paul Wendkos

The Nero Rankin Story (5/1 1/61)
The newest syndicate leader threatens reprisals against the public if Ness doesn't stop leaning on his operations
Will Kuluva, John Dehner, Joanna Moore, Richard Karlan, Brook Byron, Murvyn Vye, John Duke, Jean Carson, Barry Kelley
Written by Leonard Kantor; Directed by Stuart Rosenberg

The Seventh Vote (5/18/61)
Frank Nitti and Jake Guzik attempt to smuggle a man into the country who can help settle the leadership dispute
Nehemiah Persoff, Joseph Ruskin, George Neise, Howard Caine, Richard Reeves, Robert Cornthwaite, Gregg Dunn
Written by Richard Collins; Directed by Stuart Rosenberg

The King of Champagne (5/25/61)
Ness uncovers a plot to corner the wine market with the development of an American formula for making champagne comparable to the French product
Robert Middleton, Michael Constantine, Barry Morse, Grant Richards, Jason Wingreen, Jack Anthony, George Kennedy, Barton Heyman, Pepper Curtis, Robert G. Anderson
Written by David Z. Goodman; Directed by Walter Grauman

The Nick Acropolis Story (6/1/61)
Ness uses a three-way internal mob conflict to bust up a bookmaking operation
Lee Marvin, Constance Ford, Johnny Seven

Written by Curtis Kenyon and John Mantley; Directed by Don Medford

90 Proof Dame (6/8/61)
A Chicago mobster prominent in burlesque circles is branching out into bootleg brandy
Steve Cochran, Warren Stevens, Joanna Bames, Steven Geray, (Harry) Dean Stanton, Gilbert Green
Written by Harry Kronman; Directed by Walter Grauman

Season Three: 1961-1962

The Troubleshooters (10/12/61)
When Ness turns down a large bribe, angry gangsters attempt to frame him
Peter Falk, Murray Hamilton, Ned Glass, Vincent Gardenia, Michael Dana, Vladimir Sokoloff
Written by Louis Peletier; Directed by Stuart Rosenberg

Power Play (10/19/61)
The new head of a crime commission is also the head of an underworld syndicate
Wendell Corey, Carroll O'Connor, Albert Salmi, Mary Fickett, Paul Gonge
Written by Harry Kronman; Directed by Paul Wendkos

Tunnel of Horrors (10/26/61)
Ness goes up against a crooked cop as an amusement park is used as a base of operations for dope smuggling
Martin Balsam, Joseph Ruskin, Don Gordon
Written by John Mantley; Directed by Stuart Rosenberg

The Genna Brothers (11/2/61)
Internal family squabbling enables Ness to shut down a thriving home still operation

Marc Lawrence, Anthony Carbone, Frank Puglia, Arlene Sax, Grant Richards, Eugene Iglesias
Written by Harry Kronman; Directed by Paul Wendkos

The Matt Bass Scheme (11/9/61)
An ex-con helps Frank Nitti find a new way of getting his booze after Ness temporarily interrupts the flow
Telly Savalas, Jaynes Barron, Grant Richards, Herman Rudin
Written by David Z. Goodman; Directed by Stuart Rosenberg

Loophole (11/16/61)
Ness tries to thwart the efforts of a lawyer who is an expert in using loopholes to free mobsters
Jack Klugman, Martin Landau, George Tobias, Gavin MacLeod, Vaughn Taylor, Peter Brocco, Alexander Lockwood
Written by Harry Kronman; Directed by Paul Wendkos

Jigsaw (11/23/61)
As a counter to the Untouchables, an underworld squad has been formed to root out potential government witnesses
James Gregory, Cloris Leachman, Alan Baxter, Joe Perry, Bernard Fein
Written by George Eckstein; Directed by Paul Wendkos

Mankiller (12/7/61)
Ness turns up a showgirl with a grudge against a woman who has gone into partnership with Nitti
Ruth Roman, Grant Richards, Mario Alcalde, Mario Gallo
Written by Sy Salkowitz; Directed by Stuart Rosenberg

City Without a Name (12/14/61)
Frank Nitti enters the picture as Ness journeys east to solve the murder of a federal officer by racketeers interested in opening up their city to bootleggers and gamblers

Paul Richards, Mike Kellin, Theo Marcuse, George Keyman
Written by John Mantley; Directed by Paul Wendkos

HAMMERLOCK (12/21/61)
A respected member of the baking industry is acting as a frontman for racketeers seeking to get a piece of bakery profits
Harold J. Stone, Joan Staley, Will Kuluva, John Larch, Robert Carricart
Written by Mel Goldberg; Directed by Stuart Rosenberg

CANADA RUN (1/4/62)
Ness investigates the flow of liquor into Chicago from Canada
Simon Oakland, Arthur Hill, John Anderson, Dabbs Greer, Than Wyenn
Written by Barry Trivers and Harry Kronman; Directed by Bernard McEveety Jr.

FALL GUY (1/11/62)
Three hoodlums offer their services as "specialists" to mobsters requiring special skills to thwart Ness's investigations
Herschel Bernardi, Don Gordon, Robert Emhardt, Jay C. Flippen, Herbie Faye
Written by David P. Harmon; Directed by Bernard Kowalski

THE GANG WAR (1/18/62)
Ness investigates a gangland war after an innocent bystander is gunned down
Victor Buono, John Kellogg, Ed Nelson, Ann Whitfield
Written by John Mantley; Directed by Paul Wendkos

THE SILENT PARTNER (2/1/62)
Ness takes credit for killing a favorite of the underworld kingpin in an attempt to spare Hobson, the true gunman, from reprisals

Charles McGraw, Dyan Cannon, Allyn Joslyn, Bert Convy
Written by Harry Kronman; Directed by Abner Biberman

THE WHITEY STEELE STORY (2/8/62)
Ness goes undercover in San Francisco to bust a horse racing wire service that is also peddling narcotics
Henry Silva, Murray Hamilton, Eduardo Ciannelli, Phil Pine, Sean McClory
Written by George Eckstein; Directed by Abner Biberman

THE DEATH TREE (2/15/62)
A knowledge of gypsy customs helps Ness take on the gypsy hired by the Capone organization to head their cheap whiskey operation
Charles Bronson, Barbara Luna, Theo Marcuse, Ed Asner, Richard Bakalyan
Written by Harry Kronman; Directed by Vincent McEveety

TAKEOVER (3/1/62)
On the eve of the repeal of prohibition, a father and son are nearing a showdown over control of the Chicago beer market
Luther Adler, Robert Loggia, Collin Wilcox, Mort Mills, Leonard Nimoy, Oscar Beregi
Written by Sy Salkowitz and Theodore Apstein; Directed by Bernard Kowalski

THE STRYKER BROTHERS (3/8/62)
An arsonist is hired by a trio of brothers to destroy the building containing the evidence against them for a mail robbery
Nehemiah Persoff, Frank Sutton, Michael Strong, Joseph Bernard, Grant Richards, Buck Kartalian, Amy Freeman
Written by Gilbert Ralston; Directed by Stuart Rosenberg

ELEMENT OF DANGER (3/22/62)
A psychopath found at the scene of a warehouse holdup convinces police that he is an innocent bystander
Lee Marvin, Victor Jory, Al Ruscio
Written by John Mantley; Directed by Bernard Kowalski

THE MAGGIE STORM STORY (3/29/62)
The owner of a swank speakeasy also uses the location as an auction house for illicit merchandise
Patricia Neal, Vic Morrow, John Kellogg, Bernard Fein, John Harmon, Herman Rudin, Joseph Ruskin, Frank De Kova
Written by George Eckstein; Directed by Stuart Rosenberg

MAN IN THE MIDDLE (4/5/62)
An informant's life is endangered when his wife inadvertently exposes him
Martin Balsam, Tom Drake, Cloris Leachman, Gavin MacLeod, Mike Mazurki, Joey Barnum
Written by Harry Kronman; Directed by Bernard Kowalski

DOWNFALL (5/3/62)
Bootleg whiskey from Canada is traced to a respectable railroad family
Steven Hill, Simon Oakland, Stefan Schnabel, Milton Seltzer
Written by Robert Yale Libott; Directed by Stuart Rosenberg

THE CASE AGAINST ELIOT NESS (5/10/62)
Ness is sued for slander after challenging a public figure who tries to take over the 1933 World's Fair
Pat Hingle, Jeanne Cooper, Cliff Carnell, Joseph Turkel
Written by George Eckstein; Directed by Bernard Kowalski

The Ginnie Littlesmith Story (5/17/62)
A spinster clings to her "inheritance," the records of her deceased hoodlum uncle that could help Ness put away a group of racketeers
Phyllis Love, Don Gordon, Brook Byron, Jeno Mate, Linda Evans, Leonard Strong, Marlene Callahan
Written by Leonard Kantor; Directed by Stuart Rosenberg

The Contract (5/31/62)
Ness pursues a criminal to a gambling ship moored off the California coast
Harry Guardino, Gloria Talbott, Frank Sutton, John Larkin, Oscar Beregi
Written by George Eckstein; Directed by Bernard Kowalski

Pressure (6/14/62)
A narcotics dealer openly informs Ness of his shipments, but threatens to destroy a school full of children if the shipments are interfered with
Harold J. Stone, Warren Gates, Darryl Hickman, Collin Wilcox, Booth Colman
Written by Harry Kronman; Directed by Vincent McEveety

Arsenal (6/28/62)
A gang war threatens to break out after the discovery that no law blocks the sale of machine guns
Salome Jens, George Mathews, Kevin Hagen, Karl Swenson
Written by John Mantley; Directed by Paul Wendkos

The Monkey Wrench (7/5/62)
Using the home of a gangster's widow, Frank Nitti smuggles in brewmeisters to replace those nabbed by Ness in raids
Claude Akins, Oscar Beregi, Dolores Dorn, Cliff Osmond, Albert Szabo

Written by George Eckstein; Directed by Bernard Kowalski

Season Four: 1962-1963

THE NIGHT THEY SHOT SANTA CLAUS (9/25/62)
A showgirl helps Ness find the killer of a man gunned down while playing Santa at an orphanage on Christmas Eve
Nita Talbot, Ruth White, Murvyn Vye, Russell Collins, Isabel Jewell, Grace Lee Whitney, John Duke
Written by Mort Thaw; Directed by Alex March

COOKER IN THE SKY (10/2/62)
Chicago mobsters bring in a brewery expert from New York to construct a "Ness-proof" plant, untraceable by federal agents
Anne Jackson, Milton Selzer, J.D. Cannon
Written by John D.F. Black; Directed by Robert Butler

THE CHESS GAME (10/9/62)
A blind Boston fish merchant is using his refrigerated freight cars to smuggle champagne
Richard Conte, Murray Hamilton, Michael Constantine, Barbara Barrie, Ned Glass
Written by David Z. Goodman; Directed by Stuart Rosenberg

THE ECONOMIST (10/16/62)
An educated mobster tries to corner the whiskey market
Joseph Sirola, Ellen Madison, George Mathews
Written by Harold Gast; Directed by Paul Stanley

THE PEA (10/23/62)
Ness uses the debts of a speakeasy busboy as leverage to turn
Frank Gorshin, Sally Gracie, Albert Paulsen, Gilbert Greene, Elizabeth MacRae, Stefan Gierasch
Written by Harry Kronman; Directed by Paul Stanley

BIRD IN THE HAND (10/30/62)
Ness and the Health Department both seek a racketeer who owns a pet shop, and who has parrot fever
Dane Clark, Carroll O'Connor, Herschel Bernardi, Nan Martin
Written by Harry Kronman; Directed by Walter Grauman
The first of two pilots for The White Knights, *a prospective spin-off series starring Dane Clark*

THE EDDIE O'GARA STORY (11/13/62)
A vanished gangster returns from oblivion after three years to help his old boss, Bugs Moran, form a new organization
Mike Connors, Robert J. Wilke, Sean McClory, Meg Wyllie
Written by Carey Wilbur; Directed by Robert Butler

Long before he became a household name as private eye Joe Mannix, Mike Connors starred in *Tightrope* (CBS, 1959-1960), a fast-paced thirty-minute action series about an undercover police detective who infiltrated the world of organized crime. Though popular with TV audiences here and abroad (the series had a particularly huge following in Mexico), *Tightrope* was canceled after just one season due to a dispute between CBS and the show's primary sponsor. According to Connors biographer Bill Taylor, three attempts were made to rework the concept into an hour-long series, with Connors starring in the first two: *The New Tightrope* (ABC, 1960) and *The Expendables*, which he filmed shortly after completing production of THE EDDIE O'GARA STORY. Connors would spend the next few years alternating between movies and television before finally hitting prime-time paydirt in *Mannix* (CBS, 1967-1975).

ELEGY (11/20/62)
Ness is offered the records of a dying gangster if he will find the man's daughter before he dies

MEN OF ACTION

Barbara Stanwyck, Peggy Ann Garner, John Larch, Bill Sargent
Written by Herman Groves; Directed by Robert Butler
The first of two pilots for The Seekers, *a prospective spin-off series starring Barbara Stanwyck*

COME AND KILL ME (11/27/62)
A karate expert is training teenage boys to be killers
Dan Dailey, Ted de Corsia, Robert Bice
Written by Kitty Buhler; Directed by Robert Gist

A FIST OF FIVE (12/4/62)
A frustrated policeman forms a vigilante group which Ness must ultimately deal with
Lee Marvin, Phyllis Coates, James Caan, Roy Thinnes, Frank De Kova, Mark Alien, Whitney Armstrong
Written by Herman Groves; Directed by Ida Lupino

THE FLOYD GIBBONS STORY (12/11/62)
A famed war correspondent helps Ness solve the slaying of a reporter friend and uncover a diabolical underworld operation
Scott Brady, Dorothy Malone, Stuart Erwin, Alan Baxter, Norman Burton, Lee Krieger, Paul Langton, Jerry Oddo, Robert Bice
Written by George Eckstein; Directed by Robert Butler
The first of two pilots for Floyd Gibbons, Reporter, *a proposed spin-off starring Scott Brady*

DOUBLECROSS (12/18/62)
Ness interferes with Jake Guzik's bootlegging operation by supplying retailers with the product himself
Harry Morgan, Nehemiah Persoff, John Duke, John Kellogg, Malachi Throne
Written by John Mantley; Directed by Paul Wendkos

SEARCH FOR A DEAD MAN (1/1/63)
Ness and a representative of the Missing Persons Bureau attempt to identify a body fished out of Lake Michigan
Barbara Stanwyck, Virginia Capers, Ed Asner, Alan Dexter, Carlo Tricoli
Written by Harold Gast; Directed by Robert Butler
Second of two pilots for The Seekers, a proposed spin-off series starring Barbara Stanwyck

THE SPECULATOR (1/8/63)
A financial wizard attempts to swindle Frank Nitti in a Wall Street investment deal
Telly Savalas, Frank Sutton, Ted Knight
Written by Max Ehrlich; Directed by Alien Reisner

THE SNOWBALL (1/15/63)
A college graduate is conducting a profitable whiskey trade on various campuses, but his assistant becomes greedy
Robert Redford, Gerald Hiken, Robert Bice
Written by Norman Katkov; Directed by Alex March

JAKE DANCE (1/22/63)
Ness arranges a jailbreak for a con in hopes that he will lead him to the head of the ring that is flooding Chicago with poisoned liquor
Dane Clark, John Gabriel, Sondra Kerr, Liam Sullivan, Linda Watkins, Joe De Santis
Written by Gilbert Ralston; Directed by Robert Butler

BLUES FOR A GONE GOOSE (1/29/63)
The wife of a bootlegger falls for a trumpet player in one of the clubs supplied by her husband
Robert Duvall, Kathy Nolan, Will Kuluva, Marc Lawrence, Richard Bakalyan

MEN OF ACTION

Written by Don Brinkley; Directed by Sherman Marks

GLOBE OF DEATH (2/5/63)
Ness tries to uncover a $2 million dope shipment from the Far East
Phillip Pine, Barry Morse, Gilbert Green, Malachi Throne, Jerry Fujikawa, Cliff Osmond
Written by John Mantley; Directed by Walter E. Grauman

AN EYE FOR AN EYE (2/19/63)
Ness tries to bust an almost fool-proof scheme for selling illicit liquor involving hundreds of small merchants
Jack Klugman, George Voskovec, Frank Wilcox
Written by John D.F. Black; Directed by Robert Butler

JUNK MAN (2/26/63)
Ness jails a man for throwing a punch at him, only to learn that he is an undercover government drug agent
Pat Hingle, Joe De Santis, Edward Binns, Joan Chambers, Michael Constantine, Jerry Oddo
Written by Herman Groves; Directed by Paul Wendkos

MAN IN THE COOLER (3/5/63)
Ness is double-crossed by a man he released from prison to help
Salome Jens, J.D. Cannon, Peter Whitney, Eddie Firestone, I. Stanford Jolley
Written by John D.F. Black; Directed by Ida Lupino

THE BUTCHER'S BOY (3/12/63)
A pair of World War I veterans are running an extortion racket
John Larkin, Frank Sutton, Francine York, Barney Phillips, H.M. Wynant, Jay Novello
Written by Harry Kronman; Directed by Alien Reisner

THE SPOILER (3/26/63)
A gangster returns from hiding in Brazil to retrieve hidden loot, and must avoid the clutches of Ness as well as another mobster
Claude Akins, Rip Torn, Tim Considine, Virginia Christine
Written by Tony Barrett; Directed by Laslo Benedek

ONE LAST KILLING (4/2/63)
Rival hoodlums doublecross each other, then throw false clues to Eliot Ness
Don Gordon, Harold J. Stone, Jeanne Cooper, Johnny Seven, Woodrow Parfrey
Written by Harold Cast; Directed by Alien Reisner

THE GIANT KILLER (4/9/63)
A convicted racketeer suspects that his son-in-law set him up
Paul Richards, Torin Thatcher, Peggy Ann Garner, Karl Lukas, Patty Regan
Written by George Eckstein; Directed by Leonard Horn

THE CHARLIE ARGOS STORY (4/16/63)
When Ness refuses to track down the son of a dying mobster, two of the man's Aides take up the search for their own reasons
Robert Vaughn, Kent Smith, Patricia Owens, Stefan Gierasch, Christopher Dark, Stanley Adams
Written by Harry Kronman and Robert Yale Libott

THE JAZZ MAN (4/30/63)
Ness impersonates a slain musician and travels to New Orleans to trace the source of narcotics being shipped to Chicago
Simon Oakland, Robert Emhardt, Jacqueline Scott, Cliff Carnell, Steven Geray, Robert Ellin, Robert Bice
Written by David Goodman; Directed by Vincent McEveety

THE TORPEDO (5/7/63)
Utilizing the failing nerve of an aging hitman, Ness turns a pair of bootlegging operations against each other
Charles McGraw, John Anderson, Gail Kobe, John Milford, James Griffith
Written by Ed Adamson; Directed by Ida Lupino

LINE OF FIRE (5/14/63)
The mentally disturbed brother of a ganglord ignites a gang war
Sherwood Price, Ed Nelson, Joe De Santis, Ford Rainey, Grace Lee Whitney, Richard Bakalyan
Written by Tony Barrett; Directed by Robert Butler

A TASTE OF PINEAPPLE (5/21/63)
Mobsters flee Chicago to establish alibis, leaving behind a psychopathic war veteran hired to kill Ness
Tom Tully, Edward Binns, Jeremy Slate, Robert Yuro
Written by Will Lorin; Directed by Alex March

Related:

The Lucy Show: LUCY, THE GUN MOLL (3/14/66)
Lucy is hired by a federal agent to stand in for a lookalike nightclub singer who is the girlfriend of a just-released-from-prison mobster
Robert Stack, Bruce Gordon, Steve London, Walter Winchell (voice)
Written by Bob O'Brien; Directed by Maury Thompson

The Untouchables (1987 theatrical feature)
Kevin Costner, Sean Connery, Robert DeNiro, Andy Garcia, Charles Martin Smith, Richard Bradford, Jack Kehoe, Billy Drago, Brad Sullivan, Patricia Clarkson, Vito D'Ambrosio, Steven Goldstein, Peter Aylward, Don Harvey, Robert Swan, John J. Walsh, Del Close, Colleen Bade, Greg Noonan, Scan

Grennan, Larry Viverito Sr., Kevin Michael Doyle, Mike Bacarella, Michael P. Byrne, Kaitlin Montgomery, Aditra Kohl, Charles Keller Watson, Larry Brandenburg, Chelcie Ross, Tim Gamble, Sam Smiley, Pat Billingsley, John Bracci, Jennifer Anglin, Eddie Minasian, Tony Mockus Sr., Will Zahrn, Louis Lanciloti, Vince Viverito, Valentine Cimo, Joe Greco, Clem Caserta, Bob Mariana, Joseph Scianablo, George S. Spataro, Melody Rae, Robert Miranda, James Guthrie, Basil Reale

Written by David Mamet; Directed by Brian DePalma

The Return of Eliot Ness (11/11/91)

Ness goes back into action when a G-man turns up dead in a gangster moll's apartment and the post-Prohibition power struggle begins between the mob bosses

Robert Stack, Jack Coleman, Philip Bosco, Anthony DeSando, Lisa Hartman, Charles Durning, Michael Copeman, Ron Lea, Frank Adamson, Shaun Austin-Olsen, J. Winston Carroll, George Chuvalo, Michael Kirby, Dwight Bacquie, Rummy Bishop, Walker Boone, Frank Canino, David Clement, Cindy Cook, Shaun Cowan, Tony Craig, Richard Cumock, Daniel DeSanto, Louis diBianco, Bob Dickenson, Eric Fink, Rod Heffernan, Doug Lennox, Jamie Jones, David Michael Mullins, Nicholas Pasco. Bryan Renfro, Timm Zemanek

Written by Michael Petryni; Directed by James Contner

Made for television feature

SECOND SERIES
41 EPISODES, SYNDICATED EPISODE GUIDE

Season One, 1993

PREMIERE (2 hours)
Treasury Department agent Eliot Ness and Chicago mob boss Al Capone begin their legendary battle for control of the streets of Chicago
Michael Parks, Joe Gazaldo, Byrne Piven
Written by Christopher Crowe; Directed by Eric Laneuville

FIRST BLOOD
Ness is forced to question his mission against Capone when the work of the Untouchables brings about the deaths of two men
Joe Gazaldo, David Pasquesi
Written by Jacob Epstein and Ken Solarz; Directed by Aaron Lipstadt

MURDER INK (2 parts)
Ness and the Untouchables discover a corrupt chief of police and reporter while plotting to shut down one of Capone's breweries, and ultimately find a shocking web of illegal financial deals involving very important men
Del Close, Earl Brown
Written by David Israel; Directed by James Quinn (Part 1), Cliff Bole (Part 2)

DEAL WITH THE DEVIL
Capone expands his control of the streets of Chicago by helping a struggling union leader fight a powerful local dairy
Philip E. Johnson, Ron Seattle, James Andelin
Written by Jack Thibeau; Directed by James Quinn

A TALE OF TWO FATHERS (2 parts)
Capone and Ness find themselves unlikely allies in the desperate search for a child killer
Danny Goldring, Robert Breuler, Peter Bums, Carla Tamburrelli, Chuck Huber, David Pasquesi
Written by Andrew Mirisch; Directed by Steve DeJamatt

THE SEDUCTION OF ELIOT NESS
Seduced by the promise of success and fame, Ness allows one of his men to risk his life by infiltrating Capone's organization
Eden Atwood, Mark Morettini
Written by John Schulian; Directed by Colin Bucksey

CHINATOWN
A smitten Al Capone drags a beautiful Chinese woman into his bloody, violent world... with tragic consequences
Ping Wu, Keone Young, Sen Shu Kuang, Joe Krowka, Vivian Wu
Teleplay by Jack Thibeau and Steve Bello, story by Jack Thibeau; Directed by John Nicolella

PAGANO'S FOLLY
Pagano risks everything when his innocent sister is forced into prostitution by Capone's thugs
Monica McCarthy, Gary Houston, Shea Farrell, Ellen Karas, Kara Zediker
Written by LeMar R. Fooks; Directed by Colin Bucksey

Pretty Boy Tommy Irish
Ness struggles to save an ambitious young boxer from the poisonous influence of Al Capone's organization
Jeffrey Jenkins, Jenny Bacon, Steve King, Sam Barkan, Nathan Davis
Written by Jack Thibeau; Directed by John Nicolella

Framed
When the man who killed his wife is brutally murdered, Mike Mafone is blamed for the crime
Kate Buddeke, Debra Sharkey, Paul Dillon, James Schneider, Kate Goehring, Bill Larson, Patrick Clear, Gene Janson, Michael Sassone, Kevin Michael Doyle, Donald Herion
Written and Directed by Charles Robert Garner

One Way Street
Capone's glamorous life captivates a boy living in poverty, and Ness puts his own life on the line to keep the child from falling under the mobster's spell
Tracy Letts, Barbara E. Robertson, Lily Monkus, William J. Norris, Cristina Allan, Frank Dominelli, Rafer Weigel, Will Clinger, Kimberley Furst, George Carson
Written by Kenneth A. Rudman; Directed by Mario Di Leo

Betrayal in Black & Tan
Ness teams with a black gambling kingpin to prevent Capone from taking over a numbers racket on Chicago's South Side
Ernest Perry Jr., Ken Earl, Candace Coleman, Jim Jackson, Cuba Gooding Jr.
Written by Michael Lazarou; Directed by John McPherson

A Man's Home is His Castle
Capone's brief affair with an unstable actress puts his entire family in danger

Maria Sucharetza, Tom Guarnieri, Christopher Pieczynski
Written by Jack Thibeau; Directed by John Nicolella

HALSTED HOLLER
A Kentucky whiskey distiller and his family meet with disaster when they inadvertently cross paths with Capone
Tony Mockus, Harry Hutchinson, Fern Persons, Michael Nicolosi, Patrick Clear, Chelcie Ross
Written by Jack Thibeau and Loyal Truesdale; Directed by Vern Gillum

ATLANTIC CITY
Capone clashes with Meyer Lansky and Charles Luciano just when he wants to forge a stronger bond between their operations
Marc Grapey, David Darlow, Thomas James White, Thomas C. Simmons, Eric Winzenried, Robert Wood, Joseph R. Ryan, Bill Visteen, Byrne Piven, Paul Amandes
Written by Steve Bello; Directed by John McPherson
Paul Amandes is the brother of series star Tom Amandes

Season Two: 1993-1994

STIR CRAZY
With Al Capone in prison, Ness and the Untouchables prepare an all-out strike against the Mob
George Dzundza, Rob Riley, John Malloy, John Beasley, Jon Polito
Written by Steve Bello; Directed by Vern Gillum

RAILROADED
While preparing for his boxing match against Capone, Ness and the Untouchables stage a daring attempt to catch Nitti with a shipment of Canadian liquor
George Dzundza, Mark Hutter, John Beasley, Gunnar Branson, J. Patrick McCormack, Neil Flynn

MEN OF ACTION

Written by Alfonse Ruggiero Jr.; Directed by John McPherson

THE CRUCIBLES
Capone's men attempt to arrange his early release from prison while Ness's wife and daughter are stalked by a crazed assassin
George Dzundza, Daniel Mooney, John Malloy, Minnie Martin, Afram, Bill Williams, Ron Perlman
Written by Jack Thibeau; Directed by Vern Gillum

CAPONE'S RETURN
In a last-ditch effort to defeat Chicago mayor "Big Bill" Thompson, Ness uses Capone's return from prison to turn Capone and Nitti against each other
Rob Riley, David Darlow, Marc Grapey, Thomas James White, Tom Guamieri
Written by Loyal Truesdale; Directed by John McPherson

RADICAL SOLUTION
Determined to regain control of Chicago's streets, Capone targets for death the newly-elected mayor
Rob Riley, David Engel, Richard Henzel, Martin Charles Warner
Written by Brad Markowitz; Directed by Colin Bucksey

THE GENERAL
When Chicago is placed under martial law, Ness clashes with the military general who has been hand-picked to run the operation
Ronny Cox, Richard Pickren, Sam Derence, Nick Kusenko
Written by Jack Thibeau; Directed by John McPherson

CUBA (2 parts)
While Ness celebrates a string of victories over the Chicago mob, Capone retakes control with an ambitious plan to expand operations to Cuba

Paula Korologos, Yul Vazquez, Ismael (East) Carlo, Rick Snyder. Mitchell Litrofsky, Ned Schmidtke, Lee R. Sellars, Tom Guarnieri, B.J. Jones
Part 1: Written by Alfonse Ruggiero Jr.; Directed by Colin Bucksey
Part 2: Written by Steve Bello and Brad Markowitz; Directed by John McPherson

Attack on New York
Trying to stop a suspected Capone takeover of the New York Mob, Ness clashes with a politically ambitious New York prosecutor
Charles Martin Smith, Silas W. Osborne, Thomas James White, Marc Grapey, David Darlow
Written by Jack Thibeau; Directed by Aaron Lipstadt

Mind Games
Ness is led to believe that he has been in a coma for a year, his wife and child are dead, and Capone is in prison
Peter Syvertsen, Minnie Martin, Amy Carlson
Teleplay by Steve Bello and Brad Markowitz, story by Brad Markowitz and Barbara Nance; Directed by Mario Di Leo

The Skin Trade
Robbins falls for a furrier's daughter who makes a deal with Capone in hopes of saving her father's business
Gina Gershon, Eric Simonson, Richard Fire, Gerry Becker
Written by Morgan Gendel; Directed by James Quinn

Only for You
A beautiful singer becomes a target when Capone's plan to take over a local radio station goes awry
Melissa Justin, Bruce Norris, Roger Mueller
Written by Sheldon Renan; Directed by Cliff Bole

Legacy

A teen takes the law into his own hands after one of Capone's thugs gets away with killing the boy's policeman father

Robert J. Steinmiller Jr., Vince Viverito, Gory J. Barlog, Mary Kate Schellhardt

Written by Dan Peterson; Directed by James Quinn

Stadt

Ness fears Malone is losing his mind when he becomes convinced that his nemesis, a Nazi thought to be dead, is murdering Germans in Chicago

Mark Lindsay Chapman, Hollis Kesnik, Kevin Quigley, Mark Benninghofen

Written by Jack Thibeau; Directed by John McPherson

Til Death Do Us Part

Malone is targeted for murder by two gangland factions just as he reaches a decision to dramatically change his life

Karen Valentine, Minnie Martin, Michael Sassone

Written by Alfonse Ruggiero Jr.; Directed by Vern Gillum

The Last Gauntlet

While transporting a teenage prisoner, Ness learns how unfair the system can sometimes be when he finds out the truth about the boy's crime

Shannon Cochran, Matt Scharff

Written by David M. Wolf; Directed by John McPherson

Family Ties

The Capone "family" loyalty is tested when Frankie Rio's younger brother blows his cool and kills a member of a rival gang

Carol Huston, Todd Tesen, Tony Mockus Sr., Paul Makkos, Tom Guarnieri

Written by David Shore; Directed by Vern Gillum

The Fever
The brutal murder of an old friend and his own son's illness force Al Capone to re-evaluate his life of crime
Joe Guzaldo, Tom Guarnieri, Roxann Biggs
Written by Steve Bello and Brad Markowitz; Directed by Danny Aiello III

Voyeur
Ness falls for a beautiful call girl while investigating a blackmail racket linking Capone to several noted court judges
Famke Janssen. Kevin Gudahl, Tim Perot
Written by Jack Thibeau; Directed by Mario Di Leo

Omerta
Untouchable Paul Robbins takes on the Old West when he travels to a frontier town to bring back a captured Capone thug
Jim Andelin, Gerald Prendergast, Tony Crane
Written by Loyal Truesdale; Directed by Cliff Bole

Apocalypse in Chicago
Robbins defies Ness's orders and investigates Capone's connection to a plan to take over Chicago's railroads
Will Zahrn, Ned Schmidtke, Alien Hamilton, Mark Morettini
Written by Tim Iacofano; Directed by Tucker Gates

Bury My Heart at Starved Rock
While investigating the robbery of one of Capone's banks, Ness finds himself drawn to the Indian who committed the crime
Joseph Runningfox, Brian Frejo, Joe D, Lauck, Scan Grennan
Written by Morgan Gendel; Directed by Vern Gillum

Death & Taxes (2 parts)
With the end of Prohibition looming, Ness and the Untouchables launch an all-out assault against Capone

Byrne Piven, Al Ruscio, Ned Schmidtke, Darcy DeMoss, Gerry Becker, Darcy DeMers, Cathy Schenkelberg, Chic Vennera, Bernard Beck, Jeff N. Strong, Kyle Colerider-Krugh, Paul Cook, Richard Fire, Rick LaFond, Barren Bochat

Part 1: Written by Steve Bello and Brad Markowitz; Directed by John McPherson

Part 2: Written by Alfonse Ruggiero Jr.; Directed by Tucker Gates

HARRY O
(ABC, 1974-1976)

Forty-four episodes, plus two 90-minute pilots

Starring	David Janssen as Harry Orwell
Also Starring	Henry Darrow as Lt. Manny Quinlan (first thirteen episodes)
	Anthony Zerbe as Lt. K.C. Trench (last thirty-one episodes)
With	Tom Atkins as Sgt. Frank Cole (recurring role, first thirteen episodes)
	Paul Tulley as Sgt. Roberts (recurring role, last thirty-one episodes)
	Kathrine Baumann as Betsy (recurring role, first season)
	Farrah Fawcett-Majors as Sue Ingham (recurring role, last thirty-one episodes)
	Les Lannom as Lester Hodges (recurring role, second season)
	Bill Henderson as Spencer "Spence" Johnson (recurring role, second season)

Executive Producer:	Jerry Thorpe
Created by:	Howard Rodman
Produced by:	Robert E. Thompson
	(first thirteen episodes, first season)
	Buck Houghton
	(last nine episodes, first season)
	Robert Dozier (second season)
Theme by	Billy Goldenberg

Prime time network television teemed with Westerns throughout the 1950s and '60s. By the early 1970s, however, the landscape had changed. Hour-long crime dramas were in vogue, led by *The FBI* (ABC, 1965-1974), *Mission: Impossible* (CBS, 1966-1973), and *Mannix* (CBS, 1967-1975). Networks and studios alike sought new ideas for police and detective shows that could stand out from the crowd, but still have enough proven wrinkles to appeal to TV audiences (and, to some degree, network sponsors). So it was that, sometime in 1972, Warner Bros. began developing the concept for the private eye series that eventually became known as *Harry O* (ABC, 1974-1976).

According to *Harry O* historian Steve Aldous,[13] Mark Tuttle, then-head of program development for Warner Bros., put together an outline for a series about Frank Train, a retired cop who was "the youngest guy to ever make detective in the Los Angeles Police Department. He has a bullet in his back, close enough to his spine for doctors to be reticent to operate. Despite the fact he had seemingly recovered after three weeks and was willing to return to work, regulations stated he could not, and he was retired at 80-percent disability with the bullet still in his back. So he lives on his police pension in a beach house [that] represents the simple life he leads. He is a loner and has few friends... Despite the cold exterior, there is a desire to see things put right. [When he takes on a case], he invests himself fully into helping a client with a genuine need or pain."

Though he possessed noble qualities as a detective, Frank Train, as initially conceived, did not ooze warmth. As Aldous noted, the outline also described Train as a "hard guy who likes

---

13 Aldous, Steve, "The Origins of Harry O," Stevealdous.co.uk/tv-articles/the-origins-of-harry-o, originally published online on January 7, 2023. Aldous is also co-author, along with Gary Gillies, of the forthcoming *Harry O Viewing Companion* (scheduled to be published by McFarland Books in the fall of 2024).

straight-talking," but uses women "and enjoys them about like he does a can of beer on a cold day." Nevertheless, believing that the character had enough potential to appeal to male viewers, Warner Bros. approached Howard Rodman (*Naked City, Route 66*), the award-winning writer/producer of more than 1,000 teleplays, screenplays, and radio shows, to develop *Frank Train* into a pilot. While Rodman fleshed out many aspects of the original outline, he also had his own ideas about where the series should go, including the addition of two characteristics that would ultimately distinguish his character from other TV detectives: an unfinished sailboat, named *The Answer* (more on that below), and a predilection for taking public transportation.

As he explained in *Murder on the Air* (Mysterious Press, 1989), Rodman found his initial inspiration for what eventually became *Harry O* from an entirely different source: Nathanael West's classic novel of the underside of Hollywood, *The Day of the Locust*.

> There is a page or two describing this guy walking up Sweetzer—that slope between Santa Monica and Sunset Boulevard—on a very hot day. He's a door-to-door salesman going through bungalow courts and he's got his jacket off, his thumb through the hanger loop holding it over his back, and his shirt is all wet... That is the image I used to create Harry O. I mean that literally. That's where I started.

Rodman's vision of the Train character, whom he renamed Lou Chambers, was a lone-wolf private eye "whose hard-knocks-won cynicism," as crime fiction historian J. Kingston Pierce once put it, "vies constantly with his hopes for a better life—for himself as well as others." Though still a former L.A. cop hobbled by a bullet near his spine, Rodman's Lou Chambers owned a gun, but rarely used it; he didn't own a car, relying instead on the buses to go in and out of the city. He lived near the ocean—alone, but not lonely (he goes to bed with a lot of different women). Though he wasn't particularly friendly, he was a good friend to those who knew him. He was different (for television, at least), yet he was also rooted in the tradition of the literary gumshoes of Raymond Chandler and Dashiell Hammett. In fact, Rodman's title for the script, *Such Dust as Dreams Are Made On*, was itself an homage to Sam Spade's classic line in *The Maltese Falcon,* "This is the stuff that dreams are made on"(which director John Huston cribbed from Shakespeare's *The Tempest*).

Warner Bros. submitted Rodman's script to ABC Television in late October 1972. According to Aldous, at some point the protagonist underwent another name change: Lou Chambers became Harry Orwell. As Aldous noted, Rodman's copy of the original Warner Bros. outline included a handwritten note from Rodman indicating that "because Warners owned *Dirty Harry*, we changed [the name a second time] to Harry O."[14]

The project, by any other name, soon went into the capable hands of producer/director Jerry Thorpe (*The Untouchables*), who would win an Emmy Award in 1973 for his work on *Kung Fu*, another Warner Bros. property. Thorpe and Rodman discussed several possible leads, including Telly Savalas. Savalas, however,

---

14 As part of his research for his January 2023 article, Aldous reviewed Howard Rodman's personal papers, which are stored at the Wisconsin Center for Film and Theater Research in Madison, Wisconsin. In so doing, Aldous clarifies a matter that had been raised in prior accounts about the history of *Harry O* (including this article, when it was first published in 1997): whether Warner Bros. originally conceived the Harry Orwell character as a means of adapting *Dirty Harry* (1971), one of the studio's hottest properties at the time, as a weekly television series. Rodman's comments, as cited by Aldous, not only put that notion to rest, but suggests that the only connection between the two projects is that both characters have the same first name.

became unavailable once he signed to do *The Marcus-Nelson Murders,* the TV-movie that eventually led to *Kojak.* Thorpe and Rodman struck gold, however, when they decided on David Janssen—perhaps the greatest television actor of all time.

As noted earlier, the Harry Orwell in *Such Dust* is much different than the character who would eventually personify much of Janssen's personality. He's grouchier, more hard-boiled, kind of chauvinistic, and considerably more of a "man's man" in the early going. In fact, when Janssen's name finally came up, Thorpe initially thought he was wrong for the part. "I thought he was too elegant," he confessed. "He had a kind of 'movie star' quality, like a Clark Gable, which I didn't think would work for this particular character. Clearly, I was wrong. And I soon became a very big David Janssen fan."

Wrote Howard Rodman in 1980: "Little by little, I began to understand who Harry Orwell would be if David played him. [Soon] I was never able to separate Orwell from Janssen—the actor from the role he played. Harry O came out of my mind to begin with, but when David took over, there was never any question about who knew Orwell better. David did. So when he said, 'What I want to do is…' it was never a star insisting on having his own way, it was a statement of the way Harry Orwell saw it.

"If I hadn't been there from the beginning, I wouldn't have understood that the life of Harry O came out of David. It was David's vitality, David's soul, that showed on the screen each week."

Such Dust, wherein the gunman who disabled Harry hires the P.I. to find his missing junkie girlfriend, features an impressive supporting cast: Sal Mineo, Will Geer, Margot Kidder, and Martin Sheen. Also appearing in small roles were Cheryl Jean Stoppelmoor (better known as future *Charlie's Angel* Cheryl Ladd) and Les Lannom, who later played would-be private eye Lester Hodges in the *Harry O* series.

The pilot was filmed as a 90-minute movie. According to Aldous, ABC originally asked Rodman to format the pilot script to fit a 60-minute time slot; Rodman submitted a draft to that effect in early November 1972. A few weeks later, the network then asked Thorpe and Rodman to flesh out the script to ninety minutes. "As I recall, Howard came in long, as he almost always did (and I say that as an ardent fan of his, believe me)," Thorpe explained to me in 1997. "The television hierarchy at Warners decided, rather than cutting out a lot of material, that we'd add another five or so pages and make it a 90.[15]

"One major reason Warners wanted David Janssen was that his TV-Q [audience recognizability factor] was so very strong at the time. They felt that [given Janssen's prior success with ABC and *The Fugitive*] they could probably talk the network into picking up the tab for the extra 30 minutes and airing the pilot as a *Movie of the Week*. More importantly, they were convinced that, even if ABC didn't pick up the tab, they could still recoup the additional costs by selling *Harry O* as a 90-minute movie, in foreign markets and syndication, on David's name alone. It was a numbers decision, pure and simple. And while ABC didn't buy the extra half-hour, Warners certainly did recoup." It was a shrewd move on the studio's part. The 90-minute *Harry O: Such Dust as Dreams Are Made On* played constantly in TV markets worldwide for more than three decades before it was released on DVD circa 2012, along with the rest of the series.

A look at the final shooting script for *Such Dust* indicates that apparently two endings were filmed—one presumably for

---

15 Per Aldous, ABC originally asked Rodman to format the pilot script to fit a 60-minute time slot; Rodman submitted a draft in early November 1972. A few weeks later, the network then asked Thorpe and Rodman to flesh out the script to ninety minutes, in the event ABC decided to air the pilot as part of its Movie of the Week franchise. Rodman accommodated the network and delivered an updated script just before Christmas 1972.

the hour-long broadcast version, the second for the 90-minute overseas version. In the first ending, Harry shoots down the mysterious Broker (Mineo) during the showdown at the paint factory, then arrests his own client (Sheen), much to the young man's surprise. "You gave me [$1,400] to find somebody named Marilyn Bedestrum, and [gesturing to the girl] there she is," explains Harry. "[But four years ago], you and your friend broke into a drug store and robbed it. You killed one cop and you shot another. And there's no statute of limitation on murder."

A separate section of the script (clearly marked "Part Two") lays out the second ending. After slapping the cuffs on Harlan (Sheen), Harry engages in a shoot-out with the Broker. This time, the Broker gets away, while Harlan is killed in the crossfire. After taking junkie Marilyn (Kathleen Gackle) to the hospital to dry out, Harry chases down the Broker, both by foot and via motorcycle, in an excitingly-filmed finale. All of the above, plus a few additional scenes featuring Kidder (as Helen, the woman whom Harry picks up at the bar) and Marianna Hill (as Mildred, Harry's neighbor and occasional lover), appear in the 90-minute version of the pilot.

Harry O: Such Dust as Dreams are Made On aired on March 11, 1973 as part of a special edition of *The ABC Sunday Night Movie* featuring two 60-minute pilots: *Harry O*, airing at 9pm, followed by *Intertect*, starring Stuart Whitman as a former FBI agent who now runs an international detective agency. As Sunday nights were traditionally the most-watched night of the week for all three networks at the time, this also tells us that ABC had high hopes for *Harry O*'s prospects as a series. The lukewarm reaction of most TV critics, however, promptly dashed those hopes. "The pilot's intent seemed to be an approximation of the mood and motivation of the Dashiell Hammett-Raymond Chandler school of private eyes, but one assumes it read better than it played," commented *Daily Variety*. "Janssen's semi-sullen interpretation of the lead did not look too much like a character viewers could grow fond of." The trade also cited several script gaps that were "[apparently] the result of the hour-long running time."

In fairness, *Such Dust* is much more cohesive when viewed in its entirety. Still, even in its abbreviated form, the pilot wasn't bad—it just didn't stand out. "It was just a little too close to the conventional private eye genre," adds Thorpe.

The failure of a pilot to sell usually spells the end of the project. But there have been exceptions to this basic rule of television, and *Harry O* is one of them. While the Harry Orwell character may have come across as sullen, David Janssen himself tested well before the ASI audience that previewed the pilot. A Los Angeles-based research organization, ASI arranges for members of the public to screen network TV pilots before broadcast. The audience responds to the program by rotating a special dial located on the armrests of their chairs. The composite responses are recorded electronically and correlated second-by-second with the content of the show.

"The ASI audience really liked David," recalls Thorpe. "That was the impetus for why we made the second pilot." Indeed, according to *TV Guide*, the test audience wanted to see Janssen "firm and capable, with a good amount of toughness, but, underneath, sensitive, understanding and a 'bleeder' for the problems of others—qualities that make him vulnerable on several levels." These, of course, were many of the same qualities that endeared Janssen to television viewers worldwide during his four seasons as the Fugitive.

Convincing ABC to finance another pilot was another matter. When asked to provide the network with a memo outlining the merits of the project, Howard Rodman responded with a thirty-page document discussing the philosophy of *Harry O* (the series and the character) in detail: Harry Orwell "had to be a guy who was totally honest, the sort of guy who would listen to you, and then say calmly, 'That's bullshit, because…'—whatever the reality of 'Because...' happened to be," Rodman began.[16] "I liked that. I liked it because it was reassuring. One of the qualities of the world I live in is that nothing is fixed and steadfast anymore. Everything changes so fast from day to day, that I have to learn new rules. Even 'changing against change' is change. What verities remain then? Well, certain ways we like people to behave – like a man who says, 'Bullshit is bullshit.'"

In other words, Harry O was a man of old-fashioned values. He was also a kind of anachronism. As David Janssen himself once put it: "What we have here is a show of the '70s using a character of the '40s. The man himself, Harry Orwell, is my own age. He's a part of today, but he seems to relate more to the '40s and maybe the '50s. [You see that in] the clothes I wear, for instance. The button-down shirt, the narrow tie, the narrow lapels on the sports jacket—little things, subtleties, but they add up to the sum total of the man."

Rodman felt that Harry's experience as a policeman was both a boon and a potential source of concern. While he knew that a police background would establish Harry as a figure of authority, he also knew that "a cop has a drawback for a series which requires audience empathy. Because almost as much as an audience wants stability and effectiveness, it rejects too much stability and effectiveness because that makes the audience feel the guy is arrogant, or too perfect. 'Too perfect' is a serious charge against a hero in fiction, since individuals in an audience, including thee and me, aren't perfect at all. 'Too perfect' is somebody you can't identify with."

While the Harry Orwell in *Such Dust* wasn't necessarily "too perfect," he was certainly aloof, a man who kept behind a shell that prevented the other characters (as well as, of course,

---

16 All quotes from Rodman's treatment originally appeared in *Murder on the Air*, which referenced excerpts of the otherwise unpublished document as part of its chapter on *Harry O*.

the viewers) from coming inside. Rodman later remedied this by introducing the voice-over narrations that would become one of the series' endearing trademarks.

"Harry O is a man who has to have compassion," continued Rodman. "He has to have feeling. Again, it's a matter of balance. For on the one hand, he must seem to be cool, self-contained, and invulnerable. [Yet what also must] open up to the audience, what the audience must be able to discover for itself, is a secret that none of the bad guys will ever uncover—that Harry is vulnerable and caring and has pity and compassion."

Jerry Thorpe underscores this point. "I learned a lot about Harry O, and about David Janssen, in that first pilot," he said. "When we were planning the second pilot, I remember pitching the importance of tapping into the David that I knew by that time, to make the character more interesting and more vulnerable—which we did, I think, in *Smile Jenny*."

In *Smile Jenny, You're Dead*, the second pilot, Harry falls for his client, a beautiful young model named Jennifer (singer/actress Andrea Marcovicci) who is being stalked by the mentally imbalanced young photographer (creepily played by Zalman King) who has murdered both her estranged husband and current lover. Harry rescues Jennifer, but loses her nonetheless when the emotionally fragile woman walks away at the end of the story. It's a crushing moment for Harry, who realizes the chances for true love increasingly diminish as he continues to grow older. Though he maintains a stoic expression, Harry lets the audience know just how badly he aches through his final voice-over:

> *Days happen to you...and sometimes I wish I could go back to when I was seventeen again. When I was seventeen, I once said, "A woman is like a bus—let her go. There'll be another one along in five minutes." But that was a long time ago...*
>
> *Goodbye, Jennifer.*

Harry O's use of voiceover narration remains one of the high points of the series. While some mystery writers believe that voiceover narration and network TV are an oil-and-water mix, Quinn Martin, for one, used it successfully on three of his hit series (*The Untouchables*, *The Fugitive*, and *The FBI*). Indeed, depending on the writing (and the voice-acting abilities of the performers involved), voiceover narration can be a great way to convey certain points, enhance aspects of the main character (assuming he or she is the narrator), and further connect viewers to that character. Darren McGavin, both in *The Night Stalker* and *The Outsider*, and Tom Selleck on *Magnum, p.i.* excelled at voiceover narration, while Robert Urich, when he starred in *Spenser: For Hire*, never sounded comfortable doing it.

David Janssen was so good at performing Harry's voiceovers that he practically made it into an art form. Janssen's inflections never failed to capture the mix of self-deprecating humor, wit, world-weariness, and life perspective that were not only essential to the Harry Orwell character, but made him interesting to watch every week.

Harry Orwell was definitely unlike other TV private eyes, particularly since he really didn't have to work. While his disability pension didn't make him rich, it sustained him enough to live the lifestyle he wanted—which often didn't require more than a run on the beach, a few hours fishing, some putzing around with his boat, then maybe reading a good book. He was content with simple pleasures, like having a few good friends or watching the sunset every night. Though he didn't work for free, he didn't always work for money: in one episode [DOUBLE JEOPARDY] he let his client (played by Kurt Russell) pay off his fee by working on his boat for a few days. But he could also afford to do an occasional case "on the house," if he had a client he truly believed in, or if he felt, as is the case in THE ADMIRAL'S LADY, that he'd somehow let the client down. Jim Rockford would *never* do that.

The stories, in turn, unfolded at a leisurely, almost novelistic pace that allowed the audience to immerse themselves in the lives of Harry and the different characters he'd meet. "We're not laying out a complete biographical background on Harry O, as is often done with series leads," said Janssen in 1974. "We'll find out more about him as the series goes on. We do know that he lives alone in a small beachfront house. He has a car that doesn't run, but he figures, why should he have it repaired when he could just as easily hop a bus?" Indeed, as Janssen also put it, "Harry's a part-time investigator and a full-time human being."

As a full-time human being, Harry had hopes and dreams that sustained him throughout the disappointments that sometimes came his way. As Rodman explained to the network, those dreams were personified by what would become one of the show's more memorable characters: Harry's boat, *The Answer*.

> Harry, like everyone else, has an unfulfilled, inchoate hunger. A boat like that takes you away (my homage to Clifford Odets, whose irrelevant third acts always took his protagonists to that far place). Even though, no matter how long the series would continue, the boat would never be finished. Because, like everyone else, Harry has answers which never come to reality, has dreams which remain dreams. The boat is simply a statement of what he's after—both in the specific of a detective's work, and in general, as a human being trying to find out what kind of world he's living in. And that answer is never finished because it's always in the making. It's always under construction.

"You don't see too many allegories on network television," added Jerry Thorpe. "But that was the particular beauty, and the genius, of Howard Rodman. The man had DaVinci's IQ—I'm sure it was over 200. I loved sitting down and talking with him."

Janssen also spoke enthusiastically about how the use of Harry's boat could open the door to different kinds of stories. "[Harry] can get the built and set off on a cruise to the island," the actor told the *Portland Oregonian*, "or we could have a couple of love stories with no crimes involved." (However, the former premise was not likely to occur, given Rodman's intent that *The Answer* would remain unfinished, "no matter how long the series" continued.)

Harry's hopes, dreams, and eternal search for answers were likewise captured in the thoughtful music of Billy Goldenberg, the Brooklyn-born composer who began his career as a rehearsal pianist on Broadway before landing work as musical director such acclaimed TV specials as *Petula* (NBC, 1968) and *Elvis: The 1968 Comeback Special* (both of which were produced and directed by Steve Binder). In 1968, Goldenberg became assistant to Stanley Wilson, director of music at Universal Television, and began "scoring episodes of *It Takes a Thief* and *The Name of the Game* and landing several major TV-movie assignments," noted Jon Burlingame in *Music for Prime Time: A History of American Television Themes and Scoring* (Oxford University Press, 2023). Among those plum assignments was the music for *Ransom for a Dead Man* (NBC, 1971), the second pilot for *Columbo* and the one that sold the series.

Film historian Gary Gerani is also the writer and director of *Romantic Mysticism* (2022), a feature-length documentary on the life and music of Goldenberg. "If you're a musician working in television, you're gonna wind up doing themes," Gerani said on *TV Confidential* in 2020. "But Billy approached [the music he did for television] like a great musician. He wasn't necessarily just looking to do catchy little themes. Of course, the most distinctive thing about his *Columbo* scores [was that] the music was always based on the villains, because the villains were larger than life. They were the focus of the story. But that was also storytelling. Because by focusing all your music on the villains, and ignoring your hero, that's the way

Columbo [shines]. You can't possibly think this nerdy little guy is going to outwit the super powerful, super smart, super rich villains. So even Billy's score [for *Ransom for a Dead Man*] plays along with that idea and ignores him. That was brilliant, brilliant thinking… and very typical of the way he approached his work [at Universal].

"Another example of that is *A Clear and Present Danger* (NBC, 1970), the pilot for *The Senator* with Hal Holbrook, one of the most important TV shows of that era.[17] The pilot, which was a two-hour movie, had the Hal Holbrook senator character dealing with air pollution. That was the theme of the pilot. Given the nature of the material, Billy just kept his music to, like, very limited sound effects, to keep it very real. Then, once *The Senator* went to series, Billy told the producer, "There should be no music in this—I mean, I'm the composer, I'm talking myself out of a job here, but it's best for the material here.[18] [The series would] be more real, more biting, more topical, and seem more serious without music.'

"He was absolutely right," added Gerani. "For Billy, it was always about the work."

Burlingame also notes that, though Goldenberg's original contract with Universal expired in 1971, the composer always

---

17 Coincidentally, Howard Rodman also wrote the script for *A Clear and Present Danger*.
18 This wasn't the first time that Goldenberg "talked himself" out of a credit. As Steve Binder has noted on many occasions (including a 2016 interview with me on my radio show, *TV Confidential*), Goldenberg and lyricist Earl Brown wrote "If I Can Dream," the original song that Elvis Presley performed at the end of the *1968 Comeback Special*. After watching Presley rehearse the song, and recognizing immediately how much it meant to him on a personal level, Goldenberg knew that, once Elvis performed "If I Can Dream" on the special, the song would belong to Elvis forever. So he erased his name from the music sheet—a decision that likely cost Goldenberg millions of dollars in royalties. But that also speaks to how selfless Goldenberg was, both as a musician and as a person.

considered Universal to be like "home" because his career in film and TV composition started there. Indeed, he often returned to Universal as a freelance composer because he was a favorite of the studio (and, particularly, director Steven Spielberg). By 1973, however, Goldenberg was also freelancing for other studios, including Warner Bros. That accounts for how he was available to score both *Smile Jenny, You're Dead* and the *Harry O* series. For the former, Goldenberg provided a haunting, minimalist score that mostly came into play in the tense sequences featuring Zalman King as the sociopathic killer. For the theme music for the latter, Goldenberg created a somber, almost melancholy anthem that captures the essence of Harry Orwell as a "full-time human being" who happens to make his living as a private eye. (Goldenberg also provided original scores for eleven episodes for the *Harry O* series, including the premiere episode, GERTRUDE.)

Though ABC liked the basic concept of *Harry O*, it did have its reservations. "They thought no dramatic series could survive without 'hard action,'" Rodman said in *Murder on the Air*. "They would rather have seen Harry drive a car, carry a gun, and not be hampered by the bullet in his back." In other words, ABC wanted the show to be "different," but with the same trappings as other private-eye shows. Known in the television business as "the jello wall," this particular mindset would ultimately prevail over the course of the show's first season.

Still, ABC not only ordered the second pilot, but commissioned seven scripts for possible episodes and paid Janssen a handsome holding fee to ensure his availability. *Smile Jenny, You're Dead* aired as a two-hour *Sunday Night Movie* on February 3, 1974. Clu Gulager co-starred as Lt. Milt Bosworth, Harry's police contact. Other guest stars included Howard da Silva, John Anderson, Tim McIntire, and a twelve-year-old Jodie Foster.

"The Harry O character is an interesting human being," noted *Variety* in its review. "Janssen gave the role a well-shaded, often effectively underplayed interpretation." The trade paper also commended Rodman's script for "focus[ing] on character development of the feature's leads, rather than the hardcore detective action of most such series." Producer/director Thorpe's trademark "painstaking attention to detail" was also noted.

Harry also has a car in the second pilot, although we never actually see it (it's in the body shop). However, by the time the series began, the car became more visible, probably as a concession to the network. ABC didn't want to lose out on having the General Motors Corporation as a sponsor. The ancient Austin-Healey MG rarely fared better than it did in *Smile Jenny*—it frequently didn't start, and even broke down once in the middle of the street while Harry was on a case [in Coinage of the Realm]. Visiting his mechanic became as much a part of Harry's life as riding the bus. Harry would have three mechanics over the life of the series: Roy Bardello, played by Mel Stewart (*Scarecrow and Mrs. King*); Clarence, played by Hal Williams (*Sanford and Son*, *227*); and Spencer "Spence" Johnson, played by Bill Henderson (*Trouble Man*). A one-time member of the San Francisco-based comedy improv group The Committee, Stewart had played Arvin Granger, Harry's police contact in the first pilot. (He was also a cast member of *Turn On*, the infamous comedy series, created by George Schlatter, that ABC notoriously canceled in February 1969 in the middle of its premiere broadcast.) Williams had previously starred as Sgt. Earl Danning in the San Diego episodes, while Henderson played a street contract known only as "Teak" in the San Diego episode Eyewitness.

ABC was once again last among the three major networks heading into the 1974-1975 television campaign. Being last is not necessarily a bad thing—because there's nowhere else to go but up, you can afford to experiment once in a while. In announcing its lineup of new shows for the fall, ABC said that many of its new shows would have a "non-L.A." look to them. *The Night Stalker* with Darren McGavin took place in Chicago; *Kodiak* with Clint Walker was set in Alaska; *Paper Moon* with Jodie Foster and Chris Connelly was based in 1930s Kansas. In addition, the network also announced that several of its new programs would also be filmed on location. *Kodiak* was lensed in Oregon, while *Paper Moon* was actually shot in Kansas.

Harry O was also going to be filmed outside of Los Angeles—the only question was where. ABC suggested Seattle or Honolulu. Seattle wouldn't work, it was determined, because the rainy climate would cause too many production delays. Honolulu was out because Jack Lord and *Hawaii Five-O* were already firmly established on the Islands.

Executive producer Jerry Thorpe suggested the city of San Diego. "I'd shot a TV-movie down there a few years earlier [*Dial Hot Line,* the pilot for the *Matt Lincoln* series with Vince Edwards], so I knew the terrain," he recalled. "It's very scenic, and I thought it would make an appropriate place for someone like Harry Orwell to live." Thorpe showed *Dial Hot Line* to ABC Entertainment head Marty Starger; Starger liked what he saw and gave Thorpe the go-ahead.

Thorpe knew there would be two major problems indigenous to shooting exclusively in San Diego. The first matter concerned a rule imposed by the Screen Extras Guild requiring that any film location less than 300 miles from Los Angeles must bring in extras from Los Angeles. At the time of the show, screen extras could cost a studio as much as $55 per day; factor in travel expenses and per diem, however, and the fee could jump as high as $125 per day per extra. Depending on the setting, of course, there often could be as many as thirty to forty extras at work in any given scene, so you can see how quickly this particular cost can add up.

Thorpe met with SEG representatives before commencing production and came away with the impression the Guild "would give us some relief by softening its policy," he continued. "Once we started shooting, though, we learned that wasn't going to be the case. So instead of casting extras from the local area, we had to bring them down from L.A, which amounted to additional costs we hadn't originally budgeted."

The other major red flag focused on the lack of experienced film technicians in the San Diego area. Cities such as New York or San Francisco, where many movies and TV series have been filmed over the years, have established labor pools, so a production company shooting there can hire as many as half of its entire crew from the local area. But this wasn't an option in the case of *Harry O*, since, with a few exceptions, San Diego had never been used extensively as a location city before; consequently, Thorpe had to bring down crew members from Los Angeles and house them for the entire time the series was based in the border town.

According to an item in the *Los Angeles Times*, the series was originally budgeted at $205,000 per episode that first year, "with the extra $5,000 as a consideration toward the cost of shooting away from Los Angeles." The *Times* also reported that while Warner Bros. "knew in advance it would be at least $30,000 an episode into deficit financing," the studio believed *Harry O* was a bankable property with hit series potential, "which would allow them to negotiate better terms for [the] next season."[19]

Later on, the show would also have to deal with the San Diego Board of Health, which claimed that the catering company providing food for the cast and crew violated many of the city's health codes. Exacerbating the matter was the lack of a city

---

19 While Warners had risked deficit financing with *Harry O* once before (shooting the first pilot as a 90-minute movie, with an eye toward international distribution), it seems unlikely that the studio would have willingly bankrolled a series that would cost them thousands of dollars each week—regardless of how big a hit *Harry O* could become. Like most sound companies, major motion picture studios are usually in business to make money.

commission or ombudsman assigned specifically to work with film companies to iron out these and other kinds of problems. (The city would eventually have such a position in place, but not until long after *Harry O* left town.)

Originally, Clu Gulager was going to continue as Lt. Milt Bosworth, a man who somehow always felt threatened by Harry's unassuming presence. Harry always tried to get Bosworth to relax. "[Riding the bus] gives you a chance to think," he tells him in the second pilot. "You ought to try it sometime, Milt."

But when Gulager opted not to do the series, Howard Rodman reshaped the character in the image of Henry Darrow, who was perhaps best known as Manolito on *The High Chaparral*. Darrow's Manny Quinlan was, like Bosworth, a by-the-book, somewhat uptight cop who bristled whenever Harry became entwined in an actual police investigation. Unlike Bosworth, however, Manny liked Harry, though his friendship with the P.I. sometimes got him in trouble with the brass. Manny trusted Harry and usually cooperated with him because he knew that Harry would always return the favor by bringing him in on the kill. Manny was a good cop in his own right, but his arrest record probably wouldn't have been as impressive without Harry's help. *(Henry Darrow shares his insights into the character and the series in the accompanying stand-alone interview.)*

Harry O was also marked by the innovative camera style of director/producer Jerry Thorpe, long recognized in the industry for his exciting sense of the visual. "One of the things that evolved, as my style was evolving, was that I began to stage exclusively in forced perspective—that is, 'up and down stage,' as opposed to 'stage left and stage right,'" he explained. "That eliminated the use of master shots, or wide angles, which I felt the audience had a hard time reading in television, because of the size of the screen.

So I usually had something predominant in the foreground—I'd shoot from behind the actors, or over their shoulders, or I'd have them walking toward the camera, then I'd cut. I also liked to use props that way—a lamp, a table, a telephone, something in the foreground that would give the audience the feeling of perspective."

Thorpe's camera style can be traced to the 1965 spy movie *The Ipcress File*, a textbook example of how forced perspective works, directed by Sidney Furie. "That was a very stylishly made movie," he said. "Some of it was a little far out for that time—for example, he used hardly any wide-angle shots, which was unheard of for a feature motion picture. But it's an absolute visual feast, and I soon began practicing and incorporating some of the things I saw into my own work."

One of Thorpe's earliest efforts using forced perspective is *The Cable Car Murder* (1971), a two-hour pilot filmed in San Francisco that is itself a visual gem. Besides utilizing the sweeping and swooping camera movements he borrowed from Furie, Thorpe introduced many other techniques (such as slow-motion and double exposure) that he would hone to perfection by the time he made *Kung Fu* and *Harry O*. *The Ipcress File* is available on home video; *Cable Car Murder* airs in syndication under the title *Crosscurrent*. It's worth watching both of these movies to get a sense of how *Harry O*'s visual style developed.

Thorpe met with *Harry O*'s directors, particularly at the beginning, and encouraged them to shoot in forced perspective as much as possible. "The reason for that," he explained, "has to do with one of the findings we discovered at the ASI testing back in '73. We noticed that during those scenes in the [first] pilot where there were long shots, the audience lost interest – the needle would drop to nowhere. But the minute they saw somebody big in the foreground, where they could zero in on their eyes and expressions, the needle would jump back up again." The executive producer found an eager protégé in Richard Lang, who'd worked with Thorpe as an A.D. on both the *Harry O* and *Kung Fu* pilots. "He was a really talented guy," added Thorpe. "We talked about filmmaking and TV philosophy constantly for two or three years. We were just blessed having him." Lang, who died in 1997, eventually helmed seventeen of *Harry O*'s forty-four episodes.

Thorpe also insisted on filming his TV series and movies in natural locations (both interiors and exteriors), as opposed to shooting inside a soundstage, as much as possible. "When I began directing," he explained, "I wanted to develop a dynamic style for television, and I didn't think I could do that within the confines of the soundstage. The camera can go in all 360 degrees, but you can't always shoot it 360 degrees on a studio set. Sometimes, you can't even shoot up and down. I found those kinds of constraints to be overwhelming, especially since I felt that camera movement was very important. So I tried to stay away from that by using natural settings. Of course, sometimes you run into those same problems on a natural set, but I've often found that the camera solves those problems for you. Plus, when you're shooting inside an actual office, or home, as opposed to shooting inside an 'office set' on a soundstage, you'll often find a unique object, or knickknack, that's much more interesting than any of the properties available to you at the studio. You can use that in the shot."

Among the more prominent San Diego landmarks featured in the early episodes are the U.S. Naval base, Midway High School, the San Diego Sports Arena, Belmont Park, the NTC Maritime Museum, and Tiffinanny's Delicatessen.

Another natural setting was the San Diego public transportation system. The bus sequences were not only filmed aboard real city buses, but were coordinated around the city's actual transit schedules. For example, look back to the scene in GERTRUDE in which Harry outfoxes the intelligence agent assigned to tail him by exiting the bus—then re-embarking one block later. That sequence was timed around that particular bus's regularly scheduled stops.

According to art director Serge Krizman, there were also plans to film the sequences with Manny Quinlan inside the actual headquarters of the San Diego Police Department. When that proved impractical, however, the show converted part of the suite where *Harry O*'s production offices were housed to resemble a typical police station. "But it was always a tight fit," recalled Krizman, who was also art director on *The Fugitive*. "We'd load all the cameras, plus all the lights and so forth, up to this little second-story room. It was a standard-sized office, with eight-foot-high ceilings—how they managed to all stick those lights up there, I'll never know. By the time we were ready to shoot, it got to be very cramped, and very hot. I remember poor Henry Darrow was always struggling not to sweat inside those nice-looking suits he had to wear. But we made it work."

Krizman also designed the only other regular "set" used on the show: Harry's beachfront shack, an actual house built along the shore of Coronado Island. The walls of the house were constructed with special hinges that enabled the walls to be opened up, while the house itself stayed in its frame. This in turn gave the camera crew the room they needed to film interiors from anywhere throughout the house without constraints.

Krizman recalled some of the thought that went into the design of Harry Orwell's house: "It had to look like the home of a bachelor (which, of course, is what he was). It had to be practical, but without any warmth (meaning, without any 'woman's touches'). That's why there were hardly any warm colors in the interior. I did not want it look to like a 'well-lived-in' or even a 'happy' home—because he was a loner, kind of like the character Janssen played in *The Fugitive*. So to me, that called for some 'coldness,' both in terms of the choice of colors, as well as in the way the house was furnished.

"Once you got outside, though, you burst right into nature. It was very bright, with that unique 'sun presence' that you wouldn't otherwise have in Santa Monica, because of the smog.

The water was 100 feet from his home. The water is also a different color down in San Diego, a crisper, sparkling shade of blue, which created another kind of contrast to the starkness inside his home. Then, of course, you had the boat, and all the other junk he had lying around.

"When the house was finished, I showed it to Jerry Thorpe, and I asked the crew to demonstrate how the walls opened up, and so forth. He was very pleased. He said, 'Well, unless the weather causes us some problems, this is an engineering marvel.' I was very flattered to hear that."

The show received special permission from the City of San Diego to keep the house standing permanently, as opposed to taking it apart at the end of each shooting day, for as long as the series was in production. In fact, even after production relocated to Los Angeles, the house remained intact for a few months as a kind of tourist attraction before it was finally torn down in early 1975. The exterior was sprayed with a special finish that protected it from the elements.

There were a few early production snafus, though. Filming on the first segment [GUARDIAN AT THE GATES] was delayed slightly when one of the guest leads had to be recast after one day's shooting. Janssen sustained numerous bumps and bruises, including an injury to his forehead that was later written into one of the episodes [ACCOUNTS BALANCED]. One of the grip trucks accidentally smashed the front gate of a private residence used for location shooting in one of the early shows (the studio's insurance policy covered the damage).

Harry O premiered with GERTRUDE (written by Howard Rodman), starring Julie Sommars (*Matlock, The Governor and J.J.*) as a ditzy, slightly prudish young woman who hires Harry to locate her equally peculiar brother Harold (Les Lannom), a career Navy man who leaves but one left shoe (civilian) as a clue to his whereabouts. The combination of mystery, whimsy, beautiful photography, and crisp performances (Janssen and Sommars are delightful together) scored well with critics and audiences alike. GERTRUDE finished with a 19.6 Nielsen rating, and a 34 share, both solid audience numbers. The second broadcast [GUARDIAN AT THE GATES, with Linda Evans and Barry Sullivan] was another thoughtfully executed character study that also scored well (a 32 audience share).

Despite the promising start, however, both Warners and ABC had concerns about *Harry O* as the season progressed. The studio continued to worry over the show's deficit financing (nearly $40,000 over budget per episode, according to another item in the *Los Angeles Times*). More specifically, Warners knew that the creative control of a series ultimately lies where the production is based—and in the case of *Harry O*, that was on location in San Diego, not at the studio in Los Angeles. "I think what really happened was that the management in Hollywood finally woke up and said, 'Look, we're not making any money off this show, because they're not renting anything,'" said Serge Krizman. "We were not renting any stages. We did not use any of their people while we were down in San Diego. We had our own construction crew, our own operating crew, our own administrative crew. My boys had a very nice shop, where they could build all the things we needed. We had everything we needed down there. It worked beautifully.

"I really believe that once they realized they were losing revenues, that motivated them to think, 'We've got to bring them back up here,' because, as I said, we did not have to pay any stage fees. I don't know how much they were at the time, but it would've been something like $2,000-3,000-4,000 a day, plus the generators, plus the electricity, plus the security cop at the gates, etc. It was all pro-rated for each show. And we had none of that to pay in San Diego."

Added Jerry Thorpe: "Actually, the Warner Bros. overhead [40 percent], which is the awful number, was applied even when we down there in San Diego—as is the case with all studios making television series. So, it really boiled down to stage rental, and the construction of permanent sets [once we moved back to Los Angeles], versus paying for actors, and extras, and per diems, and hotel rooms, and overtime. From the studio's perspective, the cost of the show became prohibitive."

The studio probably would have justified the costs, though, had *Harry O* become a breakaway hit like its Thursday night lead-in *The Streets of San Francisco* (itself an expensive show to make, because it was filmed entirely on location in the Bay Area). After six broadcasts, however, *Harry O* ranked 45th out of eighty shows, averaging a 17.2 rating and a 30 share. Though these numbers were certainly respectable, from ABC's point of view they were nonetheless disappointing because the show's audience, while steady, was not growing—and, in fact, the six-week averages were down 12 percent from the opening night figures. The network particularly felt that the leisurely pace of the storylines was not hooking enough viewers.

By this point, the show was on hiatus, having completed production of the initial order of thirteen episodes. After discussing the situation with Tom Kuhn, Warners' V.P. in Charge of Production, Thorpe met with Marty Starger at ABC to talk about the future of *Harry O*. "The studio felt, and I quickly realized, that if we didn't change the tone of the show somewhat, ABC would remain disenchanted," recalled the exec producer. "So I sat down with Marty, and we basically made a tradeoff.

"I said, 'Look, I see a lot of wonderful qualities in David Janssen. He's very vulnerable, he has a lovely sense of humor, self-deprecatory, he's humble. He has a lot of qualities that we aren't really tapping. He's always been a fairly internal performer—until you tapped into his sense of humor, and then he just lights up.' I then brought up GERTRUDE, which had just aired, as an example of where I wanted the show to go. He and Julie Sommars were terrific together. So that was the goal.

"I said to Marty, 'We'll make the show more melodramatic [which is what the network wanted] —but you'll have to promise me that you'll let me bring more humor to the show, and panache, so that we could at least hold onto some of the character elements that we had in the first thirteen episodes.' And that was the deal we made."

By the time it resumed production, *Harry O* had evolved from an unconventional drama [about a man who happened to be a private investigator] to a show with more traditional private-eye trappings. The episodes now began with Harry already on the case, instead of going through the motions of being hired. Harry's voice-overs were pared down and revamped (the introspective musings were replaced with straightforward, keep-the-plot-moving narrations). Except for a brief scene in SOUND OF TRUMPETS (which was actually footage lifted from one of the San Diego episodes), Harry no longer rode the buses, which meant there were more car chases and squealing brakes and tires than before. As another concession to the network's demand for "hard action," the bullet in Harry's back miraculously disappeared, enabling our hero to become more dynamic or acrobatic when necessary.

Harry also carried a gun more often, though he still preferred using non-violent means to work his way out of trouble. The show's reflective theme music was also jazzed up with a new Billy Goldenberg composition featuring hot guitar licks and a driving percussion. All of these changes, ABC believed, would give the storylines the kind of "running start" that could better take advantage of the enormous *Streets of San Francisco* lead-in.

Just as production was relocated to Los Angeles, so, too, did Harry himself, with the switch in locale explained over the course of two episodes. In FOR THE LOVE OF MONEY, Harry has to spend a few weeks in L.A. on a case, so he rents an apartment;

there, he befriends his neighbor Betsy (Kathrine Baumann), an airline stewardess with a boyfriend named Walter whom Harry hears a lot about but never actually sees. When Harry learns [in SOUND OF TRUMPETS] that his home in San Diego is being torn down to make room for a new highrise, Betsy helps him find a new beachfront house, 1101 Coast Road in Santa Monica (which happens to be right next door to *her* new place). Betsy and her roommates Gina (Barbara Leigh, a.k.a. Mildred in the second pilot) and Linzy (Loni Anderson) frequently pop in for a visit—usually wearing nothing more than bikinis. Harry never seemed to mind.

Gradually, though, Betsy disappears, and fellow stewardess Sue Ingham (Farrah Fawcett-Majors, one year away from *Charlie's Angels*) takes over as Harry's neighbor in the episode DOUBLE JEOPARDY. Though various other women come in and out of Harry's life, it is Sue who becomes Harry's steady love interest for the balance of the series. (Her dog Grover, a hulking white and black-spotted Great Dane, is another matter. Grover doesn't like Harry, no matter how often our hero feeds him when Sue's out of town.)

Though Fawcett was still far from an accomplished actress at the time, she played off of Janssen very well. Both actors liked each other, and that warmth definitely comes across in their scenes. "That was another of David's essential qualities that we wanted to tap into," added Jerry Thorpe. "He was very genteel toward women, very gallant, and kind. That was something I recognized right away, and so the relationship between Harry and Sue was kind of based on that."

Art director Serge Krizman also designed several permanent sets, including a new home for Harry, and an intricately-built police station located on Soundstage 4 at the Burbank Studios. "The set we used in San Diego, nuisance as it was to shoot in, somehow had more of a 'homey' feeling, which I felt was closer to the original tone of the show," said Krizman. "Whereas the one

I designed at Warners was an elaborate thing, with Lt. Trench's office, and the holding cell, and the interrogation room, and so forth. That, to me, is also indicative of some of the changes that were made to the show when we moved."

The police set became another kind of "co-star," as it was utilized frequently throughout the Los Angeles episodes. When he wasn't trading barbs with (or mooching coffee from) Lt. Trench, Harry was often paying a visit to his client-of-the-week in the station's holding cell. "It was a rather 'workable' set," beamed Krizman. "In fact, I remember Jerry was very excited when we first showed it to him. He said, 'I can't wait to work this into our stories.'"

Though it wouldn't have been impossible to imagine, reassigning Manny Quinlan to Los Angeles at the same time Harry moved north probably would've looked contrived. As a matter of logic, a new character had to be brought aboard. More to the point, however, is this basic fact of life in television: when a series struggles in the ratings, sometimes cast changes are made if the producer thinks that doing so might make the formula work. That explains why Henry Darrow was replaced by Anthony Zerbe.

"First of all, I think Henry is a marvelous actor, and indeed, that's the very reason I hired him," explained Thorpe. "He's also an internal performer. David Janssen was an internal performer. They were both very good, but the two characters weren't working off of each other, in my opinion – meaning, there wasn't enough of a contrast between the characters that could generate the kind of spark needed to grab the audience. That's why we made the change."

Thorpe felt that, for the show to more fully exploit Janssen's unique abilities as a performer, he needed both a character who was the antithesis of Harry Orwell and an actor who could provide a counterpunch to Janssen's low-key style. Enter the versatile Zerbe, who brought his unique theatricality to the role of Harry's new foil, Lieutenant K.C. Trench.

ANTHONY ZERBE: I hadn't seen the show yet by the time the offer came in to my agent, so I asked to take a look at the pilot, and maybe one or two shows, so that I could get a feel for what they were doing. They did just that, and I soon became very interested. It looked like a neat show to become involved with. I liked the writing, and I saw what a master David Janssen was at playing this laid-back, nonchalant guy. And I thought, the only line that occurs to me would be, 'Take out the pauses, Harry, we're in the big city'—which I would say to him as the window's going up. Meaning, 'I don't have time for you. I've got an entire office to run.'

I remember when I first met David. I'd read over my dialogue for the scene we were going to do [for the episode FOR THE LOVE OF MONEY]. I'd made changes to some of my lines, to make them more elaborate, in a way that I felt would work for the character, that I felt I could accomplish. The writers were trying to write to that, but at that point, since this was my first show, I felt I had the inside track on that, since I was actually doing it.

A lot of times, actors will change things, but very rarely will their changes affect the other actor's lines. However, in this case, in order to facilitate this particular aspect that I was felt important for my character, the change I made was going to completely alter David's line in that scene.

Richard Lang was directing, and he said, "Let's run through it." And so, I met David. He was very nice, and he said, "I'm sure glad you're doing this, and this is great," and he was very warm. And we started to do the scene, and I knew my lines, because I was prepared to do it. And David's reading it off the script, so I'm thinking, "Well, what do I do, go back to the way it was written before?" And I thought, "No, let's just hang with it." So we get to the line that I say, the one that makes the line that he's *reading* on the page, his response, absolutely impossible. And I say that line. There's just the slightest beat, then he improvises the next line, and goes right on.

So, I thought, "All I can say is, I love this guy." I mean, he didn't say, "Whoa, whoa, whoa, what's going on here?" or "Why are you so off the script?" He didn't even bat an eye. It was like, "Okay, I see what you're doing. You wanna do that, okay." It was all instantaneous.

David did that all the time. He would give you the space to do something like that, and he would absolutely ask the same of you in return. But the fact that he did it that way, that day, in that initial moment of our first contact, was so extraordinary. I think that was the key to why our relationship on the show just took off.

He was the star of the show, but he was in no way dictatorial. Perhaps you could call him a 'benign dictator,' but in the best sense of that, because he himself did not want to be dictated to. The way that he managed the set was that it needed to be loose, and fun, and easy, and spontaneous—or it didn't work for him. That didn't mean he didn't work hard. That didn't mean there wasn't tension, when there needed to be tension. But the working atmosphere was terrific, because it allowed everybody else to be loose, the cast, the crew, the entire company. People loved to work for him. He was a brilliantly witty man.

They used to give me a lot of exposition, because David didn't want to always learn all that stuff—but that would always catch up to him, sooner or later, because he had to explain this, or do that. He was real smart, real fast, but he wouldn't necessarily glance at this stuff. Instead, he'd glance at it and think that he couldn't do it. One morning, we were shooting a scene, and he kept fouling up the dialogue. After about take four or five, I said, "Janssen, what're you even *doing* here?" And he said, "Well, I really came for lunch." And I said, "Well, you've been out to lunch all morning!" And he said, "I play laconica on the beach at Santa Monica." And it was *that* fast. It was that fast. And everybody just cracked up.

We were shooting this scene out in Malibu, for the first show I did. We're walking down the road, and there was this big hedge. The cameras were rolling, and we start walking and talking (I, of course, have most of the dialogue), and he starts nudging me into this hedge. I keep talking, he keeps pushing, and finally, when the scene's over, I look at him and say, "What are you *doing*?"

He said, "Look at the sun." While the camera was moving, he had kept both of us in the light, so we got the shot we needed. And I know that sounds nuts, but if we had done the way it was originally prescribed, we would have lost the light, and we wouldn't have gotten the shot, because we would have gotten into something where there would be a big light change. David did stuff like that all the time.

Though Trench respects Harry's honesty and appreciates his experience as a former cop, the lieutenant admittedly has mixed feelings about their relationship. He's constantly frustrated by Harry's casual manner and independence ("A really good detective is an organization man, yet you *never* share your information"). He chides Harry for relying more on intuition than hard evidence ("I don't trust hunches"), even though he knows that, more often than not, Harry's hunches about a case are right on the mark. "That," confesses Trench to Harry, "is why I have mixed feelings about you."

"Trench had his way of doing things, and he was very successful at it," added Zerbe. "Then suddenly he looks over his shoulder, and he sees this guy Orwell is gaining on him, and that's the fun of it.

"Trench really loves Harry, but he knows Harry's way is not his way. And he knows that Harry needs a Trench, and that Trench definitely needs a Harry. It's a kind of symbiotic relationship. Harry bemuses Trench, and even exasperates him, but ultimately Trench loves him."

Michael Sloan wrote seven episodes of *Harry O* for the second season (SHADES, REFLECTIONS, THE MADONNA LEGACY, BOOK OF CHANGES, HOSTAGE, RUBY, and VICTIM), all of which feature classic moments between Zerbe and David Janssen. "They were both very close, and that really comes through in the dialogue," Sloan said on *TV Confidential* in June 2020. "My favorite Trench line, of the ones I did, had Harry coming into his office, where he sees Trench shining his shoes. Trench [in an uncharacteristically welcoming manner] says to Harry, *'Orwell, come on in. Tell me what's on your mind.'*

"Harry looks at him and says, 'Are you feeling all right?'

"And Trench says, 'No, I just thought I'd try it out for size and see if I liked it. *I don't.* Goodbye, Orwell.'"

Trench's protégé was Sergeant Roberts (Paul Tulley), a still-wet-behind-the-ears young cop who never talked much—but then again, he was smart enough to know he didn't have to. Roberts picked up a world of experience simply by watching Harry and Trench in action.

Sloan, the creator of *The Equalizer* film and TV franchise and the author of the best-selling *Equalizer* novel series, joined *Harry O* in late 1974, around the time when the series had moved production from San Diego to Los Angeles. Earlier that year,

Sloan was an actor and aspiring screenwriter living in London when he decided to write a spec script for one of his favorite American series, *Columbo*. (The premise: What would happen if the lieutenant matched wits with an accomplished stage magician who commits murder to hide a dark secret from his past?) Sloan finished the script, but didn't know what to do with it because he had no screenwriting credits at the time. Sometime later, however, while visiting his family in Los Angeles, Sloan met with an agent who promised to deliver an outline of Sloan's script to then-*Columbo* story editor Peter S. Fischer. To Sloan's unexpected delight, Fischer called Sloan a few days later to let Sloan know that he liked Sloan's idea and thought it might make a good story. (What Fischer didn't tell Sloan: the series desperately needed a script that could go into production almost immediately.) Long story short: Though Sloan had to return to London, Fischer not only conveyed his story notes to Sloan via telephone, but soon commissioned Sloan to develop his idea into a teleplay. That fortuitous set of circumstances launched Sloan on a television career that would make him one of the most prolific writer/producers of his era.[20]

Upon returning to the U.S. later in 1974, a similar bit of serendipity brought Sloan to the attention of *Harry O* producer Robert Dozier. "Bob came up with the great quintessential *Harry O* line," Sloan recalled in 2020 on *TV Confidential*. "Harry is in Trench's office, talking about the case or whatever, then there's a pause. Trench looks at him and says, '*Orwell, you have managed to rekindle my lack of interest.*' That was my favorite line of the show."

---

20 Sloan's script, which Fischer later entitled Now You See Him, is not only one of best *Columbo* episodes ever made, but marked the only time in which the series bought and produced a script from an outside writer—meaning, a writer who was either not on staff on the series or not on Universal's list of approved television writers.

The shift to Los Angeles introduced another character whom Jerry Thorpe believed would enhance the show. Thorpe thought that Les Lannom, who had previously appeared as the slow-witted brother in GERTRUDE, worked well with Janssen in that episode, so he decided to bring Lannom into the series in a similar capacity, as another means of tapping into Janssen's humor. Lannom began appearing as Lester Hodges, a silver-spooned would-be criminologist whose well-meaning stupidity usually got Harry in Dutch with Lieutenant Trench. A typical Lester misadventure was MISTER FIVE AND DIME [from the second season], in which Harry's investigation into the kidnapping of an elderly counterfeiter leads to embarrassing ramifications involving Trench, the FBI, the Treasury Department, and the Mexican Secret Service. The episode is also a good measure of what separates Lester from Harry—besides experience and common sense, of course. While Lester is content with rescuing the old man (which Harry does), Harry knows that if he doesn't clean up the mess he made for Trench, the lieutenant will likely have him deported.

Lester doesn't understand. "But, Harry, you're a U.S. citizen. He can't do that to you."

Harry sighs. "That's how bad it is."

The series also continued to tap into Harry's vulnerability in more demonstrative ways. Whereas Harry's humanity had been conveyed subtly early on (usually via the voice-overs, and through Janssen's own tortured expressions), it was now being dramatized in stories like ELEGY FOR A COP, in which Harry avenges the murder of Manny Quinlan. "I don't have many friends," he grieves in that episode. "You take away one of my friends, you take away a piece of me."

ELEGY was one of the first instances in television history in which a regular character in a series is killed off. M*A*S*H, of course, did the same thing with ABYSSINIA, HENRY (McLean

Stevenson's last appearance as Col. Henry Blake, broadcast March 18, 1975), as did *Nichols* a few years earlier with ALL IN THE FAMILY, wherein James Garner's rascally sheriff is wasted by a gunman played by Anthony Zerbe. Though the *M*A*S*H* episode is the only one that seems to be remembered these days (doubtlessly because, unlike *Harry O*, *M*A*S*H* was a Top Ten hit back then), it is worth noting that ELEGY aired several weeks *before* Stevenson's swan song (on February 27, 1975).

Harry O fans also know ELEGY FOR A COP as "the show with a lot of scenes from the first pilot." See our episode guide for *Harry O* for the back story on that. And though it spelled the demise of his character, Henry Darrow singled out ELEGY as his favorite episode because of the heroic nature of Manny's death. For more on that, see our stand-alone interview with Darrow that accompanies this piece.

Though *Harry O* may have lost much of its original identity with all the changes in format, at the same time it gained a wonderfully new kind of quirkiness. Sometimes the storylines could be farcical, sometimes very touching, sometimes hard-hitting— sometimes all in the same show. It went smoothly because everyone shared the same understanding. And the viewers responded. By the end of the 1974-1975 season, *Harry O* was averaging an increase in total audience of over 10 percent from its first-half figures, and picked up another ten notches in the overall series rankings. For the year, the show finished tied for 38th place [out of seventy shows], with an average rating of 18.5—good enough to merit renewal from the network.

The second season featured several stand-out episodes. Harry clears Trench of a trumped-up murder charge in ANATOMY OF A FRAME, while the lieutenant returns the favor in A.P.B. HARRY ORWELL (in which Janssen once again finds himself playing a fugitive when Harry busts out of jail in Act IV). Harry's vulnerability is further explored in REFLECTIONS (an unlikely reunion with his ex-wife touches off bittersweet memories of their marriage), EXERCISE IN FATALITY (Harry becomes so consumed with avenging the murder of an old flame that he nearly commits a tragic error), and DEATH CERTIFICATE (Spence dies in a car explosion intended for Harry). Lester Hodges returns to plague Harry and Trench in LESTER TWO and THE MYSTERIOUS CASE OF LESTER AND DR. FONG, the latter episode a pilot for a Les Lannom spinoff series (co-starring Keye Luke, Master Po on *Kung Fu*) that never materialized.

A.P.B. HARRY ORWELL is also known as "the peanut butter episode," as Anthony Zerbe explained, because of a delightful sequence he and Janssen improvised at the top of the show. "We were both in his kitchen to do this scene which was mostly exposition, when I noticed this jar of peanut butter on the set. So I said, 'Hey, David, let's start eating peanut butter, and we'll get completely incomprehensible—except to each other, because for some reason, we'll both understand each other.' And he started doing it! It was hilarious." Although the producers considered overdubbing this sequence, Janssen and Zerbe prevailed upon them to leave the scene the way it was because they didn't want to lose that "authentic peanut butter feel."

Zerbe and Janssen ad-libbed another priceless moment in that particular scene. "Trench was supposed to come into his house, and he was carrying his mail—I don't think I had a line about the mailbox, but I said, 'Your mail...?' as if he hadn't checked his mailbox for three weeks. Then we did a little thing about Orwell not balancing his bank statements for three months, before finally easing into the rest of the exposition."

A.P.B. HARRY ORWELL is also the episode that won Zerbe the Emmy Award for Best Supporting Actor for the 1975-1976 season. When the nominations were announced, the producers originally wanted to submit the ANATOMY OF A FRAME episode to the Television Academy's blue-ribbon panel, which would make the final decision. But Zerbe insisted on sending A.P.B. "I said, 'If I have any say in this, I want it to be the peanut butter show,' because that was more indicative of what had been created," he recalled. "They said, 'But you're featured in the other show. This is one of the ones that's really about you.' I said, 'It doesn't matter. The work in the peanut butter show is the real relationship [between Harry and Trench]. That's the real character.'" Indeed, Trench walks a tightrope throughout that episode (particularly after Harry breaks out of jail), balancing his personal friendship with Harry with his sworn duties as a police officer.

So, what's it like to win an Emmy?

> ANTHONY ZERBE: It feels… great! It's nice that a group of your peers watched your work, and felt you could be awarded. But I've always been clear about this: It's not just me. The fact that I stood up and got it, and they named me, just speaks to everybody that was involved on the show—the writers, Richard Lang and the other directors, Jerry Thorpe, and definitely David. And when people do thank the people around them, it's very genuine. I mean, that's why you're there in the first place. And, you know something? It's all just fun. I didn't put all that much stock in it, because I figured, "Hey, I got nominated. If I win, great. If I don't win, that's great, too." And David sent me a lovely telegram when I won.

While the audience numbers for the second season were slightly lower (an average Nielsen rating of 17.3, down one point from the first year), they were not significantly different overall from those of the first year. The series was winning its time slot consistently. Why, then, was *Harry O* canceled after only two years?

The answer to that dates back to the end of the first season, when Fred Silverman replaced Marty Starger as president of ABC Entertainment. Fresh off a tenure at CBS that saw the Eye Network finish No. 1 for five consecutive seasons, Silverman brought an aggressive approach geared toward catapulting ABC, the perennial No. 3 network, to the top. "He was looking for shows that he thought had the potential to be runaway hits," explained Jerry Thorpe. "That was his philosophy. He didn't want to settle for the 'average.' He wanted to take chances with shows that could really elevate the network's standing—which was exactly what ABC needed to do at the time."

Silverman looked at the numbers and decided that *Harry O* was, at best, a "good little show," as opposed to a show with great big potential. In reporting the show's cancellation in April 1976, *Variety* noted that "while *Harry O* was the best of the lot [of the shows that were axed], ABC determined that the ratings for the show were as good as it could get," and that the numbers "would simply stagnate in the future." (Of course, by today's standards, a show with *Harry O*'s audience figures would be considered a Top Ten hit.)

According to TV writer/producer Lee Goldberg, Silverman's decision was also personal. "I worked with Fred for several years as an executive producer on *Diagnosis Murder*. One day I asked him why he canceled *Harry O*," Goldberg recalled. "He told me that it was too dour and dull, that Janssen looked like he had a headache in every scene. But the big reason he cancelled it was out of pure spite. When Silverman was at CBS, he wanted to renew *O'Hara: U.S. Treasury* for a second season, but Janssen refused to come back. Fred really resented him for that.. so he cancelled *Harry O* to get even."

Whatever the rationale was, it took ABC "a long time to make up their mind," added Thorpe. "They went back and forth for about a month before they finally decided to drop the show." Silverman did, in fact, have ABC in first place by the end of the 1976-1977 season.

It's too bad, though, that the plug was pulled on *Harry O* prematurely, because the show had some fun ideas in store for the third season. "I had an idea," recalled Zerbe, "where Janssen and I would go camping, and get drunk—then all of a sudden, we'd discover a bomb or something, and we'd have only three minutes to disable it. We'd be fumbling around looking for a screwdriver, and Janssen's trying to read the directions, and so forth. In the hands of our writers, a situation like that would work, and it would be funny. We also talked about seeing more of Trench's family, and maybe having Harry come back onto the force to take care of some unfinished matter. There were a million places to go."

Harry O has enjoyed a remarkably lengthy afterlife in reruns, both on national late-night television and in local markets and superstations—even though only forty-four episodes were made, nowhere near the "magic number" (one hundred episodes) that usually guarantees eternal success in syndication. After a two-year run on *The CBS Late Movie* (1979-1981), the show went into syndication in 1982 and continues to be distributed internationally to this day. Both pilots likewise aired frequently for the next two decades on local stations and such national cable networks as TBS and Lifetime. The entire series was then released on DVD circa 2012.

Harry O holds up well today, both as detective fiction and as pure entertainment. Aside from a reference to Willie McCovey playing for the San Diego Padres in one of the early episodes (EYEWITNESS), and maybe some of the fashions, not much dates the series as being from the mid-1970s. The humor still works (especially in the scenes between Janssen and Zerbe), while Harry remains someone whose adventures you like following, sixty minutes at a time. Plus, being a lone wolf, he is a classic literary type.

In a sense, it's fitting that *Harry O* ended when it did. There probably could not have been a more appropriate way to send off the show than the "tag" segment of what turned out to be the final episode [VICTIM]. Harry finally buys Trench a new bag of coffee (the department had been out of coffee since Harry finished off the last batch a few days before). Though the lieutenant appreciates the gesture, he still has a lot of work to do, so it's business as usual: "Goodbye, Orwell."

"Goodbye, Trench," says Harry, as he strolls past Sergeant Roberts.

"Goodbye, Harry," says Roberts. Freeze-frame.

"David Janssen was a wonderful guy," Michael Sloan said on *TV Confidential* in June 2020. "He and I got on quite well for a while. In fact, the last time I saw him, I was having lunch at Le Ser [a restaurant in Beverly Hills] when I ran into David, and he said, 'Let's have lunch.' That was on a Wednesday. He passed away on Friday, two days later.

"That was really sad, because he smoked too much and he drank too much. But had a wonderful life, and he was a wonderful guy to me."

David Janssen died of a heart attack on February 13, 1980 at age forty-eight. Howard Rodman died on December 4, 1985. But their mutual creation still lives on. Somewhere right now, Harry Orwell is walking along the beach—his jacket off, his thumb through the loop as it hangs over his shoulder, an answer never finished because it's ever under construction.

INTERVIEW WITH HENRY DARROW

ER: How did you become involved with *Harry O*?

HD: Well, as far as I know, the show was ready to go with the character "Milt Bosworth," which was the original name for the character. And it was Clu Gulager—Clu and I, I think we came into town around the same time, sometime in the '50s, and he wound up under contract at Universal, and I wound up busting my butt for the next thirteen years until I got lucky with *High Chaparral*.

But Clu didn't want to do the show. I have no idea why. In the meantime, I had just lost out to Earl Holliman in another police show, called *Police Woman*.

ER: With Angie Dickinson, right?

HD: Yeah. Because I remember David telling me he was at the screening with her – or at least, they discussed it, and that they looked at films of mine, and films of Earl, and she chose Earl. So, somehow, that might have remained in the back of David's mind, because next thing I know, I get a call.

I knew there'd been a *Movie of the Week* on the show, and Clu was in that, so they probably assumed that he was going to continue. But he said no, and I stepped in, and all of a sudden there was a character called "Manuel Quinlan."

ER: Given your strong identification with "Manolito" on *High Chaparral*, do you think it was just a coincidence that your character on *Harry O* was also named "Manny?"

HD: I've often wondered about that myself. Sometimes Linda Cristal would call me "Manolo" when she was ticked off at me – she would go "*Manolo…*" Whereas "Manolito" meant everything was cool. So I'm just assuming they came up with that combo. And with "Quinlan," certainly, you've got to think a little bit of Tony Quinn's name thrown in there, with that wonderful Mexican-Irish mix.

So then, all of a sudden, there I was, in seersucker blue-striped summer suits, and dark shirts, and white ties, or light ties, and they gave me a great haircut, and I wore shades that were tinted – regular glasses that were tinted.

ER: And you looked really cool!

HD: Yeah. [*Laughs.*]

ER: Did you pick out your own wardrobe?

HD: Nah, they took care of all of that. I have incredibly bad taste. I usually don't care what I wear…

ER: Now, when you were doing *Harry O*, did you live in San Diego, or did you commute back and forth?

HD: No, I lived down here. It was like a six-month gig. We did twelve or thirteen episodes, and I had a great time.

It was a really special time. It was different than the other series I've done, where there are four or five other regulars, and you get to know more about what's happening with your TV family than you do your own, because of the number of hours you spend together on the set. But with *Harry O*, you had just the main star, David, and you had my character. It was a unique situation.

ER: You guys clicked, and it showed on-camera. It was always believable that your characters were longtime friends, or went back a-ways, or whatever their relationship was supposed to be on the show.

HD: Yeah, we hit it off well, right from the beginning. And it was funny, because my character was sort of "by the rules" and all of that. I remember there was talk about expanding the character, and maybe having him run for councilman, or mayor, and meeting his family. But it wasn't in the cards, and that really isn't *Harry O,* anyway. *Harry O* is Harry O. He always got involved with a beautiful, incredibly attractive woman, and he hung out at the beach.

And his voice-overs... I mean, he's the master of voice-overs. I think the one that I can recall starting that was Dick Powell in those black-and-white movies of the '40s. Dick Powell was wonderful at voice-over. And Tom Selleck did a good job with *Magnum.* But I think, when you look at all the different voice-overs people have done throughout the years, that David was the master of them all.

ER: They were another way in which he made the show special. Because while it was a good detective show, it was also mostly a show about a guy who happened to be a detective.

HD: That's exactly it. It was one of the best-written shows ever done, especially whenever Howard Rodman was involved. Because Howard gave him a lot of little quirks, which David turned into wonderful moments of television. Like those shots of him sitting in his little car, waiting for it to start... and waiting... and waiting...

And, of course, he always had his tie loose around his neck, with the blue shirt unbuttoned, and the gray jacket open. That was his thing.

Once, when we were shooting a tag for one of the episodes—it may have even been the first show I did. We were down at Coronado Island, and Harry and Manny are talking by the steps in front of his house on the beach. And as I recall, one of the directors came up to me and said, "Hank, keep the energy going, so you can keep David going." Because, let's face it: we were working long hours, 14-hour days, six-day shoots for each episode. David would have to be on the set all day, from the first shot to the last, whereas I was in and out. At most, I had maybe a four-or-five-day week per show.

So, David's dressed like Harry, with his tie loose, and everything. And so I sort of unloosened *my* tie, and opened my shirt, and stepped back and became a little like Manolito, the character I played on *High Chaparral*. And it was like CUT!

Jerry Thorpe was directing. He was also exec producer (he'd hired me), and I guess he and David may have been partners on the show. He says, "Henry, can I talk to you?"

"Sure, Jerry."

"This is Harry O. And David does that. You're Manny. Manny is an uptight kind of guy. And we can't have two guys doing the same thing here…"

And I thought, "Oh, okay…" [*HD and ER laugh.*] I still don't remember whether they used that take with my shirt buttoned, and the tie up, or whether they left the one with the tie open.

ER: Well, if it was the first show, I think they used the one with your shirt buttoned, and the tie done. But I can also think of a couple other tags where Manny drops by the house, and his tie's undone.

HD: A-ha!

ER: Speaking of *High Chaparral*, Leif Erickson did one of the early shows, didn't he?

HD: Yeah, that's right, Leif went down there. In fact, we were up on the penthouse someplace there, and it got real quiet, we put the TV on, and Nixon resigned.

ER: Oh, wow! [*Laughs.*]

HD: [*Laughs.*] Yeah, you just triggered that. I remember Leif saying, "Yeah, that sonuvabitch, they got 'im—good! Get 'im outta there!" Yeah, that's right. I remember that now.

ER: I guess that's one of those moments where everyone remembers where they were.

HD: Yeah, exactly, in that particular case. But I met a lot of other wonderful guest stars that were there, like Stef Powers, and then you bump into them years later, and you reminisce about doing the show with David. A lot of people enjoyed him, and liked him. He had a really good reputation.

ER: The newspaper accounts I've read say there were two official reasons for why *Harry O* moved from San Diego to Los Angeles: low audience numbers, and the studio thought the show was too expensive to film down there. But there was never any reason given for the decision to drop your character. Any thoughts on this matter?

HD: I think both of those things are true. Because we followed *Streets of San Francisco*, and they'd hand over to us like a 36 or 37 share—and then we'd drop down to 30 or 31. That's a pretty big drop. Of course, now, 30 or 31 would be fabulous.

ER: Yeah, I know—it'd be a Top Ten show. [*Laughs.*]

HD: You betcha! [*Laughs.*] But back then, they could play with that, and say, "Well, that's it."

And the reason they dropped my character was, they figured, since there was going to be a whole new change of locale (which, actually, was sort of similar, because it was Malibu), they couldn't take Manny with him. It wasn't like it was the Armed Forces, where you travel around the world. And so, they came up with that episode, where they killed Manny.

But that is my favorite episode, in a sorrowful kind of way, because of the irony of my character being killed, on camera. Throughout the years, several policemen who've seen that show have told me that's how they remembered being shot themselves, or some of their friends. They'd think, "Wow," after I looked down to see where I'd been shot in the stomach. Because they're thinking, "Aw, shit, I just bought it. It's over for me."

And then, at the end of the show, there's the irony of David being the one who goes into a bar and puts up that bottle of tequila and [*slipping into a perfect Janssen intonation*] says, "In case any of yer friends come in, let 'em have a drink on Manny…"

I still can hardly watch that tag. It was just too much. And I couldn't handle going to his funeral because of it. I just thought, "No…"

I know David fought for me. I noticed that the behavior toward me had changed, for about a few days before I found out. He finished shooting at around 10 in the morning that day. I wasn't supposed to finish until around four or five, but he waited for me—which he didn't have to do—in order to tell me himself. We got drunk at one of the local pubs. He apologized, and he said, "Hank, I fought for you. I wanted you to go up there with me." But they told him, "You don't understand. You go solo, or you don't go."

It wasn't meant to be. They paid me off for the second half of the season, and then they brought Anthony Zerbe onto the show.

I once asked ABC for a copy of my last episode. I finally got one, years later, from a friend. I found out there was a fan club, I asked for a copy, and I'll be damned, they sent me one. Every now and then, I'll take a look at it.

ER: I've always liked the camaraderie between you and Janssen—although I've also liked the camaraderie between him and Zerbe. But it's really two different things.

HD: Oh, absolutely. And Anthony's a marvelous actor. We worked together on a piece called *Attica,* which had to do with the prison break at Attica State Prison in '71. Charlie Durning was in it, and George Grizzard, and Anthony, and myself, and a host of other actors. I played Herman Badillo, who was the Puerto Rican New York Congressman who went up there. We shot that, I guess, around '79, long after *Harry O.*

We've had this running joke over the years, which had to do with my reading for him for some Shakespearean thing—this would have been after we did *Attica.*

ER: That's right, he's directed a lot of theater festivals, and things like that.

HD: Right. So I'd have to read for the part of a gardener, or the part of a spear carrier, and I would say, "Well, you know, I've done all of these plays." And he'd say, "Yes, yes, Henry. But can you do one line for me in a good Shakespearean tone?" [*ER laughs.*] And that became a kind of put-on that we would greet each other with whenever we'd bump into each other.

ER: There seemed to be a little bit of improvisation between you and David as you did your scenes together.

HD: Yeah, it was loose. It was pretty loose, to be honest. I mean, I'm always "around the book" of a script, whatever it is.

Usually, David's philosophy was, "If I can't memorize it," referring to himself, "there's something wrong with the writing." Meaning, something's not clicking, it's not put in the right way—for him. And most of the time (usually, all of the time), he was right.

And I find, for myself, if it's put in such a way, and it just doesn't flow, there's something wrong here—I wouldn't know what, but David would. He could analyze scripts. He had a good feel for scenes, and material. But, yeah, there was some improvisation, now that I come to think of it.

ER: The one show I'm thinking of—this is one of my favorite scenes of the entire series. There's a scene with you and David, you're at this nice restaurant, and he's got a Band-Aid on his head, because apparently a light or a boom hit him, or something like that. And so, that's like the running gag on that show: everyone's asking Harry, "What happened to your forehead?" And Manny's one of the few guys who doesn't pay attention to it. So Harry says, "Manny, aren't you gonna ask me what happened to my head?" Manny finally plays along: "Okay, Harry, what happened to your head?" And Harry says, "An alligator bit me!"

HD: [*Laughs.*] Yeah, that's right. And he did nail himself. We were going up the steps or something, and BAM! he just walked into that, and *Ho-lee shit*, there it was—it was a good-sized lump. I'd forgotten how they worked that into the show.

ER: You did an interview with Diane Albert a few years ago, and at one point, while you were discussing *Chaparral* and your camaraderie with Cameron Mitchell, you mentioned that there were a number of times where he'd do something in a scene, and you'd laugh out loud—only it'd be *you* laughing on-camera, not your character.

HD: Yeah. I had a lot of good times with Cam.

ER: As I read that, I thought about many of the scenes with you and David on *Harry O*, and I was wondering whether there might have been a little of that going on there, too.

HD: Sure, there were a couple of moments like that. Like, whenever we had scenes in my office, David would come in, and he'd start fiddling with the stuff on my desk. He'd always pick up a pencil, make a note, something like that. One time, I ended up breaking all the pencil points, and then putting them all back in the pencil case. David came in, sat down, picked up a pencil, started to write—and then BLEAH! He said, "Hey, how'd this happen?" And I said, "Geez, I don't know..."

He also liked to play with the paper clips. So, one time, I connected them all. He started picking one up, when all of a sudden, he had a string of paper clips about eight inches long... So he yelled, "Cut!" And he knew it was me.

ER: They tried out several different actors to be Manny's sidekick on the show.

HD: That's right. First there was Charlie Haid, who's now a director. Then we had Hal Williams for a couple of shows, then finally Tom Atkins. I still bump into those guys occasionally—in fact, I was over at Haid's house sometime last year.

ER: That's right. He only did one show, maybe two at most.

HD: He had that horrible high voice back then—oh my God! [ER chuckles.] And he didn't have too much experience going for him.

ER: Well, of course, he took that high voice and went all the way to the bank, with Renko.

HD: Boy, you better believe it!

ER: 'Course, the interesting thing about Atkins was, at the time, I think, he was commuting back and forth, doing *Rockford*, around the same time he was doing *Harry O*.

HD: I'll be darned!

ER: Yeah. He was kind of a well-meaning doofus on your show.

HD: Exactly.

ER: But he was a totally different character with Jim, on *Rockford Files*. He was more of a hard-ass. But he was good in both.

HD: Oh, that was neat then, for him. I didn't know that, at the time.

ER: Any other thoughts about the show, or working with David Janssen, that you'd like to share?

HD: Just that it was, again, a great experience for me, all the way around. There was a hockey team down there back then, the San Diego Mariners, and they sort of made me the team mascot. One night a bunch of the players got us in to see the Ali/George Foreman fight on closed-circuit TV. They were showing it on this huge massive screen at their arena.

ER: Oh, yeah, that's right. That's what they did, before the days of pay-per-view, and all that.

HD: That's right, exactly. Exactly. And we caught the fight with these guys. And I mean… [*Chuckles.*] These are a bunch of hard drinkers. I mean, holy cow! [*ER laughs.*] And I could hold my own, and so could David, but all of a sudden your body says, "No, no. No more…"

I don't know what might've led to that massive heart attack he had, or if he'd ever had heart trouble before—if he did, he never told anybody, which would seem to be par for the course for him, I would imagine. He always seemed to fear that he wasn't going to work anymore, though. Like he'd say, "Where's my next job gonna come from?" And you'd say, "God, David, you're like Jimmy Garner—you're one of the top guys. You can do whatever you want."

ER: Don Freeman had a great line about Janssen, and it was along the same lines. He remembered talking to him around the time of the show, and David said, tongue in cheek, "Look, I never went to college. This is all I can do

	to make a living." [*HD laughs.*] I mean, there he was, one of the top guys, and he's saying, "This is all I can do to make a living..."
HD:	He got a kick out of life. He had his own style, his own way.

And he had that incredibly wry, dry sense of humor. On his birthday, I'd buy him not the best year, but the second-best, of the finest wine or champagne. Let's say it's '66 or '68. '66 is the best, so I'd give him a '68 bottle of Dom Perignon. And he'd say, "Oh, '68. They didn't have any '66?" [*ER laughs.*] But he'd do it with a straight face. I'd say, "No." And he'd say, "Okay." [*Laughs.*] And that would be that! You couldn't get back at him.

He had T-shirts made for everyone in the production company: "*Harry O* starring David Janssen." So I made up some T-shirts of my own, "Henry Darrow is Manny Q," and I set up this incredible gag.

One day, we were shooting around Balboa Park. It was lunchtime, and David was seated at one of those long picnic tables there, and he was being interviewed by Don Freeman. There were about eight, ten, twelve members of the crew milling around. David didn't know this, but they were all wearing the "Manny Q" T-shirts underneath their *Harry O* shirts. Meantime, I arranged for a limousine, and even asked the studio cop to give me a police escort. So all of a sudden, the siren blares, the limo pulls up, one of the guys rolls out the red carpet, and I come out of the limo. I'm wearing my "Manny Q" T-shirt, and I walk over to where David's being interviewed to say hello. At that point, everybody else takes off their *Harry O* shirts to show off their "Manny Q" shirts.

And without skipping a beat, he turned and said, "You guys are all fired." [*ER laughs.*]

[*Smiles.*] But you never got the feeling that it impressed him. He just stayed in character. He wouldn't give you that recognition for it—he'd do that later, when you were having beers with him.

I had a wonderful time on that show. It was a special event.

HARRY O EPISODE GUIDE

Harry O: Such Dust as Dreams Are Made On (60 min.; 3/11/73)
The man whose bullet disabled Harry from the police force four years earlier hires Orwell to find his missing girlfriend
Martin Sheen, Sal Mineo, Marianna Hill, Will Geer, Kathleen Gackle, Lawrence Cook, S. John Launer, Garry Walberg, Nate Esformes, Les Lannom, Margot Kidder, Mel Stewart, Mike McGreevey, Jack Kosslyn, Wesley Lau, Sarah Fankboner, Bill McLean, Joe Hoover, Barry Delaney, Donald Eiber, Van Kirksey, Ethel Hazen, Cheryl Jean Stoppelmoor (Ladd), Sylvia Hayes, Tim Haldeman, Robert C. Anderson
Written by Howard Rodman; Directed by Jerry Thorpe

Smile Jenny, You're Dead (a.k.a. See Roy Take a Picture) (120 min.; 2/3/74)
Harry looks into the murder of a policeman's son-in-law and soon becomes emotionally involved with the cop's daughter, who happens to be the chief suspect in the killing
Clu Gulager, Andrea Marcovicci, John Anderson, Howard da Silva, Zalman King, Martin Gabel, Tim McIntire, Jodie Foster, Harvey Jason, Barbara Leigh, Victor Argo, Ellen Weston, Chet Winfield
Written by Howard Rodman; Directed by Jerry Thorpe

Season One, 1974-75

GERTRUDE (9/12/74)

Harry joins forces with a slightly daffy blonde, whose search for her missing brother involves a dangerous assortment of characters and a half-million dollars in diamonds

Julie Sommars, Fred Sadoff, Michael McGuire, Clay Tanner, Mel Stewart, Les Lannom, Bill Stevens, Jon Lormer, Jim Bohan, Joseph Johnson

Written by Howard Rodman; Directed by Jerry Thorpe

Nominated by the Mystery Writers of America Edgar Award for Best Television Episode of 1975

THE ADMIRAL'S LADY (9/19/74)

Harry races against time to thwart a deranged killer stalking the wife of a retired admiral

Leif Erickson, Sharon Acker, John McMartin, Ellen Weston, David Moses, Sally Carter Ihnat, Charles Haid, Al Checco, Milt Kogan, Lucas White, Stacy Keach Sr., Tom McFadden

Written by Del Reisman; Directed by Paul Wendkos

GUARDIAN AT THE GATES (9/26/74)

Business mixes with pleasure for Harry, whose search for a would-be killer draws him into a romance with the daughter of the intended victim

Barry Sullivan, Linda Evans, Anne Archer, Richard Kelton, Katharine Woodville, Michael C. Gwynne, Edith Diaz, S. John Launer, Gordon Jump

Written by Stephen Kandel; Directed by Jerry Thorpe

Known around the world for her iconic screen roles opposite Michael Douglas in *Fatal Attraction* and opposite Harrison Ford in both *Patriot Games* and *Clear and Present Danger*, Anne Archer began her screen career by appearing in just about every crime drama and private-eye series in the 1970s, including *Harry O*. She remembered David Janssen as being "extremely charming, very professional, just good people," she said on *TV Confidential* in May 2023. "No outsized ego, where you felt that everybody had to cater to the ego on the set—he was a real professional [who was] interested in getting a great product and treated other actors with a lot of grace and professionalism."

MORTAL SIN (10/3/74)
The seal of the confessional must be preserved as Harry goes after a deranged killer who confessed his crimes to a priest
Laurence Luckinbill, Walter McGinn, Carol Rossen, Charles Drake, Barry Cahill, John Doucette, Mary Murphy, Phillip Pine, J. Edward McKinley, Dan Barrows, G.W. Bailey, Marion Ferree, Frances Burnett
Teleplay by Stephen Kandel and Robert Malcolm Young, story by Robert Malcolm Young; Directed by Paul Wendkos

The daughter of Oscar-winning director Robert Rossen (*The Hustler, All the King's Men*), Carol Rossen had completed production of *The Stepford Wives* (1975) around the time she filmed this episode. "I did a lot of work with David, both on *The Fugitive* and on *Harry O*," she told me in 1990. "Both he and Quinn Martin were good people, and it was good to work [on both his series] because the people were respectful of each other, and good to each other, and loyal to each other. Those are virtues and values that are not exactly described often in Hollywood, and they're always appreciated when you run into them as a professional person. You remember that more than you remember [any particular storylines].

"Essentially, what I recall, when I think about experiences, is the spirit of the set, and the 'soul' of the set. And that was a very sweet, sweet place. Good people."

COINAGE OF THE REALM (10/10/74)
The carnival atmosphere of an amusement park adds a bizarre twist to Harry's attempt to save a little girl's life and prevent a gangland murder
Joan Darling, David Moses, Kenneth Mars, David Dukes, Dawn Lyn, Florence Stanley, Granville Van Dusen, Edward Walsh, Julio Medina, Danny Wells, Archie Hahn, Ed Gilbert, Joseph Angarola, Casey MacDonald
Written by Elroy Schwartz; Directed by Richard Lang

Best known to TV fans as Dodie Douglas on the last four seasons of *My Three Sons* (ABC/CBS, 1960-1972), Dawn Lyn began her acting career at age four and continued to act in movies and television throughout her teenage years before pursuing other interests, including running her own business in San Francisco, and an accomplished career as a voiceover artist with the Avalon Community Theater Radio Troupe in Southern California. Her other screen credits include *Shoot Out* (opposite Gregory Peck), all three *Walking Tall* movies (as Buford Pusser's daughter), and a memorable episode of *Wonder Woman* from 1978 that also featured Leif Garrett, Lyn's real-life older brother.

"Working with David Janssen was so much fun," Lyn said on *TV Confidential* in August 2016. "He was absolutely wonderful—just a really, genuinely nice person who seemed to enjoy children in general. Because, you know, some, some actors are like W.C. Fields; his reputation was 'Get this kid away from me!' But David was not like that at all.

"I've got a great behind-the-scenes story for you. In the episode, if you remember, I was a dialysis patient. So I'm in the hospital most of the time (and, yes, they sewed up my gown in the back, thank you very much!). One day, they call lunch, and David comes up to me. Now this guy was a playful kid at heart. *Just horrible.* He comes up to me with these *huge* syringes—I mean, I've never seen any bigger. And, of course, they didn't have any needles in them, just the syringe. And David says, 'Here, I got an idea.' And so we went and filled them with water, and then we ran around the set, squirting people with water—and then we're like, 'Nyah, nyah, you can't squirt us back—we're in wardrobe! You can't retaliate, we're in wardrobe....'

"David Janssen was great. He really was great. It was a really, really nice atmosphere on the set. He is one of those greats who has a special place in my heart."

Eyewitness (10/17/74)
A slaying in a black ghetto finds Harry relying on a blind "eyewitness" to zero in on the killer
James McEachin, Rosalind Cash,, George Spell, Margaret Avery, Hal Williams, Ty Henderson, David Moody, Leonard Simon, John Hawker, Edmund Cambridge, G.W. Bailey, Adrian Ricard, Bill Henderson, Leonard Simon, Renny Roker, Nathaniel "Jetihadi" Taylor, John Gruber
Written by Herman Groves; Directed by Richard Lang

Korean War veteran and Purple Heart recipient James McEachin worked briefly as a police officer in New Jersey before curiosity brought him to Los Angeles, where he found work as an artist and repertoire producer for such labels as Liberty Records (where he worked with such artists as Otis Redding and the Fury). By the late 1960s, he had embarked on an acting career, working steadily in television for more than forty years, including many of the shows produced by Jack Webb, as well as such films as *Play Misty for Me* (starring opposite his longtime friend Clint Eastwood). Known to fans of the *Perry Mason* reunion movies as Lieutenant Brock, McEachin also starred as private eye Harry Tenafly in *Tenafly* (NBC, 1972-1973), the first network TV drama with an African-American actor as the solo lead.

Though he had played all sorts of characters on TV at this point in his career, McEachin had particularly vivid memories of his appearance in Eyewitness. "I played a pimp," he said with a laugh when reminiscing about this episode in 2013. "We shot that one down in San Diego. I wore a maroon coat and had a Cadillac that was about as long as a truck! I also remember David and I going to a nightclub together before one of the scenes we shot. That was a lot of fun."

This episode almost marks the first of five appearances by Bill Henderson, the jazz singer who enjoyed a successful recording career in the 1960s before segueing into movie and TV acting in the 1970s. About a year before *Harry O* went into production, Henderson had made his film debut as Jimmy, the pool room owner, opposite Robert Hooks in the Blaxploitation classic *Trouble Man* (1972). "Bill Henderson was a wonderful human being," Hooks said on *TV Confidential* in April 2019. "Most people knew him as a singer—and while he was not as popular as a lot of singers at the time, he was a fabulous singer. *Boy*, could he sing. But a lot of people didn't know he was also an actor. Bill and I became very, very good friends doing *Trouble Man*. I loved him."

In his one scene opposite David Janssen in Eyewitness Henderson plays a street operative named Teak who meets Harry at a pool hall and slips him some vital information. While that's more likely a coincidence than an homage to his character in *Trouble Man*, it is fun to note nevertheless. Henderson joined the cast of *Harry O* in the second season, making four appearances as Harry's new mechanic, Spence.

SHADOWS AT NOON (10/24/74)
Harry commits himself to and becomes trapped in a mental institution when he struggles to rescue a strange young woman from a murderous plot to steal her inheritance
Guy Stockwell, Diana Ewing, Michael Strong, Bob Hayes, Marla Adams, Jack Mullaney, Walker Edmiston, Diane Shalet, David Moses, G.W. Bailey, Joseph Hoover, Logan Field, Roger Creed, Corley Lawrence, Cal Haynes
Written by Robert Dozier; Directed by Paul Wendkos

Robert Dozier was the story editor on *Harry O* for the first season before becoming the show's producer in the second. The son of television producer William Dozier (*Batman*, *The Green Hornet*) and screen legend Ann Rutherford (*Gone with the Wind*), he was responsible for bringing Michael Sloan to the *Harry O* fold. "Bob was also married to Diana Muldaur," Sloan said on *TV Confidential* in June 2020. "I was very close to Diana, and I adored her. She did a lot of work for me over the years [including a recurring role on *McCloud*, one of Sloan's first credits as a TV producer]. She's a very special lady."

BALLINGER'S CHOICE (10/31/74)
Illicit romance leads to murder as Harry follows the trail of a married publisher having an affair with a sixteen-year-old girl
Juliet Mills, Tim McIntire, Paul Burke, Ken Johnson, John McLiam, Lisa Gerritsen, Mel Stewart, Victor Caroli
Written by Gene Thompson; Directed by Jerry Thorpe

SECOND SIGHT (11/7/74)
Harry is drawn into an extraordinary mystery when he follows a trail of murders forecast by a novelist suffering from hysterical blindness

Stefanie Powers, Mitzi Hoag, Michael Baseleon, Anne Seymour, Henry Oliver, Martin Brooks, Millie Slavin, Frank Ramirez, David Moses, Robert Doyle

Teleplay by Gene Thompson and Barry Trivers, story by Barry Trivers; Directed by John Newland

Stefanie Powers starred as Jennifer Hart, the distaff half of the jet-setting, crime-solving husband-and-wife team on *Hart to Hart* (ABC, 1979-1984) and, before that, as April Dancer in *The Girl from U.N.C.L.E.* (NBC, 1966-1967). In the decade in between those series, she was a marquee guest star on many top TV shows and TV-movies, including *Harry O*. "I was working on so many television shows in those days, I'd literally be working on one show, and at lunchtime, I'd go to the next studio to get a fitting for the next show, which would start the day after I finished the one I was working on," Powers recalled with a laugh on *TV Confidential*. "I was a very busy girl back then."

MATERIAL WITNESS (11/14/74)

Pressed into service by the police, Harry must protect an eyewitness against attempts to assassinate her before she can testify against a murderer

Barbara Anderson, James Olson, Mike Farrell, John Evans, Jerry Douglas

Written by Richard Danus; Directed by Barry Crane

FORTY REASONS TO KILL (2 parts; 12/5/74, 12/12/74)

Harry unearths a deadly power struggle when he investigates the murder of an old friend and finds himself the prime suspect in a second killing

Joanna Pettet, Craig Stevens, Broderick Crawford, Hillary Thompson, Eric Christmas, Kevin Hagen, Ned Romero, Bill Quinn, Paul Benedict, Lou Frizzell, Wayne Grace, Al Couppee,

Craig Campfield, Mary Maldonado, Eleanor Zee, William H. Bassett, Pedro Martinez, Don Freeman
Written by Stephen Kandel; Directed by Daryl Duke

ACCOUNTS BALANCED (12/26/74)
Harry probes the mystery of an accountant leading a double life as a paid killer
Robert Reed, Gerrit Graham, Linda Marsh, Tammy Harrington, John Crawford, Luis Goss, Marie Moneen, Vernon Weddle, Pam Randolph, Isela Edwards, Fielding Greaves, Mike Travis, Larry Leigh, E.J. Andre, Jerry Hardin, James Jeter, Charlie Briggs, John Duke Russo
Teleplay by Michael Winder and Herman Groves, story by Michael Winder; Directed by Robert Michael Lewis

THE LAST HEIR (1/9/75)
Harry investigates a murder and finds his suspects being killed one by one at the desert mansion of an eccentric recluse
Jeanette Nolan, Katherine Justice, Clifford David, Whit Bissell, Irene Tedrow, Sylvia Field
Written by Gene Thompson; Directed by Richard Lang

FOR THE LOVE OF MONEY (1/16/75)
The payoff is murder when Harry investigates a burglary that a secretary engineered with her cheating boyfriend
Mariclare Costello, Sharon Farrell, Joe Silver, Bernie Kopell, Fred Beir, Kathrine Baumann, Don Haggerty, Sabrina Scharf, Frances Fong, Don Eitner, Beau Cecchino, Paul Tulley
Teleplay by David P. Harman, story by Skip Webster; Directed by John Newland

THE CONFETTI PEOPLE (1/23/75)
Harry tries to unravel the mystery of a mentally disturbed young man who's convinced that he's murdered his own brother, twice

Diana Hyland, Marsha Hunt, Harvey Jason, Scott Hylands, John Rubinstein, Scott McKay, Kathrine Baumann, Marvin Dean Stewart, Kay E. Kuter, Cynthia Towne
Teleplay by Mann Rubin and Herman Groves, story by Mann Rubin; Directed by Richard Lang

Mann Rubin wrote the screenplay for *Warning Shot* (1967), a thriller that not only ranks among the best theatrical movies that David Janssen ever made, but has wrinkles that will make you think of both *The Fugitive* and *Harry O*. In *Warning Shot*, Janssen stars as Tom Valens, an L.A. police sergeant who finds wrongly himself accused of manslaughter after shooting and killing a man during a stakeout. Though Valens saw the suspect wielding a gun, no gun was found at the scene of the crime. When the dead man turns out to be a respected doctor with no criminal record, Valens is suspended. To clear his name, he conducts an investigation on his own time and meets a host of "only in Los Angeles" characters along the way before he finally solves the case. In that respect, Valens becomes an ad-hoc private detective, not unlike Harry Orwell.

Rubin's other screen credits include episodes of *Studio One, Mannix, The FBI, Mission: Impossible, The Rockford Files,* and *The Fugitive.*

Sound of Trumpets (1/30/75)
Harry is hard-pressed to protect a former jazz great from a knife-wielding killer
Jim Backus, Cab Calloway, Julius Harris, Henry Corden, Ron Soble, Brenda Sykes, Alan Manson, Hal Williams, Betty Cole, Ken Renard, Kathrine Baumann, Cynthia Lynn
Teleplay by Larry Forrester and Robert Pirosh, story by Robert Pirosh; Directed by John Newland

SILENT KILL (2/6/75)
Harry runs into a deadly conspiracy when he tries to clear a deaf man charged with arson and murder
James Wainwright, Kathy Lloyd, Gail Strickland, Lawrence Pressman, Charles Wagenheim, James McCallion, Len Wayland, William Sylvester, Jed Allen, Jack Riley, Tom Scott, Roberta Dean, Lou Fant, Tim Haldeman, Walt Davis Goodrich, Everett Creach
Teleplay by Stephen Kandel, story by John Meredyth Lucas; Directed by Richard Lang

The adopted son of Academy Award-winning director Michael Curtiz (*Casablanca*), John Meredyth Lucas worked extensively as a writer, director, and (occasionally) producer in network television for more than five decades. *Star Trek* fans know him best as a writer, director, and producer on the original series, including such classic episodes as OBSESSION, THE GAMESTERS OF TRISKELION, A PIECE OF THE ACTION, ELAAN OF TROYIUS, and PATTERNS OF FORCE.

Harry O was not Lucas' first collaboration with David Janssen—he co-produced, along with Wilton Schiller, the first few episodes of the final season of *The Fugitive* (ABC, 1966-1967), plus he directed two of the last episodes of that series (including CHANGING OF THE HABIT, which Lucas also wrote). "Writing for *Harry O* was like writing for David Janssen," Lucas told me in 1990. "It's the same character, basically. Personally, Janssen was a nice guy."

DOUBLE JEOPARDY (2/13/75)
Harry takes on an unusual client when he tries to protect a murder suspect from syndicate killers
Kurt Russell, Will Kuluva, Ben Piazza, Audrey Totter, Joel Lawrence, Marianna Heller, Hal Williams, Nancy Stephens,

Mary Munday, Paul Brinegar, Ellen Chute, Emily Chute, Renata Vanni, Wonderful Smith, Robert Cleaves, Richard Carlyle, Linda Dano, Ed Call, Roger Creed, Sonny Shields
Written by Marvin A. Gluck (billed as "M. Gluck"); Directed by John Newland

LESTER (2/20/75)
The nude body of a murdered college girl sends Harry on the trail of a psychotic killer
Jamie Smith Jackson, Richard Schaal, Les Lannom, Esther Palmisano, Scott Newman, Lynette Mettey, Ken Sansom, Norma Connolly, Rand Bridges, Allen G. Norman, Karen Gomey, Tracy Fink
Written by Robert C. Dennis; Directed by Richard Lang

ELEGY FOR A COP (2/27/75)
Harry assumes an undercover identity to avenge the murder of his close friend, police lieutenant Manny Quinlan
Sal Mineo, Carmen Zapata, Margaret Avery, Kathy Lloyd, Clay Tanner, Mel Stewart, Julio Medina, Jennifer Lee, Rodolfo Hoyos, Olan Soulé, Raymond O'Keefe, Cris Capen, Paul Harper, Kenia Torres Hernandez, Sarah Fankboner, Nate Esformes
Written by Howard Rodman; Directed by Jerry Thorpe

Harry O fans know ELEGY FOR A COP as "the show with a lot of scenes from the first pilot." Approximately thirty minutes of the episode consists of footage from *Such Dust as Dream Are Made On*—most of which was culled from the sequences that were filmed specifically for the 90-minute overseas version of *Such Dust* (as explained earlier), but which did not air on ABC. Some important expository scenes, however, such as the late-night meeting between Harry and the Broker (Sal Mineo), were lifted from the original 1973 hour-long broadcast and edited into this episode.

The reason for recycling this footage from the pilot had a lot to do with economics. "As you know, we were terribly over budget at the time, because of the deficit we ran in San Diego,' producer Jerry Thorpe explained to me in 1997. "I was trying hard to hold costs down, while at the same time maintain the quality of the production we'd established in the first half. So I suggested at one point that we do a show that incorporated that 'second part' of the pilot story into a new storyline. It seemed like a way to recoup some of that deficit (because we would not need an entire six-day shoot to film the new scenes) without compromising on the episodes we were making currently. And Howard Rodman did a really incredible job of weaving that stuff into a new story."

Indeed, the seamlessness of the entire production, coupled with the poignant nature of the story itself, makes ELEGY a truly remarkable episode. It is far and away the best show of the series.

STREET GAMES (3/13/75)
Harry seeks to find and protect a teenage dope addict before she is killed by a ruthless narcotics overlord
Claudette Nevins, John McMurtry, Ketty Lester, Maureen McCormick, Phillip Sterling Jr., Lezlie Dalton, Tony Alvarenga, Stanley Clay, Ray Vitte, Lani O'Grady, Trent Dolan, John Lawrence, W.T. Zacha, Vince Martorano, Anthony Mason, Jean Leabetter, Bill McLean
Written by Herman Groves; Directed by Richard Lang

Ketty Lester earned a Grammy nomination for Best Female Solo Vocal Performance for her 1962 international No. 1 hit single, "Love Letters," and her album that year of the same name. After more than a decade of performing in nightclubs throughout the U.S., the UK, and Canada, she won critical acclaim for her performance opposite Ruby Dee in the 1968 film *Uptight* (directed by Jules Dassin). That opened the door to a career as a movie and TV actress, though Lester continues to sing today. Fans of *Little House on the Prairie* know her as schoolteacher Hester Sue Terhune, while her other film roles include Juanita, the wise-cracking, but ill-fated, cab driver in the 1972 blaxploitation classic *Blacula*.

Lester immediately clicked with David Janssen, particularly in the sequence in which Harry asks Lester's character, the owner of a bar, whether she knows how to make a banana daiquiri. "You find some people that you can work with, that you can just walk in and there they are, and you feel that this is a natural situation, [like] 'I can work with this person,'" she said on *TV Confidential* in February 2022. "You go over it, and you see them, the way they do every scene, and you know then what you can do with them when it comes to your time."

Lester added that there were two other actors with whom she felt that kind of connection: Moses Gunn, her co-star on *Little House on the Prairie* (and, a few years before *Prairie*, the *FBI* episode EYE OF THE STORM), and comedian Bernie Mac, Lester's co-star in *House Party 3*.

Season Two, 1975-1976

ANATOMY OF A FRAME (9/11/75)
Harry fights to clear his friend, Lt. Trench, when the police detective is framed for the murder of a narcotics informant
Rene Auberjonois, Harold J. Stone, John Harkin, William Sylvester, Margaret Avery, James McEachin, Rand Bridges, Gordon Jump, Laurie Kennedy, Christine Avila, Al Hansen, Gary Sandy, James Hong, Macon McCalman, Royce Wallace

Teleplay by John Meredyth Lucas, story by Herman Groves; Directed by Jerry Thorpe

James McEachin previously appeared as Teezer Strock in EYEWITNESS. "David Janssen was my favorite guy to work with," he said on *TV Confidential* in February 2013. "David was a piece of work. Great guy. Fun guy."

ONE FOR THE ROAD (9/18/75)
Hit-and-run murder injects Harry into the investigation of an alcoholic woman attorney who suspects that she herself may be the killer
Carol Rossen, Robert Loggia, Larry Hagman, Christopher Allport, Frederick Herrick, John Zaremba, Richard Roat, Lindsay Workman, Trent Dolan, Susan Adams, Ron Gwynne, Jim Boles, Ann Noland, Peggy Doyle, Jean Leabetter
Written by Norman Strum; Directed by Harry Falk

Carol Rossen previously appeared in MORTAL SIN. "I think of David with great love, and caring, and I'm terribly sorry that he's not with us anymore," she told me in 1990. "I mean, that's how I feel. That's my memory, that's how I feel."

LESTER TWO (9/25/75)
Kidnapping, smuggling, and a double-cross force Harry to team up with eccentric young criminologist Lester Hodges in an 8,000-mile search for stolen diamonds
Les Lannom, Ina Balin, Clifford David, Richard Venture, Eric Server, Maria Grimm, Loni Anderson, Roger Etienne, Alain Patrick, Paul Harper, Rhonda Bates, Mary Angela, Ed Deemer, Marilyn Child
Written by Robert C. Dennis; Directed by Richard Lang

SHADES (10/2/75)
Harry confronts race hatred and blackmail in his attempt to clear a businessman's housekeeper of murder
Anjanette Comer, Lou Gossett, Lincoln Kilpatrick, Linden Chiles, Maidie Norman, Bill Henderson, Thayer David, David Moody, Junero Jennings, G.W. Bailey
Teleplay by Michael Sloan, story by Eugene Crisci and Ron Jacoby; Directed by Richard Lang

After a stellar career on Broadway from 1955 and throughout the 1960s (including productions of *Desk Set*, *A Raisin in the Sun*, and *My Sweet Charlie*), Louis Gossett, Jr. worked steadily in movies and on television throughout the 1970s, including an Emmy Award-winning performance as Fiddler in the groundbreaking miniseries *Roots* (ABC, 1977), before his breakthrough role opposite Richard Gere in *An Officer and a Gentleman* (1982), for which he won the Academy Award that year as Best Supporting Actor. One of the few actors to win both an Oscar and an Emmy, Gossett had starred in a series of his own a few years before appearing in this episode (*The Young Rebels*, a Revolutionary War drama that aired on ABC in the fall of 1970). Nevertheless, he remembered his appearance on *Harry O* as a "learning experience" about continuity in television.

"I played a gangster in that episode," Gossett said on *TV Confidential* in December 2020. "One of the scenes had me eating barbecue [when Harry] came to see me. I didn't know much about movies, so I had lunch [before we shot that scene]. Now we had to do ten takes of this scene of me eating barbecue. I had never been so full of barbecue in my life—because [with each different take], I had to duplicate it and match it for the major shot and the close-ups across the board. I had so much barbecue in my system, by the time I went home that day I almost fell asleep at the wheel!"

That experience aside, Gossett enjoyed working with David Janssen. "He was one of my favorites," he said. "He was quite a man. Quite a man."

PORTRAIT OF A MURDER (11/20/75)
Harry fights to prove the innocence of a mentally impaired teenager accused of homicide
Adam Arkin, Katherine Helmond, Jeff David, William Traylor, Lou Frizzell, Alan Feinstein, Rose Gregorio, Allan Miller, Don Hanmer, Paul Harper, Erica Yohn, Amy Botwinick, Jeff Cadbury
Written by Robert C. Dennis; Directed by Richard Lang

THE ACOLYTE (10/16/75)
Harry follows a murder trail that leads him to a religious sect and a plot to defraud a mentally disturbed woman
Bettye Ackerman, Sam Jaffe, Kristina Holland, Severn Darden, John Calvin, Alan Oppenheimer, Joe Melt, Joshua Shelly, Barry Atwater, Peter Brocco, Clyde Kusatsu, Barbara Leigh, George Reynolds, Christopher Barrett
Teleplay by Larry Forester and Robert Blees & Dorothy Robinson, story by Robert Blees & Dorothy Robinson; Directed by Harry Falk

MAYDAY (10/23/75)
A pilot's widow hires Harry to prove that the death of her husband—in a crash that a Senator "miraculously" survived—was murder
John Crawford, Geoffrey Lewis, Maggie Blye, Linda Kelsey, Ned Wilson, Bruce Kirby, Hildy Brooks, Robert Reisel, June Whitley Taylor, Ron Stoker, Ivan Bonar, Eddie Fontaine, Jack Colvin, Macon McCalman, Sondra Blake, Claire Brennan, Barbara Leigh, Dave Morick, Raymond Singer
Written by John Meredyth Lucas; Directed by Jerry London

John Meredyth Lucas also wrote the teleplays for Silent Kill, Anatomy of a Frame, Death Certificate, and, along with Michael Sloan, Victim, the final episode of the series. Though he did not direct any of his scripts for *Harry O*, Lucas helmed many of the episodes that he wrote for other TV series (including *The Fugitive* and the original *Star Trek*).

"I directed a lot of my own stuff, but I've never written a scene and then shot it exactly as I wrote it," Lucas told me in 1990. "Because you find targets of opportunity—something that you see [as you prepare to direct the show] that is changeable, such that it makes more sense to change the background. Now, I know some writers regard anything that they've put on paper as having come from Mount Sinai. This [can be] a problem when [a writer tries to establish]what the Writers Guild refers to as the 'primacy of the first writer'—meaning, what they wrote is what they wrote and [you can't] change anything. However, I never had that problem [as a writer/director] and I can't believe it's too much of a problem today because there are so many writer/directors."

Tender Killing Care (10/30/75)
When Spence's elderly father suddenly dies after complaining of medical neglect and improper care in the nursing home where he was a resident, Harry tries to prove negligence
Kenneth Mars, Bill Henderson, Bill Overton, Richard Stahl, Janet Brandt, Allan Rich, Raymond Chao, Jester Hairston, Howard Hesseman, Tim Haldeman, Robert Ito, Esther Koslow, Bruce Solomon, Bo Kaprall, Louis Williams, Lee Duncan, William H. Knight
Written by Norman Strum; Directed by Richard Lang

Howard Hesseman (*WKRP in Cincinnati*, *Head of the Class*), Richard Stahl (*It's a Living*), and Mel Stewart (one of the three actors who played Harry O's mechanic) all came into prominence as members of The Committee, the comedy improvisational group that began in San Francisco in the early 1960s.

A.P.B. HARRY ORWELL (11/6/75)
Harry is framed for murder and must break out of jail to prove his innocence
Lesley Ann Warren, Michael C. Gwynne, Fred Sadoff, Bill Henderson, John Lupton, Joyce Easton, Richard Stahl, Dan Priest, Bob Hackman, Don Eitner, John Dennis, Dan Barrows, John Lawrence, Rosana Soto, Skip Riley, Clay Tanner, Robert Gooden, John O'Leary
Teleplay by William R. Stratton, story by Alfred Brenner; Directed by Richard Lang

GROUP TERROR (11/13/75)
Harry masquerades as an alcoholic to join a therapy session and unmask a psychopathic killer
Linda Lavin, Joanna Pettet, Carol Mallory, Don Stroud, Jay Robinson, Mills Watson, Liam Sullivan, Mark Miller, Mary Robin Redd, Georgie Paul, Geoffrey Scott, Matilda Calnan, John Holland, Dave Shelley, John Mark Robinson
Written by Dennis Landa; Directed by Russ Mayberry

REFLECTIONS (11/20/75)
Harry plots a dangerous course to rescue his ex-wife from a storm of blackmail and murder
Felicia Farr, Peter Donat, Andrew Robinson, Randy Powell, Claudette Nevins, Kermit Murdoch, Fred Schweiwiller
Written by Michael Sloan; Directed by Richard Lang

EXERCISE IN FATALITY (12/4/75)
A hotheaded policeman is accused of murder, and Harry is hired to find his missing pregnant daughter, who is a witness to the true identity of her boyfriend's killer

Ralph Meeker, Nora Heflin, Karen Machon, Anazette Chase, Ray Vitte, Asher Brauner, Carl Crudup, Bill Deiz, Cynthia Avila, Lani O'Grady, Claude Earl Jones, Leda Rogers, Ray Ballard, Richard Foronjy, Gene Woodbury, Lauren Jones, Amy Joyce, Bea Silvern, Irene Gilbert
Written by Kenneth Realman; Directed by Russ Mayberry

The Madonna Legacy (12/11/75)
Harry looks for a clue of murder in the apparent suicide of an alcoholic ex-cop
Christine Belford, John Colicos, Dennis Redfield, Phyllis Love, Gwen Amer, Charles Shull, Jack Riley, Sabrina Scharf, Jane Lambert, Joseph Stern, Doria Cook, Paul Bryar, Derek Murcott, Carol Bagdasarian
Written by Michael Sloan; Directed by Richard Bennett

Mister Five and Dime (1/8/76)
After receiving a frantic telephone call from a female classmate who has been arrested for passing counterfeit money, Lester Hodges asks Harry to help him solve the case
Michael Pataki, Les Lannom, Glynnis O'Connor, Michael McGuire, J. Pat O'Malley, Charles Siebert, Margaret Avery, Paul Jenkins, Booth Colman, Ed McCready, Douglas Dirksen, Julio Medina, Russell Arms, Cass Martin
Written by Robert C. Dennis; Directed by Richard Lang

Book of Changes (1/15/76)
The owner of a plush gambling club is murdered, but not before leaving her young protégé with an envelope containing instructions to hire Harry to find her killer
Barbara Rhoades, Joanne Nail, Russell Wiggins, Richard Kelton, John S. Ragin, Rita Gam, David Healy, Barbara Cason, Jack Mullaney, Byron Mabe, Patsy Garrett, Susan Woolen, Llynn Storer

Teleplay by Michael Sloan and Michael Adams, story by Michael Adams; Directed by Russ Mayberry

PAST IMPERFECT (1/22/76)
Harry helps a young woman save the life she has made for herself from a ruthless man out of her past
David Opatoshu, Susan Strasberg, Tim McIntire, Granville Van Dusen, Edward Power, Edie Adams, George Chiang, Mario Gallo, Nancy Bleier, Randy Powell, Larry Gelman
Written by Stephen Kandel; Directed by Richard Lang

Singer/actress Edie Adams not only was married to Ernie Kovacs from 1954 until he died in 1962, but worked tirelessly to acquire and preserve the pioneering comedian's work in television "because she knew what Ernie did was special and worth saving," Adams' son, Josh Mills, told me in 2024. Known for her iconic commercials for Muriel Cigars ("Why don't you pick one up and smoke it sometime?"), she made her film debut in *The Apartment* (1960), opposite Jack Lemmon (who himself had starred with Kovacs in *Operation Mad Ball* and *Bell, Book, and Candle*). Adams remained close friends with Lemmon and his second wife, Felicia Farr—the actress whom we saw earlier this season as Harry's ex-wife in REFLECTIONS.

HOSTAGE (2/19/76)
Harry helps the police in their effort to disarm a dangerous bandit barricaded in a liquor store
John Rubinstein, George Murdock, George Loros, Ayn Ruymen, Bruce Glover, Quinn Redeker, Linda Gitlin, Priscilla Pointer, Colleen Camp, Don McGovern, Tim Thomerson, Jack Stauffer, Fritzi Burr, Hank Stohl, Charles Knapp, Robert Yuro, June Whitley Taylor
Written by Michael Sloan; Directed by Jerry London

Tony Award winner John Rubinstein (*Pippin, Children of a Lesser God*) previously appeared in THE CONFETTI PEOPLE. He worked steadily in network television throughout the 1970s, often cast as troubled young men (such as the one he plays in HOSTAGE) before starring as Jack Warden's straight-laced, often exasperated son in the short-lived, but fondly remembered private eye series *Crazy Like a Fox* (CBS, 1984-1986). The son of acclaimed pianist and composer Arthur Rubinstein, John Rubinstein studied theater and music at UCLA and composition at the Julliard School in New York. He also happened to write the music score for HOSTAGE.

THE FORBIDDEN CITY (2/26/76)
Harry investigates the death of a friend and finds himself surrounded by the mysterious justice of the Orient
Ramon Bieri, Tina Chen, Benson Fong, Frank Michael Liu, James Hong, Herb Voland, Jerry Hardin, Clare Nono, Suzanne Astor
Written by Robert C. Dennis; Directed by Richard Lang

VICTIM (3/4/76)
Two men rape a young girl. When the police refuse to prosecute her assailants, she hires Harry to help prove their guilt
Cynthia Avila, Eugene Roche, Michael Lerner, Cal Bellini, Richard Hale, Ron Joseph, Anna Berger, Jon Lormer, W.R. Zacha, Brian Baker
Teleplay by John Meredyth Lucas and Michael Sloan, story by John Meredyth Lucas; Directed by Richard Lang

RUBY (3/11/76)
Harry goes undercover to expose a powerful auto theft organization and quickly becomes involved in murder, blackmail, and illicit narcotics
Margaret Avery, Joseph Ruskin, Tony Burton, Stanley Clay, Ty Henderson, John McMurty, Paulene Myers, John Kerry,

Edmund Cambridge, Russell Shannon, John Hawker, Michael Anthony, Randy Martin, Arnold Soboloff, Archie Hahn
Teleplay by Michael Sloan, story by Susan Glasgow and Michael Sloan; Directed by Richard Lang

THE MYSTERIOUS CASE OF LESTER AND DR. FONG (3/18/76)
Mishaps and murders abound when Lester Hodges and his mentor join forces with Harry
Keye Luke, Les Lannom, Roddy McDowall, Anne Archer, Sorrell Booke, Judith McConnell, Dean Jagger, Stuart Whitman, Barry Atwater, William Sylvester, Susan Adams, Bea Silvern, Peggy Doyle, Richard Stahl
Written by Robert Dozier; Directed by Jerry Thorpe

This episode served as the back-door pilot for *Fong and Hodges*, a prospective spin-off of *Harry O* that—had it sold and gone to series—would've starred Les Lannom as Lester Hodges and Keye Luke as his mentor, criminologist Dr. Creighton Fong

DEATH CERTIFICATE (4/29/76)
When Harry is hired to investigate malpractice, he finds himself involved in organized crime and murder
Ruth Roman, Denise Galik, Normann Burton, Kiel Martin, Thom Christopher, Bill Henderson, Richard Stahl, Rod Colbin, Hank Rolike, Susannah Brin, Susan Adams, Michael Alaimo, Robert Casper, Paul Keith, F. William Parker
Written by John Meredyth Lucas; Directed by Russ Mayberry

RUN FOR YOUR LIFE
(NBC, 1965-1968)

Eighty-five episodes, plus 60-minute pilot

Starring   Ben Gazzara as Paul Bryan

Executive Producer: Roy Huggins
Created by: Roy Huggins
Produced by: Jo Swerling, Jr.
Theme and music by   Pete Rugolo

You're in the prime of your life. Your career is thriving, and your personal life just couldn't be better.

You visit your doctor for your annual checkup—a routine thing, most years. But not this time. The doctor notices something that's far from routine. He runs some tests and soon makes an earth-shattering discovery: you have somehow contracted a rare disease for which there is no known cure. You have roughly one year left to live, perhaps as much as two.

What would you do?

You could succumb to depression, drowning your sorrows in the bottle... or worse. You might find some comfort in your own self-pity, but if you're smart, you'll soon realize all you've done is waste what little time you have left.

Or you could look at it as a challenge to dive into life, a chance to experience as much as you can for as long as you've got. In the process, you just might discover what it really means to live.

This premise and the existential questions it poses are what make *Run For Your Life* (NBC, 1965-1968) a unique television series. Whereas most prime-time protagonists are motivated by a concern for survival in some way, attorney Paul Bryan (played by Ben Gazzara) disdains survival in anything he does, because he is reconciled to the fact that the end, for him, is near.

Assuming he has the means, how does a man conduct himself when his need for the most basic of animal instincts, self-preservation, is obliterated by circumstances? In all probability, *Run For Your Life* suggests, he would attempt to live every waking instant to the utmost that his wit allows—recklessly, with total abandon.

Which is exactly what Paul Bryan does. He has no wife, no family, and no one to whom he is anything more than a good lawyer or a good friend. He's been told he will be in perfect health and be completely normal until the final two weeks. He gives up his San Francisco-based practice, sells his home, his investments, and all his possessions, and embarks on a quest to live the remainder of his life as fully as possible. He travels the world, from the most exotic locales to the poorest of countries. Whenever he finds "there are questions about my own country that I can't answer," he returns to the United States (and, often, back to his native Bay Area), and eventually comes to understand the heart of America better than any man since Charles Kuralt.

Life takes on a new dimension for Paul Bryan. He hopes "to squeeze 20 years of living into one year, or two," so he cannot linger in one place for too long. Thus, he becomes a man on the run, relentlessly racing against the time limit that has been suddenly imposed on him.

Roy Huggins, of course, originated the "man on the run" concept in network TV with *The Fugitive* (ABC, 1963-1967). While the story of Dr. Richard Kimble was winning Emmy Awards and pulling record audience numbers, rival producers scrambled to duplicate its success. In television, as in life, imitation is the sincerest form of flattery. By 1965, several *"Fugitive*-like" shows had made their premieres (*Destry, The Loner, The Man From Shenandoah*); two more followed in 1966 (*Shane* and *Run, Buddy, Run*). None of these lasted more than one full season.

The only variation on *The Fugitive* that worked, *Run For Your Life* had one advantage none of the others had: it was conceived and produced by none other than Huggins himself. "Many of my friends and colleagues saw what was going on with these imitations on *The Fugitive*, and they'd say, 'Roy, why don't you do one yourself? Everyone else is doing it, and they're doing it wrong.' Even Leonard Goldenson [then-president of ABC-TV] said that to me, only he said it after I'd already developed *Run For Your Life* and sold it to NBC. But, yes, it was a deliberate attempt on my part to copy my own concept. But how I came about doing *Run For Your Life* was entirely accidental."

Accidental, because the original idea behind the premise of *Run* did not come from Huggins himself. "It came from Jennings

Lang, who was the head of television production at Universal Studios at the time," the producer continued.

ROY HUGGINS: Jennings met with me one day, and said, "I've got a great idea for a series. A man is told he's only got two years to live. Only, when he leaves his doctor, the audience somehow learns that this is a mistake: there's nothing wrong with him. But the man doesn't know that. He thinks he's only got two years to live, and so he decides to live it up!"

I didn't say this to Jennings, but I thought it was a pretty dumb idea. Then, once I got back to my office, I sat down and thought, "Wait a minute. What if it isn't a mistake? What if the man really does have only two years to live? If that's true, then this is a really *good* idea." Because now we're dealing with an existential point of view on life.

I liked it, because it was a Rabelaisian approach to fiction, as opposed to, say, the Bunyanesque approach (as seen in *Pilgrim's Progress*, where the thing you must discover is, "you do good"). Whereas, according to Rabelais, the idea of life is to have a good time. So I thought, here's a guy who lives according to Rabelais, who faces his mortality and says, "This is what I'm gonna do about it."

I started thinking about what kind of story to tell. Around that time, Jo Swerling had read an article about chicarenos, who were young people with lots of money. They lived on the French Riviera, and they practiced the Nietzschian philosophy of "living dangerously." They jumped out of airplanes, they dived 200 feet deep into the ocean, and so forth.

I said, "That's it." A story was written that had Paul Bryan coming into contact with a chicareno [played by Katherine Crawford, Huggins' daughter in real life].

Luther Davis wrote a fine script that became the pilot, and we filmed it as a segment on *Kraft Suspense Theater*, a show I was producing at the time.

Of course, Huggins knew that, for the series to work, Paul Bryan could not be completely hedonistic. Bryan needed to become a catalyst in the lives of the people he meets in his travels; otherwise, the audience would likely become bored with his exploits after a few weeks.

In Rapture at Two-Forty, the pilot episode, Paul meets Leslie Thurston, a chicareno who loses herself in extreme adventure to win her father's approval after the tragic death of her race car driver brother, the apple of his eye. Paul realizes that in trying to live the life of her brother, Leslie is denying herself the opportunity to live life on her own terms. He decides, at great risk, "to salvage the hidden woman" in Leslie. It's a risk, because not only might Leslie fall in love with him, but he might also fall in love with her—the one pleasure of life Paul can never permit himself to have. Paul knows that kind of personal relationship increases exponentially with time, and the scars are deep once it ends (as he knows, in his case, it must).

Though Paul rarely shares his knowledge of his fate with others, he knows he must tell Leslie before he says goodbye. "I have to be with people who don't know about me, who don't really care. With you, I'd see it every day in your eyes: my time shortening. And you'd see it in mine. It's in your wet, beautiful eyes right now."

Paul leaves, taking comfort in knowing he was the conduit through which Leslie discovers something very essential about herself. "Perhaps Nietzsche meant 'emotionally,' and not just risking your neck every day," she tells her father at the end of the pilot. "I'm going to find myself a man, now that I know they exist. And I'm going to love—*that's* living dangerously. That's risk. That was the one risk I was afraid to take, but now I can't wait to take it."

Thus, as a result of a perfectly logical and believable progression of events, Paul Bryan becomes, in effect, a modern-day reincarnation of the classic Western hero – the mysterious stranger who drifts from town to town, graces the lives of those he meets, and makes each town "a little better than it was" by the time he leaves. Given the circumstances, the audience can understand why Bryan must occasionally terminate his involvements abruptly: he has no choice. The audience can therefore root for Paul without feeling guilty.

"Let's face it," admitted Huggins. "Without that death sentence looming over him, a man like Bryan, who drifts from place to place, who leaves people behind, etc., would be little more than a bum. You can't ask the audience to root for a bum every week. You can't ask the audience to root for a man who keeps walking out on the women who fall in love with him; that's asking them to root for a heel. Bryan's predicament changes that. The audience knows that it pains him to leave, but that he really has no choice. That makes him someone they can sympathize with."

That, of course, was Huggins' exact thinking when he conceived *The Fugitive* in 1960. Like Paul Bryan, Richard Kimble was a man who, because of extraordinary circumstances, found himself moving from town to town each week without ever losing the sympathy of the audience.

Paul Bryan was a departure from the typical Roy Huggins character in that, unlike Bret Maverick, he was a man who actively sought dangerous situations. Yet, at the same time, he was very much like Maverick, in that his motivations for embracing danger were decidedly unconventional.

> ROY HUGGINS: Bryan did things that Maverick would never have done because they were important to giving quality to his life—whereas, to Maverick, avoiding those kinds of situations was a way of achieving something that Bryan didn't have: long life. Maverick avoided

things in order to live to be ninety. Bryan jumped into things in order to live *as if* he had lived ninety years. He gets into these things because to choose otherwise would be a contradiction. He doesn't have a long time to live, so why shouldn't he get into something that gives excitement to his life? It has nothing to do with making up for lost time—that's something anybody might decide to do. But that isn't the case with Paul Bryan. Paul Bryan finds out he's only got one or two years to live. He's determined to extract the most excitement he can out of life, in order to lengthen it. Because the end result of 'living dangerously' is that you seem to be living longer, and more fully, than the guy who has a wife and kids and goes home at six o'clock. You are more alive, and it contains a sense of *extending* life, as well as making it exciting.

I know a little about this, from my own experience. When I was producing television, I would often go off on a three-or-four-thousand-mile drive and dictate stories for my shows into a tape recorder as I drove. I would only be gone for about four or five days, but by the time I came back home, it would feel as if I'd been away for much, much longer. It has something to do with time, and distance, and separation from the ordinary. Your perception of time is different. You can't believe you accomplished all that in just a few days; you feel as though it's been more like a month. But you're still exhilarated from the experience. I had Bryan discover that very early on, and even had him talk about it a couple of times on the show, for the benefit of anyone in the audience who might have missed it.

A good example of this occurs in WHO'S WATCHING THE FLESHPOT?, in a scene in which an ingenue named Marsha

(Davey Davison) chastises Paul for "wasting his time" instead of focusing on things like career and marriage.

PAUL

That's the trouble with people nowadays. Everybody's running around, "not wasting time." I've saved so much, I think it's about time I started spending some... I'm not sure that what I was doing back home was living at all. But since I left, there's never been a moment of doubt that I was alive.

MARSHA

But what have you got if you live just for today? Nothing but a lot of yesterdays.

PAUL

Is that bad? At least, they'll be nice, full yesterdays—something you won't mind looking back on.

"Now, I realize," conceded Huggins, "there's a contradiction in that line of thinking, in that many people say, 'Well, isn't that what makes life feel shorter?' And, in one sense, it does, in that you're never bored. But when the experience is over, you nonetheless feel as if you've lived much longer. I thought it was particularly important for a man like Paul Bryan to face his predicament that way."

What did Ben Gazzara bring to the package?

"Everything," said Jo Swerling Jr., *Run*'s supervising producer. "He did a brilliant job of playing that character. He gave

Paul Bryan a sense of strength, and sensitivity, on all levels of feeling, so that you could tell he had come to terms with his mortality, without feeling sorry for himself, but rather as the challenge of making the most of the time that he had left. You had the sense of a guy who was carrying a burden, but not overwhelmed by it. I thought Ben played that brilliantly.

> JO SWERLING JR.: We had kind of a bumpy time with him, at first, during that gear-up time when we first started production, after the pilot had been sold. Without mentioning any names, there were certain people who had Ben's confidence, and I don't think they really wanted him to do the show. They were whispering in his ear a lot, about how the early scripts that were being developed were 'no good.' Since they had been associates of his for some time, and we were the new guys on the block, we hadn't time yet to win his confidence, and his trust. That created some difficulties between Ben and Roy and me. But we somehow struggled through that, and got the first episode or two on the air. Then, the show started getting good ratings, and really good reviews. From that moment on, he was a pleasure to work with. He was very respectful of the material, and frequently contributed excellent ideas of his own. He was never a troublemaker. He was extremely professional, and a very fast study. He always knew his lines. He was a trained actor, and a fun guy. He created a good atmosphere around the set. He was the kind of guy who said Hello to everybody, and treated them well.

Gazzara originally saw Bryan as a nonconformist anti-hero, the kind of man who would stand on a table in the public library and scream at the top of his lungs. Huggins resisted, confident in his belief that such behavior in a series lead would only turn away the audience. When the premiere broadcast [THE COLD,

COLD WAR OF PAUL BRYAN] finished in the Top Ten, and the series proceeded to win its Wednesday 10pm timeslot on a consistent basis, Gazzara gave the executive producer his due. "By his knowledge of television, Huggins knows what works with the masses," Gazzara told *TV Guide* in 1965. "The ratings are good. So I have to bow to Huggins and say maybe he was right."

Run For Your Life went on to average a 35.3 share for its first season. The share, or "H.U.T. number," is considered the most accurate measure of audience response in network television. Of the total number of Households Using (i.e., actually watching) Television at 10:00 p.m. on Wednesdays during the 1965-1966 season, over one-third were watching *Run For Your Life.*

Gazzara also directed several episodes, "which were among the best, I think," added Swerling. "He did them with a sense of fiscal responsibility, too. Sometimes, when these series stars get the megaphone, they don't particularly care how much they're going to cost the studio. But not only were Ben's shows among our best, creatively, but he brought them all in on schedule, and on or under budget – which I thought was great.

"I was very sad, after it was all over, that he never won an Emmy. He was nominated twice for Best Dramatic Actor, as was the show itself for Best Drama, but we lost both times to Bill Cosby and *I Spy*. When we were nominated in our last year [1968], I thought it would've been nice if, after having given the awards to *I Spy* the year before, the Academy could've possibly 'spread the wealth around.' But that's the way it goes. We were always the bridesmaid, never the bride."

Pre-production for a series scheduled to premiere in September begins several months in advance, depending on exactly when the network orders the series. Back in the 1960s, the networks usually announced their fall schedules around Washington's

Birthday, which gave producers about three months to develop scripts before filming commenced in June.

As mentioned previously, for Roy Huggins, script preparation often began with one of his patented "story trips," during which time he would dictate fully developed stories, complete with notes on characterization, the nature of the relationships in the story, and actual dialogue. Upon his return, he would have his notes transcribed, revised, and then dictated a second time for clarity. Before assigning a writer to write the story into script form, he would meet with the writer and go over the story. This meeting would also be recorded and transcribed for the benefit of the writer. The writer would prepare the teleplay, then meet with Huggins once again for any input and/or revisions.

In theory, Huggins' approach was foolproof: because his stories included detailed characterizations and actual dialogue, all the writer had to do was transform it from prose to teleplay form. But it wasn't always easy in practice. The script had to reflect an absolute grasp of Huggins' concept; if it didn't, either the writer had to revise the teleplay so that it conformed with Huggins' vision, or Huggins would reassign the story (but not before going over the story in detail with the new writer).

Given the many story ideas that Huggins prepared, it might seem surprising that his name doesn't appear on any *Run for Your Live* script credits (or on script credits for any other of the many series with which he was associated). That's because he used the pseudonym, John Thomas James, which is a combination of the first names of the three sons he had with his second wife.

Huggins' meticulous approach did not sit well with everyone who worked with him: by his own admission, he can be extremely uncompromising in the area of story and script development, and he can be brutal with his criticism. But countless others in the film and television industry, including Stephen J. Cannell and Juanita Bartlett, swore by Huggins' methods because they respected his expertise in the craft of storytelling, and they recognized his desire to develop the talent he sees in them to its fullest possible extent.

> JO SWERLING JR.: Roy is really a teacher at heart. In fact, at one point in his life, he wanted to be a professor of political theory, and he actually left television for a time to work on his doctorate in that field, until he was lured back into television by Universal to produce *The Virginian*.
>
> While Roy was very easy with his praise when you did something well, at the same time, he was not shy about being stern whenever you screwed up. Roy could be tough—but in a lot of ways, that was good, because he'd always back off and say, "You know, if I thought you had no talent, I wouldn't bother. I only do this because I think you have something to offer, and that you'll learn from the experience."

Huggins saw himself as a teacher, but he also never lost sight of the practical reality that faced both his associates and himself if he didn't do his job well. "Roy used to tell me," Swerling added, "'If I say nothing, or if I only say 'That's okay,' then you're not going to learn anything—and at some point, your option at the studio won't get picked up.'

"So he was a stern mentor, but he was also a wonderful man to work with. He was marvelously creative. The way he could come up with stories bordered on the supernatural."

Sometimes, though, Huggins would only come up with a premise—a very good premise, but one that he knew wasn't fully developed yet as a story. That was the case with the story that eventually became one of *Run*'s most compelling episodes, NIGHT TRAIN TO CHICAGO.

ROY HUGGINS; One day, I brought Jo and Paul [Freeman, *Run*'s associate producer] into my office, and I said to them, "Imagine that Ben Gazzara is on a train and he meets a nun."

"Okay," they said. "What happens then?"

"Well, it turns out she's not a nun at all," I said. "Gazzara talks to her. Then, shortly after they get off the train, he sees her again, dressed in regular clothes, only she pretends she doesn't know him."

Now, we all agreed that the idea was interesting, but we couldn't come up with a good, dramatic explanation for the woman's disguise. We went on to discuss other story ideas, but I kept this particular premise foremost in my mind. In the first place, it was a wonderfully interesting way to begin an episode. We had a whole first scene. Gazzara talks casually with a nun on a train. In a few lines of casual conversation, her character is established as that of a warm and good person. Then he sees her dressed in regular clothes and she snubs him coldly: *why?*

If you can get a television audience to ask why at the beginning of the hour, if you can get the audience to become immediately interested in finding why, you've won the first battle of a television show: keeping the audience from going to the refrigerator or to another channel.[21]

Still, even after that first battle is won, the episode has to deliver. "There's nothing worse than intriguing an audience with a good, teasing first scene and then failing to deliver, giving them a half-baked, stereotyped explanation," Huggins explained, "and

---

21 Louise Sorel, the actress who played the mysterious woman whom Paul Bryan meets in NIGHT TRAIN TO CHICAGO, shares a few memories of working on this episode in the episode guide that follows.

that's just what we didn't have in this case—a good explanation, a good story to follow the first scene."

Huggins finally found a solution three weeks later, when he read a four-paragraph news story saying that a Congressional committee would soon resume its inquiry into the activities of national crime syndicates. This was all the stimulus he needed. At the next story conference, Huggins suggested that the woman disguised as a nun be the daughter of a Cosa Nostra Chieftain who has agreed to testify before a Congressional Committee. She is afraid she will be captured by her father's former colleagues and held to force him not to testify. The idea was soon expanded by Swerling and Freeman; a few days later, Huggins drafted a four-page story treatment. The treatment was then assigned to Robert Bloch, who wrote the teleplay.

> ROY HUGGINS: A series like *Run For Your Life* can go nowhere without good stories. The one thing I've always been proud of is being able to tell a good story, as well as recognize one when I hear one. You have to be alert all the time, because you can find a good story, or at least the germ of a good story, just about anywhere.
>
> We had a young film editor at the time named Patrick Kennedy. One day, I bumped into him at the studio commissary, and he said, "Roy, you've already established that Gazzara won't get involved with a woman romantically because he feels he can't stay long with anyone who knows about his terminal disease. Why don't you have him fall in love with a girl, and have her throw his own argument back at him? In other words, she rejects him, because she knows every time he looks into her eyes, he'll see someone who knows he's going to die."
>
> It wasn't until I had walked back to my office that I realized what he had given me: in one sentence, I had an outline for a complete three-act episode. I sat down,

wrote a twenty-two-page treatment, and the next day assigned a writer to do the script.

That one-sentence storyline turned out to be a hauntingly beautiful love story, THE SADNESS OF A HAPPY TIME, one of the best episodes of the series. Patrick Kennedy not only received full credit and money for the creation of the storyline of that episode, but received additional remuneration and credit when Huggins commissioned a sequel, THE WORD WOULD BE GOODBYE. Claudine Longet starred in both episodes as Bryan's one true love, an existential novelist loosely based on Francoise Sagan, author of *Bonjour Tristesse*.

Huggins' approach to executive producing was somewhat unusual, in that he focused primarily on just two aspects of production: preparation of stories and scripts, and post-production (with a particular eye on the editing of the film). Film editing requires not only a mastery of technical skills like splicing and dubbing, but an acute understanding of the craft of telling stories. If the editor is not in sync with what the producer, director, or writer has in mind, then the cut of the film may include (or exclude) footage that could alter the entire story. For that reason, Huggins oversaw the editing of all his series and TV-movies as vigilantly as he did the writing.

Huggins' methods didn't always sit well with the brass at Universal, whose Business Department frequently complained that his shows cost up to one-third more than any other show on the lot. The extra costs were always related to post-production. Huggins always believed, however, that the quality of what went on the air reflected the amount of time that he spent in post-production. More often than not, he could counter the bean counters with another set of numbers: high ratings.

While Huggins concentrated on overseeing the writing and the editing, he left most of the other areas of production in the capable hands of supervising producer Jo Swerling Jr. Beginning with *Kraft Suspense Theater* in 1965, Swerling worked closely with Huggins on every project the exec producer did for Universal until Huggins left the studio in 1980.

Swerling's responsibilities ranged from overseeing the production schedule, to meeting regularly with art directors and set designers to plan the "look" of each show, to prepping directors, to keeping an eye on the bottom line: making sure the series reached its qualitative goals each week without exceeding its budget. That could be particularly challenging on a show like *Run for your Life*, which didn't have standing sets that could be incorporated into each story, since the action always took place in a different city or country each week. But the show was able to meet that challenge by taking advantage of the wealth of resources readily available on the Universal back lot:

> JO SWERLING JR.: One of the things that helped make that possible at the time was the fact that we were shooting at a large studio, Universal, which had a great backlot and a lot of good sources for stock footage. We had a huge backlot, where you could find a 'European street' or a 'Mexican street' or a 'New York street,' and all of these elements. I don't remember how many sound stages there were at the time [that had complete sets in them]. The studio would leave these sets standing until they needed the space, to do a feature or whatever, and they'd have to tear them down, and put up something else. But then, *those* sets would remain standing.
>
> That enabled us to go around and scout these stages, pick out sets that were already built, and revamp them (as long as whoever had built them was done with them).

Or, if they needed to use them again, we would revamp them, and then they would charge the show budget to put them back the way they were.

We also used to sit down and have regular screenings of stock footage. Gloryette Clark, our stock footage librarian, who later became a film editor (and later yet, a writer and a director), was superb at finding good stock film. Whenever we'd put a script into production, we'd turn her loose looking for stuff. They had a pretty good film library at Universal, but they also had access to other studios, and other independent film libraries, and so on. Gloryette would find all sorts of good stuff for us.

For example, if we wanted to play a scene in a Moroccan marketplace, we would find ourselves a great wide angle, from some movie, of a location like that. We would look for some little identifying feature, like a colorful awning over a stand, or in front of a store. Then, on the Universal back lot, they actually had a kind of "Moroccan street," a Middle Eastern kind of thing. We would go and duplicate the awning, and stick it up on the street. So we'd go from this wide angle, with thousands of extras, in tight to a relatively confined area—but we would match this one identifiable feature, and then we'd have our 30 extras there, walking back and forth, in front of the camera, with a long lens, and so forth. It was a technique that worked really well in those days. I don't know how well you'd be able to get away with it today, when audiences have seen so much more elaborate stuff.

Perhaps that's true. But, still, considering that most of the sophisticated technology of today simply wasn't available back then, the whole thing comes across quite well—so well, in fact, that even the network brass couldn't tell the difference.

JO SWERLING JR.: Robert Kintner, who was president of NBC-TV at the time, used to brag about having two shows that were shot all over the world, *I Spy* and *Run For Your Life*. Now *I Spy* was, in fact, shot all over the world, whereas we rarely left the studio on *Run For Your Life*. Only Kintner never knew that. He believed we also shot our show all over the place—which, looking back, is probably the highest compliment he could have paid us.

The only time I ever recall going out on an overnight location was for a show we did in the first year, called OUR MAN IN LIMBO. That story had a sequence in which a light plane navigated by Paul Bryan crash-lands in the Sahara Desert. In order to film that sequence, we spent a couple of days in an area near Pismo Beach, called Oceania. It's a rather large sand dune area, the kind of place where the whole institution of "dune buggying" began. There aren't many places like that in the United States—certainly not out on the West Coast, at least. Most of the desert areas that we have around here, like Palmdale or Palm Springs, you'll find mountains and rocks, but not a lot of dunes; whereas this place we used for that show had really big sand dunes, where we could get down into them so that you can't see anything else around you. It was the perfect place for our purposes. So we shot, I think, two or three days there: we did the crash of the airplane, and all the sequences with Ben and the guest actress [Janine Gray]. But it was the only time we ever went out of town for *Run For Your Life*. We did a lot of local location shooting, around Hollywood, but the preponderance of stuff was usually shot right at Universal, and integrated into stock footage.

Run For Your Life was like *The Fugitive* in one other important way: it was an anthology series with a running character. Though Paul Bryan appeared in every story, there was never anything familiar about his settings from show to show. That allowed for endless storytelling possibilities. The worlds of art, crime, theater, business, music, sports, religion, politics, nature, war, the individual, the masses... Bryan could become involved in literally any kind of intrigue, from as basic and simple as helping a small child who lost a balloon, to as hazardous and international as negotiating (above or below the table) the escape of an important individual from behind the Iron Curtain.

As an anthology series, each week featured an attractive lineup of guest stars, including Macdonald Carey, Katharine Ross, Barry Sullivan, Suzanne Pleshette, Ernest Borgnine, Tippi Hedren, Brenda Scott, Kim Darby, Rossano Brazzi, Diana Hyland, Robert Loggia, Telly Savalas, Susan Strasberg, James Whitmore, Mary Ann Mobley, Eve Arden, Henry Silva, Carol Lawrence, Peter Lawford, Harry Guardino, Sal Mineo, Edward Mulhare, Gena Rowlands, Leslie Nielsen, Lesley Ann Warren, Carol Lynley, Roddy McDowall, Louise Sorel, Brock Peters, Ossie Davis, Anthony Eisley, Tige Andrews, Jack Palance, Sheree North, Linden Chiles, Michael Dunn, Jacqueline Scott, Peter Graves, Edward Asner, Kent McCord, Gavin McLeod, Jack Albertson, Pat Harrington, Dabney Coleman, Jack Kelly, William Windom, Cloris Leachman, Arthur Hill, Joseph Campanella, and Janice Rule (a.k.a. Mrs. Ben Gazzara at the time of the show). Several other actors returned to play the same character in multiple episodes, most notably Fernando Lamas (as Ramon da Vega, professional gigolo), Jeremy Slate (as race car driver Pete Gaffney), Martin Milner (as Mike Greene, Paul's buddy from the Korean War), Ina Balin (as Lisa Sorrow), Stephen McNally (as Mike Allen, Paul's CIA contact, a character originally played by Macdonald Carey), and Bruce Dern (as Alex Ryder, Paul's running partner, a character first played by John Kerr).

An avid long-distance runner for most of his life, Bruce Dern estimated that he was running about four thousand miles a year (usually, near Griffith Park) at the time he appeared on *Run For Your Life*. Indeed, according to Bob Rubin, an assistant director who worked with Dern several times when the actor appeared on *The Fugitive*, it was not unusual for Dern to commute to the studio occasionally by running (as opposed to driving his car). There likely wasn't a more authentic casting choice to play the Ryder character. Dern appeared as Ryder in the second-season episode THE TREASURE SEEKERS and twice in the third season (A TRIP TO THE FAR SIDE, AT THE END OF THE RAINBOW, THERE'S ANOTHER RAINBOW).

Dern, however, sustained a serious, and nearly life-threatening, injury while filming A TRIP TO THE FAR SIDE. "We were shooting the last weeks of the show, and on a Thursday night, I got thrown against the wall in a fight scene," the actor recalled in *Things I've Said, But Probably Shouldn't Have: An Unrepentant Memoir* (University Press of Kentucky, 2007). "A doorknob hit right behind my shoulder blade, which later caused my lung to collapse. It's called a spontaneous pneumothorax."

BRUCE DERN: I was in the middle of Malibu Canyon, running Friday morning. I've never been shot, but it felt like I had been shot. Instead of coming home in twenty-nine minutes to do the four miles, it took me about an hour just barely being able to limp [all while] being terrified. When I came off the hill, I went right into Dr. Hiken's office, which was near the Malibu Colony where the Bank of America building was. He was a famous marathon runner who was a family M.D. [He was a] little older than I was. He lived in the Colony.

It was almost noon, and I didn't have to go to work that day until four. I went in, and he took a picture. He didn't blanch. He said, "Look at the pictures. This is the left lung, and the screen is completely black, which means your lung is fine. The other side is completely white, which means there's no air in this lung, and the lung is flat and it's just tissue."

I asked, "Well, what does that mean?"

He said, "It's a 90-percent collapse, which means you basically have no air in your right lung…. The lung is trying to work, because it's a muscle. But it can't because the air is on top of it. That's why the pain is excruciating. And you only have 50-percent breath. If your other lung were to go down, you'd have about forty-five seconds to live. What's your day look like?"

I said, "I've got to be at work at four. I can't miss it. What's the diagnosis?"

Dr. Hiken said, "You have two choices: One is you shouldn't go to work, because if you lose the air from the other lung, you're dead. Choice two is if you have to go to work, I can give you a couple of pain pills, but I can't do anything about the fact that you're going to be breathing like this all day."

Dern elected to return to the set that afternoon; miraculously, he managed to complete his scenes without any incident. Meanwhile, Hiken arranged to have Dern escorted that night to St. John's Hospital in Santa Monica, where he would undergo thoracic surgery at the hands of Dr. Ramsay, whom Dern had first met about a year earlier while filming *The War Wagon* with John Wayne. Ramsey had previously performed lung surgery on both Wayne and Bette Davis.

The procedure took about seven hours. Though it would be several months before he could run again, Dern had recuperated enough by Monday morning to return to the set of A Trip to the Far Side. "The director of that episode, Fernando Lamas, was probably as grand a laid-back guy as I'd ever met in Hollywood," Dern said in his memoir. "I used one-sentence deliveries on everything where I had two or three sentences. I'd break the dialogue up, sneaking little breaths in between. It was all courtroom stuff, so it was plausible. Was it terrible? I think it was. But Fernando really didn't give a shit about anything except nailing the girl who was playing the ingénue."

Once he recovered completely, Dern resumed running... but not in Griffith Park. That's because Dr. Ramsey told him it was the most smog-congested area in the United States, given its proximity to the freeways. and that the sheer amount of car exhaust fumes that Dern inhaled every day likely caused the poor condition of his lungs, long before he was hit in the back by the doorknob while filming the fight scene for A Trip to the Far Side.

Several other guest stars graced *Run For Your Life* from other realms of show business: stage star Howard Keel, singers Bobby Darin and Mel Tormé, comic Don Rickles (who guest-starred in two episodes), and former middleweight boxing champion Sugar Ray Robinson.

Two notes of interest. Mel Tormé also wrote The Frozen Image, the episode in which he starred, while Who's Watching the Fleshpot?, the episode featuring Bobby Darin, was the pilot for a series that never materialized, *The Sweet Life*.

The show featured many other talented people behind the scenes. Director Michael Ritchie (*The Candidate*) and casting director John Badham (*Saturday Night Fever*) both went on to successful careers as directors of feature motion pictures. Nicholas Colasanto, better known as "Coach" on *Cheers*, directed and acted in many episodes. Jazz composer Pete Rugolo earned Emmy nominations each year for his musical score, as did cinematographer Lionel London for his work on the first season.

Run For Your Life was also marked by its use of "forced perspective," the innovative camera style first made popular by

Canadian director Sidney Furie in *The Ipcress File* (1965). "That film," Roy Huggins pointed out, "was the first big breakthrough in getting people interested in all sorts of unusual techniques— techniques that could be used in films for mass entertainment, not just for use in classes about film-making or so-called 'art' pictures.

"When I saw *The Ipcress File*, I said, 'This guy is doing things with the camera that are not difficult to do.' They weren't special effects, so they wouldn't be expensive to do. It was simply imaginative use of the camera, and of the set, and of perspective and composition. I'm sure a lot of directors were influenced by that film, as was I." The technique was perfectly suited for television, where the confines of the small screen created opportunities to "open up the box" in terms of depth.

THE SAVAGE SEASON is one of many excellent examples of how *Run For Your Life* put forced perspective to use. When we first see Ben Gazzara in this episode, he's standing behind Jill Haworth, and they're sort of framed by a circle. The circle turns out to be the cut-out hole of a 45-RPM record, which Haworth is holding directly in front of the camera. After a few lines of dialogue, Haworth pulls the record toward her, then places it on a turntable. Later in that same scene, the camera is positioned behind a drinking glass, and we see Gazzara and Haworth dancing, as if we're kneeling down and watching them from the glass' perspective.

Besides making the film visually interesting, forced perspective can also be an effective means of enhancing an important story point or heightening the drama of a particular scene. About midway through THE SAVAGE SEASON, Paul Bryan is jumped in an alley by two thugs, and is eventually knocked cold. The camera zooms in tight on Gazzara's face, as Bryan slowly slips out of consciousness. The screen then goes black, and stays that way for about twenty seconds, before Gazzara comes to.

Success breeds confidence, which often gives you room to experiment. *Run For Your Life* is also a "typical Roy Huggins production" in this respect. The series often took chances, sometimes by doing stories that addressed topical issues (such as Cold War politics, or abortion), sometimes by breaking the unwritten rule in network television that the hero of a weekly series is always right.

> JO SWERLING JR: We did an episode [in the third year] called THE KILLING SCENE, which Ben directed. It was a really potent, anti-capital punishment piece, with quite a remarkable cast, in retrospect: the guest stars were Tom Skerritt and Robert Duvall. Very briefly, Bryan comes across a news item about the pending execution of a death row inmate (Skerritt) whom he had once represented. He lost the case; though he always believed in the man's innocence, he was never able to prove it. Bryan goes back, hoping he can get a stay, and eventually comes to the very firm conclusion that he knows who did the crime—this man played by Robert Duvall. Now, during the ten or twelve years that Skerritt's been on death row, Duvall has become a model citizen: he has a wife and kids, and he owns a small business (a gas station). Bryan goes to him and says, "You can't let an innocent man go to the gas chamber." But Duvall says, "Just watch me. You don't seriously expect me to turn myself in, do you?" And he and Ben have some powerful scenes together. Finally, though, Bryan works his magic, and Duvall becomes very, very disturbed, to the point where his conscience gets to him. He can't let this guy die. He runs to the nearest police station to confess, and to say "Stop the execution." And they all dive for the telephone, and so on and so forth. The telephone rings, they get the warden, and they say, 'Stop the execution.' Only the

warden says, "It's too late. They pulled the switch thirty seconds ago."

It was really good stuff, and about as powerful a statement against capital punishment as you could possibly make—although, having said that, I must add that I would never make that movie today. You couldn't put a gun to my head and have me make that movie today, because now I'm very much pro-capital punishment. My outlook on such matters has changed considerably since 1965...

Another departure from the norm was DOWN WITH WILLY HATCH, starring Don Rickles as a down-on-his-heels nightclub comic falsely accused of statutory rape in a small rural town. After bailing Willy out of jail, Paul encourages him to take the stage again while he carries out his investigation. Though Willy is reluctant, Paul presses him: "You're innocent until they prove you're guilty. Performing tonight is the only way you have of showing this town you're not afraid of them."

Though Paul succeeds in proving the entire case against Willy was fabricated, he ultimately fails his friend in a more fundamental way. Willy takes the stage—and fails to get a single laugh from the members of the audience. Willy's frustrations boil into anger and, ultimately, confrontation. He lunges after a patron, prompting a massive brawl; by the end of the story, he is reduced to a catatonic state, and eventually wheeled away to a mental hospital. Paul is devastated. In his zeal to prove Willy innocent, he failed to recognize just how close his friend was to a nervous breakdown: "Sometimes you have to remember to deal with your friends on their terms, and not yours."

"The theme of that show," said Jo Swerling, "can be summarized in that old adage 'The road to hell is paved with good intentions.' With all good intentions, Paul Bryan gives advice to this down-and-out comedian which ends up destroying him. Now, there are a lot of people who would say that show was a bad idea, that 'you don't do that with the hero of a television series. You don't have him be that wrong.' And yet, it was a very human kind of thing, because he really meant well. He thought he was giving the guy good advice; it just turned out all wrong. That, of course, happens to all of us, sometimes."

Though some TV reference books list leukemia as the mysterious ailment that suddenly befell Paul Bryan, neither Bryan nor his doctor (Eric Mason, of the Garmes Clinic) ever indicates precisely what he has (other than, "it's one of those afflictions they name after the poor fellow who discovered it"). In truth, the exact disease was never actually named. "That's because there is no such disease," Huggins revealed. "Both NBC and the American Medical Association asked us not to specify it, because otherwise doctors all over the country would be deluged with people who thought they might have it. They said, 'Say as little about his ailment as you can,' and that's what we did. We never named it, because in fact it doesn't exist."

However, Huggins himself was often deluged with requests for an episode that found a cure for Bryan's condition. But the writer/producer steadfastly refused: "I thought such a resolution would be terribly contrived, and against the grain of what the show was about. I felt the audience would see right through that. And I really didn't want to do it, anyway."

What Huggins did want to do was produce a fourth season. "I felt we could have continued one more year. Our numbers were still good [the show averaged a 27.8 share during its third and final season]. The reviews were still good. But there was a guy running programming at NBC at the time—he didn't last long, because he was so sure that everything he ever said, or thought, was absolutely incontrovertible. He said to me, 'You can't go beyond a third year; you've been telling people he's only got two years, and you've already gone a year too long.'

"I tried to argue that the audience wasn't that literal. I said, 'Look, little Annie Rooney never grew an inch. The audience is willing to concede at least a fourth year.' His answer was, 'That audience, and the television audience, are completely different. Television audiences are extremely literal.'

"Now, he may very well have been right about that, though exactly how he knew that was another question. I don't know whether he'd actually done any research to establish the truth of what he was saying, or whether it was just his opinion. But that was all that really mattered: it was his opinion, and that's what made it right. And we were gone."

It's possible to understand NBC's decision to drop the show in one respect: *Run*'s audience numbers, though still very respectable, did go down slightly each year. Still, if the show were on today, with the same numbers that *Run* had in its third year, it's highly unlikely that any programming executive would cancel it. By today's standards, a show with a 27.8 share would be a Top Ten hit.

Still, looking at the matter literally, *Run For Your Life* ran for a total of eighty-five episodes during its three seasons on NBC. If you think of each episode as a week, then the series would have only covered about a year-and-a-half of Paul Bryan's life. A full television season in 1968 lasted twenty-six weeks; had the show continued for a fourth season, Paul would have in effect lived two years (which was the maximum prognosis he'd been given).

"That's sound logic," agreed Huggins. "But, to the network, a season equaled a year. In their thinking, he'd already lived one year too long."

Paul Bryan has lived on in syndication ever since, including a lengthy run on superstation WWOR during the early 1990s. And, according to the trade papers, he may be coming soon to a theater near you. Universal Studios has been actively pursuing a deal for a feature film version of *Run For Your Life*.

RUN FOR YOUR LIFE EPISODE GUIDE

Kraft Suspense Theatre: RAPTURE AT TWO-FORTY (4/15/65)
Learning that he has at most two years to live, Paul Bryan determines to pack as much living as possible into that time. But he nearly cuts his life short when he attempts to get close to a pretty girl who lives dangerously
Katherine Crawford, Antoinette Bower, Michael Rennie, Marcel Hillaire, Miguel Landa, S. John Launer, Louis Mercier, Stella Garcia, Albert Carrier, Joan Gibbs, George Conrad, Brasil 65
Teleplay by Luther Davis, story by Jo Swerling Jr.; Directed by William A. Graham
Besides serving as the pilot for *Run For Your Life*, this episode of Kraft Suspense Theater also marked one of the rare, non-music video or non-talk show TV appearances of Sergio Mendes, the legendary Brazilian musician whose unique blend of Bossa nova, jazz, and pop music entertained audiences worldwide for nearly six decades. He and his real-life band, Brasil 65, appear as themselves. Mendes passed away in September 2024

Season One, 1965-1966

THE COLD, COLD WAR OF PAUL BRYAN (9/13/65)
Paul follows a beautiful woman to a European ski resort, where he risks his life and fortune to expose a dictator
Katherine Ross, Robert Loggia, Stephen McNally, Celeste Holm, Jacques Bergerac, Hans Gudegast, Jacqueline Beer, Carl Esmond

Teleplay by Frank Fenton and John Thomas James, story by John Thomas James; Directed by Robert Butler, Leslie H. Martinson

"John Thomas James" was among the many pseudonyms that Roy Huggins used throughout his career

THE GIRL NEXT DOOR IS A SPY (9/20/65)
Paul's former sweetheart inadvertently involves him in international intrigue during a visit to West Berlin
Macdonald Carey, Diana Hyland, Robert Knapp, Britt Semand, Maye Van Horn, Walter Janowitz, Henry Rowland, Fay Wall
Teleplay by Luther Davis, story by John Thomas James; Directed by Leslie H. Martinson

SOMEONE WHO MAKES ME FEEL BEAUTIFUL (9/27/65)
Paul and his Mexican fishing guide, whose livelihood stems from charming lonely, wealthy women, vie for the affections of an American widow
Fernando Lamas, Alex Montoya, Tippi Hedren, Henry Beckman, Maureen Leeds, Marguerita Cordova, Mark Miranda, Vince Barbi
Teleplay by Robert Guy Barrows, story by Judith and Robert Guy Barrows; Directed by Leslie H. Martinson

NEVER PICK UP A STRANGER (10/11/65)
After picking up an attractive teenage hitchhiker, Paul becomes the target of a brutal sheriff
Barry Sullivan, Brenda Scott, Paul Newland, Vaughn Taylor, Gregg Palmer, Russell Thorson, Betty Bronson, Len Wayland, Michael Stanwood, Grace Lee Whitney, Don Brodie, Vernon Scott, Doris Edwards
Teleplay by Howard Browne, story by John Thomas James; Directed by Leslie H. Martinson

MEN OF ACTION

How to Sell Your Soul for Fun and Profit (10/18/65)
Paul becomes involved in a political incident behind the Iron Curtain when he devises a plan to help a political prisoner escape
Telly Savalas, Gia Scala, Eric Braeden (*billed here by his birth name, Hans Gudegast*), Jeremy Slate, Paul Bertoya, Davis Lewis, Robert K. Cunningham, Alexander De Noszody, George Tatar, Peter Scott, Leslie Tebani
Teleplay by Frank Fenton and John Thomas James, story by John Thomas James; Directed by Steve Previn

Our Man in Limbo (10/25/65)
Under orders from American Intelligence, Paul seeks proof that a charming friend is an enemy agent
Macdonald Carey, Janine Gray, Roberto Contreras, Don Diamond, Ed McCready, Fritz Ford
Teleplay by Paul Tuckahoe, story by John Thomas James; Directed by Leslie H. Martinson
Sequel to The Girl Next Door is a Spy

Where Mystery Begins (11/1/65)
At the request of an old law school friend, Paul agrees to take over the defense of a woman charged with the murder of her husband
Dana Wynter, Keith Andes, Cyril Delevanti, Ian Wolfe, Walter Brooke, Booth Colman, Tom Allen, Ken Lynch, Byron Morrow, Hugh Douglas, Jim Bacon, Barry Brooks
Written by John Thomas James; Directed by Leslie H. Martinson

The Savage Season (11/8/65)
Mobsters force Paul to take steps leading to murder
Jill Haworth, Henry Silva, Harold J. Stone, Gene Evans, Leslie Perkins, Lyle Talbot, Quinn O'Hara, Leslie Summers, Jack Crowder, Bob McCready, Vince Barbi
Teleplay by Frank Fenton, story by John Thomas James; Directed by Richard Benedict

THIS TOWN FOR SALE (11/15/65)
While waiting for car repairs in a small town, Paul becomes a convenient murder suspect when one is demanded
James Whitmore, Mary Ann Mobley, R.G Armstrong, Paul Fix, Sharon Hugueny, Anthony Hayes, William Blackwell, Nick Colasanto, Alan Reed Jr., Charles Irving, Ernest Anderson, George Dockstader, Claudia Bryar, Lindsay Workman, Charles Conrad
Teleplay by George Kirgo, story by Chester Krumholz; Directed by Richard Benedict

A GIRL NAMED SORROW (11/22/65)
Paul is caught up in a cloak-and-dagger operation impelled by World War II and climaxed in the Arizona desert
David Opatoshu, Ina Balin, William Boyett, Charles Waggenheim
Written by Judith and Robert Guy Barrows; Directed by Leslie H. Martinson

THE VOICE OF GINA MILAN (11/29/65)
An opera singer falls in love with Paul, creating a situation that bodes heartbreak for both
Susan Strasberg, Linda Watkins, Renzo Cesana, Vinton Hayworth, Michele Montau, Frances Fong, Al Checco, E.J. Andre, Patrick Whyte, Yuki Tani
Teleplay by John W. Bloch and Philip Saltzman, story by Philip Saltzman; Directed by William Hale

THE TIME OF THE SHARKS (12/6/65)
On a shark fishing expedition in the Polynesian Islands, Paul becomes a savior of lost souls
Howard Keel, Melodie Johnson, Dolores Dorn-Heft, Tony Bill, Bernie Hamilton, Deon Douglas, Steve Carlson, Ralph P. Hanalei
Teleplay by Frank Fenton, story by John Thomas James; Directed by Leslie H. Martinson

MEN OF ACTION

Make the Angels Weep (12/13/65)
A wife's infidelity leads to murder, and Paul returns to his hometown to clear a friend who has been charged with the crime
Carol Lawrence, Anne Seymour, Mario Alcalde, Kirk Duncan, Don Dubbins, Alberto Morin, Charles Sed, Jack Krupnick, Allen Jung, Jeff Scott
Teleplay by John Dugan, story by John Thomas James; Directed by Leslie H. Martinson

Journey into Yesterday (12/27/65)
Paul finds himself at the mercy of African jungle tribesmen when he searches for a friend
James Forrest, Ken Renard, Harold Fong, Steve Baron, Anthony Chazlo Sr., Chief Sua, Napoleon Whiting, Gerald Lynch
Teleplay by Lou Shaw, based on a story by Marc Norman; Directed by Richard Benedict

Strangers at the Door (1/3/66)
When Paul's car breaks down in an isolated small town, he hops a freight back to civilization and meets a young man who hates the world also along for the ride
Robert Drivas, Lynn Carey, George Chandler, Trevor Bardette, Kelly Corcoran, Zara Cully, Jim Boles, Burt Mustin, Tim Graham, Billy M. Greene, John Francis
Written by Tom Allen; Directed by Stuart Rosenberg

The Carnival Ends at Midnight (1/10/66)
Paul's plan to return a killer from a foreign country is complicated by one of the slain man's daughters
Peter Lawford, Anne Helm, Stella Garcia, Nadine Nardi, Carlos Rivas, Inez Pedroza, Mercedes Alberti, Edward Colmans, Tom Allen, Anthony Redondo, Angela Dorian, Anna Mizrahi, Edy Williams, Shari Mins

Teleplay by Boris Sobelman, story by John Thomas James; Directed by Richard Benedict

The Rediscovery of Charlotte Hyde (1/24/66)
Paul comes to the aid of gigolo Ramon De Vega, who has found himself victimized by one of his prospective benefactors
Gena Rowlands, Fernando Lamas, Emile Ganest, Wolfe Barzell, Ted Roter, John Lodge, Garry Walberg, Richard Angarola, Eugene Borden, Brioni Farrell
Teleplay by Harold Gast, story by John Thomas James; Directed by William Hale

The Night of the Terror (1/31/66)
A "haunted house" is the setting of a harrowing night shared by Paul and his date at the invitation of the owner
Sharon Farrell, Donnelly Rhodes, Charles Aidman, Maggie Thrett, Nancy Marshall
Teleplay by Gerald Vaughan Hughes, story by John Thomas James; Directed by Alexander Singer

Keep My Share of the World (2/7/66)
In the North African Desert, Paul walks away from romance to help another man desperately in love
Rossano Brazzi, Jeremy Slate, Louise Troy, Richard Crane, Athan Karras
Teleplay by John W. Bloch, story by Harold Livingston; Directed by Richard Benedict

In Search of April (2/14/66)
At Mardi Gras, Paul meets a fun-loving girl who promptly disappears, leading him on a search to Hollywood Park, Montreal, and Massachusetts
Carol Lynley, George Furth, Don Galloway, William Lundigan, Don Rickles, K.T. Stevens, Larry D. Mann, Gail Bonney,

Robert Wolders, Robert Easton, Robert B. Williams, Clay Tanner, Anatol Winogradoff, John Francis
Teleplay by Alvin Sargent, story by John Thomas James; Directed by Stuart Rosenberg

Carol Lynley filmed this episode shortly after completing production of *Bunny Lake is Missing* (1965). "Carol looks smashing in living color coming soon after the black-and-white *Bunny Lake*," noted Tom Lisanti in *Carol Lynley: Her Film & TV Career in Thrillers, Fantasy & Suspense* (Bear Manor Media, 2020). "[For most of that movie] she wore a dowdy raincoat over a nondescript skirt and blouse befitting her character.... Now, her high cheekbones were on full display and, coupled with the flattering eye makeup, she was strikingly beautiful in this episode."

"Ben Gazzara was a wonderful actor and fun to be around," Lynley said to Lisanti in an interview for his book. "You never knew quite what he was going to say. He had an adventurous sense of humor. He used to hang out with Fernando Lamas, who would come visit him on the set. The two of them were free and easy—I mean that verbally. Beyond that, I have no idea."

HOODLUMS ON WHEELS (2/21/66)
While visiting a resort that he frequented in his youth, Paul is captured by a biker gang who are terrorizing some old friends
John Drew Barrymore, Marsha Hunt, Karen Jensen. Norman Grabowski, James Oliver, Stuart Anderson, Leslie Perkins, Hinton Pope, GreggPalmer
Written by Halsted Welles; Directed by Richard Benedict

WHO'S WATCHING THE FLESHPOT? (3/7/66)
Paul becomes involved with thieves and beautiful women on the French Riviera

Bobby Darin, Eve Arden, Jeff Corey, Davey Davison, Jocelyn Lane, Nicholas Colasanto, Maurice Marsac, Nadia Sanders, Thordis Brandt, Peter Camlin, Maurice St. Clair
Written by John Thomas James; Directed by Leslie H. Martinson

This episode served as the pilot for *The Sweet Life*, a series that never materialized

SEQUESTRO! (2 parts; 3/14/66, 3/21/66)
En route to an out-of-the-way Sicilian village, Paul is kidnapped by a pair of brothers who plan to ransom him for money to provide a dowry for their sister
Sal Mineo, Harry Guardino, Marianna Hill, David Mauro, Mario Badolati, Luke Gerard
Written by A. Martin Zweiback; Directed by Richard Benedict

DON'T COUNT ON TOMORROW (3/28/66)
Traveling to a Communist country to enter the road races held there, Paul is yanked from a train and accused of being a spy
Roddy McDowall, Michael Constantine, Peter Brocco, George Perna, Eva Soreny, Eva Monty, Frank Oberschall, Clive Wayne
Written by E. Arthur Kean; Directed by Stuart Rosenberg

THE CRUEL FOUNTAIN (4/4/66)
While in South America to race autos, Paul is led into a trap while trying to help two invalid women
Kathryn Hays, Murray Hamilton, Jan Sterling, Robert Pine, Tom Stern, Jeff Scott, Johnny Aladdin, Amentha Dymally, Kai Hernandez, Judy Cannon, Jack Krupnick, Andres Cropeza
Written by Henry Slesar; Directed by Stuart Rosenberg

NIGHT TRAIN FROM CHICAGO (4/11/66)
Paul becomes a Mafia target when he attempts to find a woman he met on a train, who left behind her rosary and prayer book

MEN OF ACTION

Brock Peters, Louise Sorel
Teleplay by Robert Bloch, story by John Thomas James; Directed by Richard Benedict

Soap opera fans around the world know Louise Sorel best as Vivian Alamain on *Days of Our Lives* and Augusta Lockridge on *Santa Barbara*. But she also appeared in many popular prime-time series throughout the '60s, '70s, and '80s, including *Run For Your Life*. "I think I played a nun in one of those shows," she said on *TV Confidential* in September 2024. "But I totally do not remember anything else about it, except that I wasn't allowed to wear any makeup—which, of course, every actress wants to wear makeup, but if you're a nun, you have none, so to speak. I also remember that Ben Garzzara was a good actor, very professional, and, you know… a very attractive guy."

THE LAST SAFARI (4/25/66)
Paul meets a girl who also has a terminal illness and teaches her how to live
Leslie Nielsen, Lesley Ann Warren, Louise Latham, Keith McConnell, Abraham Sofaer, Ivor Barry, Jean Durand, Contessa Elizabeth Lassar
Teleplay by John W. Bloch and Mel Goldberg, story by John Thomas James; Directed by Abner Biberman

THE SAVAGE MACHINES (5/2/66)
Paul Bryan risks his life in an auto race on which hinges the success of a romance and a business
Edward Mulhare, Sally Ann Howes, Jeremy Slate, Brendan Dillon, Don Knight, Maurice Dallimore, Chris Winters
Teleplay by William Wood, story by Robert Guy Barrows; Directed by Richard Benedict

The Sadness of a Happy Time (5/16/66)
While vacationing in a Spanish village, Paul meets a novelist and they fall desperately in love
Claudine Longet, Stephen McNally, Lili Valenty, Don Diamond, Michael Stanwood, Victor Fiore, Eumenio Blanco, Margarita Cordova, Isobel Larrear, Angel Martin, Juan Talavera
Teleplay by John W. Bloch, based on a story by Patrick Kennedy; Directed by Alf Kjellin

Season Two, 1966-1967

The Day Time Stopped (9/12/66)
Paul seeks to discover the cause of a six-month period of amnesia after learning that a ski accident was only partially responsible
Carol Lawrence, Slapsie Maxie Rosenbloom, Billy Daniels, Paul Lukas, John Ireland, John Kerr, Sheree North, Anne Helm, Robert Strauss
Written by Henry Slesar; Directed by Leo Penn

I Am The Late Diana Hays (9/19/66)
Paul meets a woman in Mexico who has been hiding for several months after running away from her husband, who went to prison based on evidence she left behind that resulted in his being convicted of her murder
Diana Hyland, Jack Palance, Anthony Eisley, Laurence Hadden, JoyEllison, Paula Winslow, Ray Ballard, Isabelle Cooley, Tracy Stratford, Joe Finnigan
Written by Dale and Katherine Eunson; Directed by Michael Ritchie

The Borders of Barbarism (9/26/66)
The daughter of a British counter-spy seeks to clear her father's name and also uncover a treasure buried in Yugoslavia
Stephen McNally, Alf Kjellin, Joan Collins, Reginald Owen, Joseph Sirola, George Perna, Don Knight, Gabor Curtiz, Lawrence Montaigne, Peter Forster, Jane Betts, Alex Rodine

Teleplay by John Thomas James, based on a novel by Eric Williams; Directed by Richard Benedict

THE COMMITTEE FOR THE 25TH (10/3/66)
A wealthy and still influential ex-politician threatens to initiate an amendment abolishing gambling after he learns from Paul that his daughter is the virtual prisoner of a gambling czar
Wendell Corey, Ed Asner, Brooke Bundy, Peter Brocco, Edward Faulkner, John McCann
Teleplay by Luther Davis, story by Tom Allen; Directed by William Graham

Character actor Wendell Corey appeared frequently in movies and on television throughout the 1950s and '60s. Reportedly a descendant of John Adams and John Quincy Adams, he was active in both local and national politics during his acting career. President of the Academy of Motion Picture Arts and Sciences from 1961 to 1963, he was elected to the Santa Monica City Council in April 1965. Given that Corey played a politician in COMMITTEE FOR THE 25TH and was, in fact, an elected official at the time he filmed this episode, one could say that casting him in COMMITTEE was an example of art imitating life.

THE DARK BEHIND THE DOOR (10/10/66)
A woman turns to suicidal drinking when she suspects her husband of philandering
Peter Graves, Michael Dunn, Delphi Lawrence, Robert Nichols, Pamela Curran, Ken McWhirter
Teleplay by John W. Bloch, story by John Thomas James; Directed by Richard L. Bare

THE SEX OBJECT (10/17/66)
Paul and Ramon meet in a posh Mexican port for some fishing, but before they put out to sea they become involved with two New York career girls on a husband-hunting mission
Sharon Farrell, Fernando Lamas, Joan Hackett, Pepe Hern, Fernando Escandon
Written by Henry Slesar; Directed by Leo Penn

THE GROTENBERG MASK (10/24/66)
While Paul tries to persuade a jet-set glamour girl to return to the States from the ski slopes of Switzerland, the two suddenly become innocently involved in a murder
Elizabeth Ashley, Skip Homeier, Tom Sinacox, Henry Beckman, Pat Randall, George Furth
Written by Henry Slesar; Directed by Nicholas Colasanto

EDGE OF THE VOLCANO (10/31/66)
Paul helps a famed novelist participate in a revolution
Alejandro Rey, John Dehner, Katherine Crawford, Edmund Hashim, Len Wayland, Don Diamond
Written by David Moessinger and Ed Waters; Directed by Leo Penn

THE TREASURE SEEKERS (11/14/66)
Paul discovers that his winning sweepstakes ticket brings with it a threat to unveil the secret about his illness
Collin Wilcox, Bruce Dern, Jack Albertson, Anne Helm, Rosemary Murphy
Written by Max Ehrlich; Directed by Nicholas Colasanto

THE MAN WHO HAD NO ENEMIES (11/21/66)
Paul becomes the prime suspect in the Caribbean island murder of a wealthy socialite and sailboat racer
Kurt Kasznar, Nancy Malone, Joanna Moore, Victoria Shaw, John Lodge, Jean Durand, Ward Ramsey

Teleplay by John W. Bloch, story by John Thomas James; Directed by Michael Ritchie

A GAME OF VIOLENCE (11/28/66)
Suspicion is aroused when a heavily favored fighter suddenly collapses in the third round of a championship fight
Ossie Davis, Sugar Ray Robinson, Carol Lawrence, Tige Andrews, Jimmy Lennon, Chick Hearn, Janet MacLachlan, James B. Sikking
Written by Lou Guardino; Directed by Leo Penn

HANG DOWN YOUR HEAD AND LAUGH (12/5/66)
During a cross-country trip, Paul tries to discover the identity of a teenage runaway he has befriended, while she attempts to learn his secret
Kim Darby, Jacqueline Scott, Larry Ward, Fabian Dean, Marvin Brody
Teleplay by Adrien Joyce and Jack Curtis, story by Jack Curtis; Directed by Michael Ritchie

Best known for playing Mattie Ross, the young woman who asks Rooster Cogburn (John Wayne) to avenge her father's murder in the original *True Grit* (1969), Kim Darby began her acting career at age fifteen and worked steadily in movies and television for more than five decades. In August 1966, shortly before filming this episode, she began production on what would become arguably her most famous TV appearance: the title character in MIRI, the first-season episode of *Star Trek: The Original Series* in which the Enterprise encounters an Earth-like planet inhabited by children who all contract a fatal disease once they reach puberty.

"A part came up on the show *Run For Your Life*," Darby recalled in August 2008 on *TV Confidential*. "Michael Ritchie directed it, and he did something that directors don't do a lot today—he worked with me. He believed I could do it, but he needed to work with me, and he got the performance out of me."

TEARS FROM A GLASS EYE (12/12/66)
Paul helps a beautiful girl choose a husband during his visit to a Caribbean island resort
Donnelly Rhodes, Mary Ann Mobley, Gerald S. O'Loughlin, Bill Glover, Otis Young, Edward Ashley, Evelyn Dutton
Teleplay by Luther Davis, story by John Thomas James; Directed by Leo Penn

TIME-AND-A-HALF ON CHRISTMAS EVE (12/19/66)
After Paul's plane makes a forced landing on Christmas Eve at a small city airport, a taxi driver shows Paul the town and suddenly discovers the emptiness of life away from his family
Ernest Borgnine, Charles McGraw, Melanie Alexander, Craig Hundley
Teleplay by A. Martin Zweiback, story by Daniel L. Aubry; Directed by Michael Ritchie

THE SHOCK OF RECOGNITION (12/26/66)
With encouragement from Paul, a movie idol regains his self-respect through a test of courage
Farley Granger, Marlyn Mason, Frank Silvera, Gavin MacLeod, Jose Ramon Tirado, Walter Mathews, Eric Mason
Written by John D.F. Black; Directed by William Hale

Mexican matador Jose Ramon Tirado plays himself in this episode

FLIGHT FROM TIRANA/A RAGE FOR JUSTICE (2 parts; 1/9/67, 1/16/67)
Paul becomes a pivotal part of an international plot involving espionage, narcotics, and an American Army defector in Albania

MEN OF ACTION

Ossie Davis, Sam Wanamaker, George Voskovec, Will Kuluva, Nicholas Colasanto, Gloria Edwards, James Callahan
Part 1: Written by Joel Murcott; Directed by John Rich
Part 2: Teleplay by John W. Bloch, story by John Thomas James; Directed by Leo Penn

THE LIST OF ALICE MCKENNA (1/23/67)
Paul tries to help an old friend regain a place in society after seven years in prison for murdering her husband
Geraldine Brooks, William Windom, Cloris Leachman, Malcolm Atterbury, Mario Alcalde
Teleplay by Jerry Ludwig and David W. Rintels, story by John Thomas James; Directed by Michael Ritchie

THE FACE OF THE ANTAGONIST (1/30/67)
Paul helps defend an ex-policeman with a reputation for brutality against murder charges
Aldo Ray, Henry Beckman, Richard Anderson, Ron Russell, Paul Newlan, Alan Baxter
Written by Howard Browne; Directed by Nicholas Colasanto

BABY, THE WORLD'S ON FIRE (2/6/67)
Paul meets an old law school pal in Tokyo and becomes involved in a rough-and-tumble adventure when the friend uses him in a scheme to sell an electronic device
Jack Kelly, Suzanne Pleshette, Hans Lee, Ed Parker, Robert Ito, Kenny Endoso, Vince Eder, Hannie Landman
Written by Shirl Hendryx; Directed by Leo Penn

RENDEZVOUZ IN TOKYO (2/13/67)
Paul and his Korean War flying buddies turn the clock back fifteen years and gather for a reunion
Martin Milner, Joan Blackman, Ron Foster, Mickey Shaughnessy, Robert Pickering, Jon Cedar, Ron Foster, Garry Walberg

Written by Harold Livingston; Directed by Richard Benedict

THE CALCULUS OF CHAOS (2/20/67)
In Czechoslovakia, Paul is asked to help a scientist escape from his Communist captors
Inger Stratton, John van Dreelen, Pat Harrington, Stephen McNally, Gregory Gay, George Ives
Written by Bill S. Ballinger and Lou Breslow; Directed by William Hale

THE ASSASSIN (2/27/67)
A man suffering from the same terminal ailment as Paul wants revenge on a wealthy executive for an old college prank
Arthur Hill, Joan Shawlee, Harold Gould, Andrew Duggan, James Seay, Don Gazzaniga, Joan Swift, Sean Kennedy, Paul Sorensen, Don Corbett, Kent McCord, Harvey Gardner, Frank Baron, Jim Driskill, Harry Klekes, Sharon Dean
Written by Henry Slesar; Directed by Nicholas Colasanto

THE CARPELLA COLLECTION (3/6/67)
Paul inadvertently becomes a suspect in an international jewel theft
Helmut Dantine, Celia Lovsky, Mercedes Moliner, Alfred Dennis, Walter Alzmann, Rolf Sedan, Robert Apollo, Jeanne Rainier
Written by Robert Foster and Philip DeGuere Jr.; Directed by AlexanderSinger

A VERY SMALL INJUSTICE (3/13/67)
Paul is forced to accompany an escaped convict in his flight from a trigger-happy posse
Slim Pickens, Burr DeBenning, Louise Shaffer, Don Hanmer, Harry Carey Jr.

Written by Ronald M. Cohen; Directed by Nicholas Colasanto

EAST OF THE EQUATOR (3/20/67)
Paul helps a friend search for her long-missing, and presumably dead, husband after a painting stirs hopes that he may still be alive
Dina Merrill, Rudy Solari, Alan Bergman, Bill Glover, Peter Hobbs, Rodolfo Hoyos, Inez Pedroza, Donald Lawton, Berry Kroger
Teleplay by Henri Simoun, story by John Thomas James; Directed by Fernando Lamas

A CHOICE OF EVILS (4/3/67)
Paul intercedes for a gubernatorial candidate who meets a scandal unflinchingly on election eve
John Forsythe, Barbara Stanek, Coleen Gray, Wesley Lau, Walter Mathews, Karl Bruck, Joan Bradley, Clark Race, Horst Ebersberg, Faith Christopher, Bud Haley, Larry Anthony
Teleplay by Alvin Sargent and Rita Lakin, story by Rita Lakin; Directed by Ben Gazzara

Rita Lakin, creator of *The Rookies*, began her career in television as a secretary for Universal Studio executives Dale Sheets and Ned Tanen. One benefit of that job, particularly for aspiring writers such as Lakin, was immediate access to scripts. With the encouragement of Sheets and Tanen, she began to write; with the help of agent Mel Bloom, she made her first sale (A CANDLE IN THE WINDOW, an episode of *Dr. Kildare*, directed by Sydney Pollack and featuring Raymond Massey and Ronny Howard, that aired in November 1964). That opened the door to a career in television that would span more than twenty-five years, first as a freelance writer, then as a staff writer, showrunner, and (eventually) executive producer on many top-rated series and made-for-TV movies, including *Peyton Place*, *The Mod Squad*, and *Medical Center*.

At the time she wrote this episode, though, Lakin was still very much an anomaly, one of the few female writers in an industry dominated by men. "After I wrote an episode of *Run For Your Life*, I was asked about being the only female writer on two male-written shows," she recalled in her memoir, *The Only Woman in the Room* (Applause Books, 2015). "'Time after time, you were the only woman in the room. How did it make you feel?'

"I thought about it for a moment. 'Alone, I guess.' Why were these men acting oddly? Because I was a woman? Where were the other women writers? Were they any?"

By the time this episode aired, however, Lakin's circumstances had started to change. She was a staff writer on *Peyton Place*, where she not only learned there were indeed other female writers in television, but found herself working alongside many of them on that series.

TELL IT TO THE DEAD (4/10/67)
Paul and two attractive American women are caught up together in an Asian border war
Karen Black, Linden Chiles, Michele Carey, David Mauro, Than Wyenn, Peter Bourne, Aly Wassil, Don Rizzan
Teleplay by Luther Davis, story by Philip DeGuere Jr. and Betty Andrews; Directed by Leo Penn

BETTER WORLD NEXT TIME (4/17/67)
Paul's visit to a friend in a Veterans Hospital turns into a nightmare when the former Viet Cong prisoner escapes from the psychiatric ward, believing he is still in Viet Nam

Martin Milner, Leonard Stone, Michael Pataki, Jim Creech, Peter Chin, Ronnie R. Rondell, Kenny Endoso, James Shen
Written by Jack Miller; Directed by Michael Ritchie

THE WORD WOULD BE GOODBYE (4/24/67)
Paul resumes his romance with a French author Nicole after they meet accidentally en route to the Paris auto races
Claudine Longet, Albert Paulsen, Emile Genest, Ted Roter, Patrick Horgan
Teleplay by Don Balluck and Patrick Kennedy, story by Don Balluck and John W. Bloch; Directed by Alf Kjellin
Sequel to THE SADNESS OF A HAPPY TIME

Season Three, 1967-1968

WHO'S CHE GUEVARA? (9/13/67)
An American mercenary commandeers Paul's chartered plane, then embroils our hero into a bold plan to rescue an anti-Castro prisoner from hostile Cuba
Rita Moreno, Alex Montoya, Nico Minardos, Victor Milian, Abel Franco, Tony Giorgio
Written by Philip DeGuere Jr. and Robert Foster; Directed by Michael Ritchie

THE INHUMAN PREDICAMENT (9/20/67)
While Paul enjoys a romance with a princess, Ramon De Vega matches wits with a beautiful financier
Fernando Lamas, Vera Miles, Kurt Kasznar, Katherine Justice
Teleplay by Barry Pritchard and Robert Hamner, story by John Thomas James; Directed by Alexander Singer

THREE PASSENGERS FOR THE LUSITANIA (9/27/67)
During a sojourn to Mexico, Paul tries to solve the riddle of two thrillseeking Americans who seem to share his plight—a limited time to live

Cliff Potter, Murray MacLeod, David Lewis, Luis de Cordova, InezPedroza, Gregg Palmer
Written by Erich Faust; Directed by Richard Benedict

The Frozen Image (10/4/67)
Upset over his manager's attempts to keep him away from the gaming tables, a Las Vegas entertainer hires Paul to fill in
Mel Tormé, Michael Cole, Sandra Smith, Mikki Sharait, Joy Harmon, Nicholas Colasanto
Written by Mel Tormé; Directed by Nicholas Colasanto

Michael Cole was a year away from his breakthrough role as Pete Cochran on *The Mod Squad* (ABC, 1968-1973) at the time he filmed this episode. I interviewed him at Stanley's Restaurant in Sherman Oaks in the summer of 2010; he lit up when I asked him about working with singer Mel Tormé. "Mel wrote all those songs, 'The Christmas Song,' etc., and yet he turned to me for acting help, when we did that show," he said. "That was amazing to me."

In that same conversation, Cole told me that Marlo Thomas played a pivotal role in Danny Thomas hiring him to play Pete on *The Mod Squad*. "I did a screen test with Tige Andrews. Marlo saw the dailies and said to Danny, 'Daddy, if you don't hire Michael, someone else will and he will be a big star.' A few days later, Danny called me and said, 'Hello, star…' That's when I knew I got the part."

Trip to the Far Side (10/11/67)
Despite an agreement to go separate ways after a two-week "dating game," in Rome, a young lady persuades Paul to accompany her to Africa to join her father on a lion hunt
Ralph Bellamy, Geoffrey Horne, Marianna Hill, Bruce Dern, Don Knight

Teleplay by Paul Tuckahoe, story by John Thomas James; Directed by Fernando Lamas

THE COMPANY OF SCOUNDRELS (10/18/67)
Paul leads a movement to outlaw gambling through a constitutional amendment and, in the process, battles the underworld
Pat Hingle, Ford Rainey, Robert Yuro, Lou Frizzell, Dean Harens, Kermit Murdock
Teleplay by Howard Browne, story by John Thomas James; Directed by Michael Ritchie
Sequel to THE COMMITTEE FOR THE 25TH

AT THE END OF THE RAINBOW, THERE'S ANOTHER RAINBOW (10/25/67)
Paul helps a close friend resolve a dilemma when she is innocently involved in a conspiracy to defraud an insurance company
Anne Helm, Bruce Dern, Jeff Corey, Fabian Dean, Arch Whiting
Teleplay by Henry Slesar and John Thomas James, story by John Thomas James; Directed by Nick Colasanto

DOWN WITH WILLY HATCH (11/1/67)
A has-been comedian faces the wrath of a small town when he is charged with a statutory crime, prompting Paul to come out of "retirement" to defend him
Don Rickles, Robert Donner, Clarke Gordon, Mary Jo Kennedy, Lou Wagner
Written by Richard Baer; Directed by Richard Benedict

THE NAKED HALF-TRUTH (11/8/67)
Paul and Ramon De Vega battle two powerful Andorran families as they try to rescue a young girl believed to be an American millionaire's daughter
Fernando Lamas, Letitia Roman, Joe De Santis, Edward Andrews, Frank Puglia

Teleplay by Marc Norman and Roger O. Hirson, story by Roger O. Hirson; Directed by Michael Ritchie

TELL IT LIKE IT IS (11/15/67)
A retired jurist reacts furiously to humiliation suffered during a talk-show interview to promote his book. When he has an appearance scheduled on another controversial show, Paul comes along to try to save the judge from insults
Franchot Tone, Joan Huntington, James Daly, Michael Strong, Jackie Coogan Jr., Quinn Redeker
Written by Shirl Hendryx; Directed by Ben Gazzara

CRY HARD, CRY FAST (2 parts; 11/22/67, 11/29/67)
Paul assumes blame for a deadly multi-car crash, while a bank robber involved in the wreck stands by helplessly as his hidden loot is hauled to a police impound lot
James Farentino, Charles Aidman, Jack Albertson, Robyn Millan, Susan Clark, Anthony Eisley, Diana Muldaur, Mary Jackson, Richard O'Brien, Joan Van Ark
Written by Luther Davis; Directed by Michael Ritchie
Based on the novel *Cry Hard, Cry Fast* by John D. MacDonald

CRY HARD, CRY FAST marked the first major television appearance of Joan Van Ark, the actress known around the world as Valene Ewing on both *Dallas* (CBS, 1978-1991) and *Knots Landing* (CBS, 1979-1993). Not only that, but when I interviewed Van Ark in February 2020, she pointed out that this episode also happened to have two *Knots Landing* connections: James Farentino, the lead guest star, was married to Michele Lee (Van Ark's longtime co-star on *Knots*) at the time CRY HARD, CRY FAST was filmed, while Jack Dusick, the makeup artist on *Run For Your Life*, was Lee's father. "There was something serendipitous about Jack taking me, this young neophyte actress from New York, under his wings and showing me the ropes," Van Ark said on my radio show, *TV Confidential.* "He was a loving, generous, wonderful person who certainly knew the business, because of Michele and Jimmy and all of that. That was such a gift, to have him help me and guide me through."

THE MUSTAFA EMBRACE (12/6/67)
An American beauty, cut loose by her wealthy Moroccan husband, asks to help her leave the country with a priceless gift
Katherine Crawford, Stanley Waxman, William Sargent, Edmund Hashim
Teleplay by Robert Hamner, story by John Thomas James; Directed by MurrayGolden

IT COULD ONLY HAPPEN IN ROME (12/20/67)
Paul protects a young, guitar-playing singer when she is insulted by two youthful tourists, then decides to solve the mystery surrounding her Bohemian life
Tisha Sterling, Robert Brown, Renzo Cesana, Philip Chapin, Jeff Malloy, Sal Ponti
Written by Elick Moll; Directed by Alexander Singer

FLY BY NIGHT (12/27/67)
Paul turns detective and finds new clues which prompt police to reopen an unsolved murder case
Felicia Farr, Andrew Duggan, Jason Evers, Don Stroud, Bruce Glover
Teleplay by Robert Foster and Philip DeGuere Jr., story by John Thomas James; Directed by Richard Benedict

A DANGEROUS PROPOSAL (1/3/68)
After agreeing to negotiate a business deal for an industrialist, Paul discovers that the assignment is merely a front for a more serious matter involving a struggle for international power

Albert Dekker, Judy Carne, Carlos Romero, Mark Lenard, Marino Masé

Teleplay by Robert Hamner, story by Tom Blackburn; Directed by Barry Shear

One Bad Turn (1/10/68)

Paul is jailed in a small town on a false charge of interfering with an arresting officer, and his troubles mount as he tries to win his freedom

Warren Oates, Bert Freed, Anne Helm, Walter Brooke, Strother Martin, Jon Lormer, Michael Mikler

Teleplay by Paul Mason, story by John Thomas James; Directed by Ben Gazzara

The Rape of Lucrece (1/17/68)

A novelist invites her old friend Paul to dinner and then makes a serious accusation against him

Julie Harris, Audrey Totter, Donald Foster, Vincent Van Lynn, Michael Harris, Margo Moore

Teleplay by Chase Mellen, story by Dale and Katherine Eunson; Directed by Larry Peerce

The Killing Scene (1/31/68)

With only forty-eight hours left before execution time, Paul works frantically to save an innocent man from the gas chamber

Robert Duvall, Will Geer, Tom Skerritt, Dana Elcar, Walter Brooke

Teleplay by Robert Foster and Philip DeGuere Jr., story by Ed De Blasio; Directed by Ben Gazzara

Saro-Jane, You Never Whispered Again (2/7/68)

Searching for a missing girl, Paul finds her entrenched in the hippie movement and accused of authoring an obscene book

Barbara Hershey, Frank Marth, Austin Willis, Robert F. Simon, Michael Bell, James Oliver
Teleplay by Adrien Joyce, story by John Thomas James; Directed by Alexander Singer

THE DEAD ON FURLOUGH (2/21/68)
Paul joins an Israeli archaeological team and becomes involved in a border skirmish
Ina Balin, Eric Braeden (*billed here by his birth name, Hans Gudegast*), Ronald Feinberg, Nate Esformes, Dina Van Minnen, Shlomo Bachar, Yossi Eichenbaum
Teleplay by James M. Miller, story by Paul Freeman; Directed by Alexander Singer

BEWARE MY LOVE (2/28/68)
In Italy, Paul poses as an insurance investigator after a friend reveals doubts about her sister's death
Anna-Lisa, John van Dreelen, Michael Evans, Grant Woods, Susan Trustman, Pat Priest, Louis de Cordova
Written by Robert E. Thompson; Directed by George McGowan

CAROL (3/6/68)
A pregnant young wife seeks an abortion after her husband rejects her
Kim Darby, Ron Russell, Jana Taylor, Booth Colman, Yvonne White
Written by Robert Foster and Philip De Guere, Jr., story by Philip De Guere, Jr.; Directed by Ben Gazzara

Kim Darby previously appeared in HANG DOWN YOUR HEAD AND LAUGH. A fixture on many dramatic series throughout the 1960s and '70s (including many of the shows produced by Universal Television), she had fond memories of working with Roy Huggins. "He was wonderful to me," she said on *TV Confidential* in October 2008. "He really made me feel very, very special. He had a lot of faith in me and never underestimated me. I just remember him as being real special and having good taste."

LIFE AMONG THE MEAT-EATERS (3/13/68)
In Sardinia at the invitation of a friend, Paul tries to keep an heiress from marrying an international playboy
Anne Baxter, Jacques Bergerac, Peter Donat, Philip Chapin, Anna Capri, Judy Lang, Peter Bromilow
Teleplay by Mann Rubin, story by Robert Hamner; Directed by Robert Day

THE EXCHANGE (3/27/68)
Paul enters East Germany to negotiate the trade of a Russian spy for a millionaire held captive by the Communists
Janice Rule, Stephen McNally, David Hurst, Lee Bergere, John Bryant
Teleplay by Howard Browne, story by John Thomas James; Directed by John Llewellyn Moxey

ABOUT THE AUTHOR

Ed Robertson is an award-winning author, journalist, and media analyst who writes and edits for print media and creates, produces, and distributes audio content for broadcast media. His books on television include *The Fugitive Recaptured, 45 Years of The Rockford Files, The Ethics of Star Trek* (with Judith Barad, Ph.D.), *The Case of the Alliterative Attorney: A Guide to the Perry Mason TV Series and Made-for-TV Movies* (with Bill Sullivan), and *The FBI Dossier: A Guide to the Classic TV Series Produced by Quinn Martin and Starring Efrem Zimbalist, Jr.* (also with Bill Sullivan). He also hosts and produces *TV Confidential*, a syndicated weekly radio talk show about television that features lively conversations about all aspects of network, cable, and streaming-on-demand programming, plus interviews with special guests. Archives of previous broadcasts are available on Apple Podcasts, Spotify, and wherever podcasts are found. Follow Ed online at EdRobertson.com and televisionconfidential.com